Exploring
Mark

Exploring
Mark

A DEVOTIONAL COMMENTARY

GEORGE R. KNIGHT

REVIEW AND HERALD® PUBLISHING ASSOCIATION
HAGERSTOWN, MD 21740

The author assumes full responsibility for the accuracy of all facts and quotations as cited in this book.

All Bible texts quoted are the author's translation unless otherwise noted.
Bible texts credited to ESV are from the *English Standard Version* of the Bible, copyright © 2001, by Crossway Bibles, a division of Good News Publications. Used by permission.
Texts credited to NASB are from the *New American Standard Bible,* copyright © 1960, 1962, 1968, 1971, 1975, 1977, 1994 by the Lockman Foundation. Used by permission.
Scriptural quotations marked NIV are from the *Holy Bible, New International Version.* Copyright © 1973, 1978, 1984, International Bible Society, used by permission of Zondervan Bible Publishers.
Bible texts credited to Phillips are from J. B. Phillips: *The New Testament in Modern English,* Revised Edition. © J. B. Phillips, 1958, 1960, 1972. Used by permission of Macmillan Publishing Co.
Texts credited to REB are from *The Revised English Bible.* Copyright © Oxford University Press and Cambridge University Press, 1989. Reprinted by permission.
Scripture quotations marked RSV are from the *Revised Standard Version of the Bible,* copyright © 1946, 1952, 1971, by the Division of Christian Education of the National Council of the Churches of Christ in the U.S.A. Used by permission.

This book was
Edited by Gerald Wheeler
Cover designed by Left Coast Design
Cover illustration by Jerry Blank
Electronic makeup by Shirley M. Bolivar
Designed by Mark O'Connor
Typeset: 11/14 Bembo

PRINTED IN U.S.A.

08 07 06 05 04   5 4 3 2 1

R&H Cataloging Service
Knight, George R
    Exploring Mark: a devotional commentary.

    1. Bible. N.T. Mark—Criticism, interpretation, etc.   I. Title.

227.87

ISBN 0-8280-1837-5

Dedicated to

Kurt and Debbie Frey
and
Ed and Barbara Roy

———————

True neighbors who are waiting to help
before being asked.

Contents

Exploring the "Exploring" Idea

Exploring Mark joins *Exploring Hebrews* as the second volume in what I hope will become a series of user-friendly commentaries aimed at helping people understand the Bible better. While the books have the needs and abilities of laypeople in mind, they will also prove beneficial to pastors and other church leaders. Beyond individual readers, the "Exploring" format will be helpful for church study groups and in enriching participation in midweek meetings.

Each volume is best thought of as a devotional commentary. While the treatment of each passage will seek to develop its exegetical meaning, it will not stop there but will move on to practical application in the daily life of believers in the twenty-first century.

Rather than focusing on the details of each verse, the "Exploring" volumes will seek to give readers an understanding of the themes and patterns of each biblical book as a whole and how each passage fits into its context. As a result, they will not attempt to solve all of the problems or answer all the questions related to a given text.

In an effort to be user-friendly these devotional commentaries on the Old and New Testaments will present the entire text of each biblical book treated. The volumes will divide the text into "bite-sized" portions that will be included immediately before the comments on the passage. Thus readers will not have to flip back and forth between their Bibles and the commentary.

The commentary sections will aim at being long enough to significantly treat a topic, but short enough for individual, family, or group readings.

The translation of each biblical book is my own, and claims no special merit. Although I have based it on the original languages, in making it I have conferred with several English versions. While not being a "technical achievement," the translation has sought to take every significant translational problem and issue into consideration and to remain as close as possible to the original text of the Bible. In order to accomplish that goal the translation employs word-for-word translation wherever possible but utilizes thought-for-thought translation when word-for-word fails adequately to carry God's message from the original languages and cultures into modern English.

George R. Knight
Andrews University
Berrien Springs, Michigan

Foreword

Mark is the fastest moving of the four canonical Gospels. Compared with the other three, it features Jesus' actions more than His teachings. But even in the realm of teachings it provides important data not included in the other Gospels.

The shortest of the four biblical portrayals of Jesus' life, it was almost certainly the first written. Thus it provided a model that Matthew and Luke would follow quite closely and John to a lesser extent. Like the other Gospels, Mark gives a disproportionate amount of space to the final events in Jesus' life and to His death. From beginning to end he presents Jesus as the Son of God who would die for His followers.

The biblical author composed the second Gospel to encourage people who were facing trials and who needed comfort. It still performs that function 2,000 years later. I trust that *Exploring Mark* will be a blessing to its readers as they seek to learn more about their Lord and how to follow Him more closely.

I would like to express once again my special appreciation to Bonnie Beres, who managed to read my handwriting as she typed the manuscript; to Gerald Wheeler, who supplied his editorial expertise; to Jeannette R. Johnson, who has continued to encourage me in my writing; and to the administration of Andrews University, who have provided support and time for research and writing.

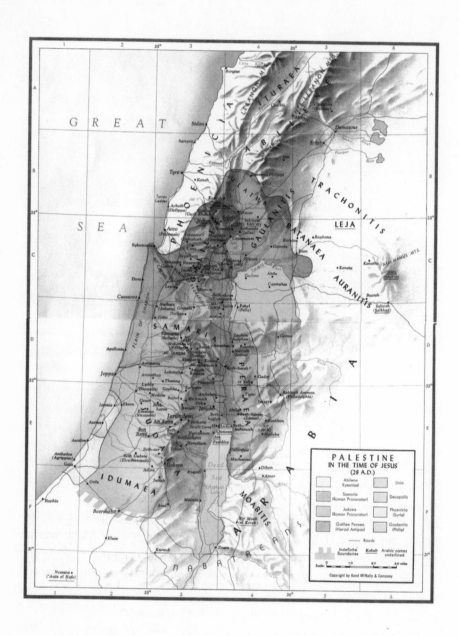

PALESTINE
IN THE TIME OF JESUS
(28 A.D.)

Abilene
(Lysanias)

Samaria
(Roman Procurator)

Judaea
(Roman Procurator)

Galilee Peraea
(Herod Antipas)

Livia

Decapolis

Phoenicia
(Syria)

Gaulanitis
(Philip)

Roads

Indefinite
Boundaries

Kokab Arabic names
underlined

Scale

0   10   20   30 miles

Copyright by Rand McNally & Company

Introduction
to the Gospel of Mark

The Gospel of Mark holds a unique place in the history of Christianity. "As far as we can tell," Ralph Martin tells us, *it is the first Christian book about Jesus Christ to be written and circulated.* With Mark's effort, as the Spirit directed him, Christianity went into the publishing business" (Martin, *Where the Action Is,* p. 5). Paul, of course, had previously written letters, but those were documents aimed at congregations or individuals and addressed quite specific concerns. Mark's Gospel, on the other hand, even though probably prepared with a specific group of Christians in mind, was "obviously intended for a more extensive class of readers, namely Christians in the Roman Empire across the Mediterranean world" *(ibid.).*

Purpose of Mark

The Gospel's very first verse clearly states the author's purpose, to write the "gospel of Jesus Christ, the Son of God" (1:1, RSV). In other words, the book is an introduction to Jesus, God's Messiah or Christ, who had come to usher in the "kingdom of God" for all who repented and believed the gospel (1:15). Thus in one sense the Gospel of Mark was an evangelistic treatise to introduce the life and ministry of Jesus.

But that introduction has a specific context in that it appears to be addressing a group of believers under threat of persecution. R. A. Guelich points out that the strained situation of Mark's audience "may well have given rise to questions about who Jesus really was and the nature of the kingdom he had come to inaugurate" (in Green, p. 524). From that perspective, the Gospel through its explanations provides a basis for their faith. The author's ultimate intention is to create disciples who will not only follow Jesus, but will have the courage to do so no matter what the consequences might be.

And those consequences were serious. After all, roughly one third of the Gospel focuses on Jesus' death. But the good news (gospel) is that death wasn't the end for Jesus. After His death came resurrection. So it would be for those who followed Jesus. They had nothing to fear if they remained true to the One who not only had gained victory over death but would eventually come "in clouds with great power and glory" to bring about the full salvation of His followers (13:26, 27, RSV).

Mark's Major Themes

A gospel by definition is a presentation of the life and work of Jesus. But the gospel accounts are not biographies in the usual sense. Rather than presenting a well-balanced sketch of His life, each of the four canonical gospels focuses on His death. That is especially true of Mark, in which one third of his gospel deals with the last week of Jesus' life.

Because of its very nature, the themes of Mark's Gospel center around the significance of Jesus. But they don't stop there since an understanding of His life is not merely an academic exercise. Thus a second thematic aspect of Mark involves what it means to believe in Jesus and to become one of His followers. The second Gospel's themes fall into several broad topics.

1. *Jesus Christ*. The central subject of Mark from the first verse to the last is the nature and meaning of Jesus. Along that line, Mark provides his readers with a series of rich images.

One is that Jesus is the *Son of God*. James Edwards correctly points out that "the divine Sonship of Jesus is the theological keystone of the Gospel of Mark" (Edwards, p. 15). Son of God occurs in the first verse of the Gospel ("The beginning of the gospel of Jesus Christ, the Son of God" [1:1, RSV]) as well as in the climactic confession of the centurion at the cross ("Truly this man was the Son of God" [15:39, RSV]). The fact of Jesus' divine identity appears not only at the beginning and end of Mark but throughout the body of the text.

A second identification of Jesus is that He is the *Son of Man*. In Mark that is the only title that Jesus employs of Himself. On the other hand, no one else in the Gospel refers to Him by that title. The title itself evidently comes from Daniel 7:13, in which "one like a son of man" comes to the "Ancient of Days" (RSV). Thus once again we find a title with supernatural connotations.

A third description of Jesus is *Christ* or *Son of David*. Christ is the Greek form of the Hebrew title "Messiah," which literally means "the anointed one." "In Mark 'Christ' refers to God's anointed king, and in particular to the messianic figure whom Jews expected to restore the throne of David and to . . . inaugurate the Kingdom of God" (Williamson, p. 9). The center point in Mark has Peter confessing that Jesus is the Christ (8:29).

Yet Mark does not present Jesus as one fulfilling the usual Jewish expectations of the one who would come as the Son of David. In place of a kingly figure, Mark sets Jesus forth as the *Servant of the Lord.* Whereas Mark pictures Jesus as having authority over such things as people, nature, and disease, he does not depict Him using that power on His own behalf. Rather, Jesus employed His authority for others. "For the Son of man . . . came not to be served but to serve, and to give his life as a ransom for many" (10:45, RSV). From the time of His baptism up through His death we find allusions to the servant of God as portrayed in Isaiah 42-54, and especially the suffering servant of chapter 53.

Our brief overview of Mark's presentation of Jesus leaves us without a doubt that he sees Him as the divine Being predicted in the Old Testament. Yet Jesus is much more than a supernatural figure in Mark. Mark also depicts Him as an intensely human person with a full range of human emotions (see, e.g., 14:33, 34).

2. *Kingdom of God.* Closely related to Jesus and His mission in Mark is the theme of the kingdom of God. In fact, the good news that Jesus brings is about the kingdom. "The time is fulfilled, and the kingdom of God is at hand" (1:15, RSV), John the Baptist declared when he introduced Jesus at the very beginning of His ministry. News about the kingdom dominates the second Gospel. We see that emphasis reflected, among other places, in the parables of the kingdom (4:1-34, the longest discourse in the first half of Mark), kingdom teaching in relation to discipleship (e.g., 9:1, 47; 10:14, 15, 23-25), and Jesus at the last supper stating that He will not drink of the fruit of the vine "until that day when I drink it new in the kingdom of God" (14:25, RSV).

3. *Eschatology*. In Mark the kingdom of God is both a present reality in the ministry of Jesus and a future hope for when He comes again to establish His kingdom in its fullness. That future hope is especially vivid in chapter 13. Vincent Taylor notes that "Mark's eschatology has a strong apocalyptic cast. Not only is the Parousia the object of his earnest expectation, but the events leading up to it and its spectacular character are strongly emphasized" (Taylor, p. 116).

4. *Christ's Passion*. As with the other three gospels, the climax of Mark is the passion week and the death and resurrection of Christ, who gave "his life as a ransom for many" (10:45, RSV). More than one student has defined a gospel as "a Passion story with an extended introduction" (Cole, p. 54). Events throughout the Gospel all lead up to the cross.

5. *Conflict*. The way of the cross was not easy for Jesus. Mark portrays His life as one of ascending conflict. It begins with the wilderness confrontation with Satan (1:12, 13), extends up through disputes with the religious leaders (2:1-3:6), and climaxes with clashes with Caiaphas and Pilate (14:53-65; 15:1-15). Beyond those conflicts are those with His family (3:20, 21, 31-35), the disciples (8:14-21, 32), and even His own self (14:32-42). Part of the author's lesson here is that if Jesus had to live in the atmosphere of conflict, so would His disciples.

6. *Discipleship*. Closely related to the theme of conflict in Mark is that of discipleship. Mark presents the way of Jesus as the path He also calls His disciples to tread with Him. Thus only a clear perception of Jesus and His life will provide disciples with a sufficient picture of what it means to follow Him. If He had conflicts, so will they, and if His life was the way of the cross, so theirs will be also. That thought becomes quite explicit in Mark 8:34, in which Jesus says that those who come after Him would have to deny themselves and take up their cross. Like Him, they must be ready to suffer and even die. A disciple is one who follows.

Unfortunately, after the first few chapters, Mark's presentation of Jesus' actual disciples is quite negative. In fact, it becomes progressively characterized by misunderstanding and an eventual betrayal. But beyond that misconception and treachery are grace and restoration (16:7). We will have more to say on those topics under the section on relevance below.

7. *Faith*. Mark intimately relates faith to discipleship and to following the suffering Son of God. Faith is a response to hearing, and Mark demon-

strates two very different faith reactions to Jesus. On the one hand are those who have a vibrant faith. Paradoxically, however, those with a healthy faith response are generally outsiders, such as a leper (1:40-42), a ritually unclean hemorrhaging woman (5:34), a Syrophoenician Gentile (7:24-30), a blind man (10:52), a centurion (15:39), and so on. On the other hand, those who seemingly have all the advantages Mark pictures as deficient in faith. Thus Jesus' family (3:31-35), his fellow citizens of Nazareth (6:1-6), the Jewish religious experts (11:27-33), and even the 12 disciples lack a healthy faith. But, suggests James Edwards, "like the blind man at Bethsaida, they, too, can be made to see, but only by the sustained presence and repeated 'touch' of Jesus (8:14-26)" (Edwards, p. 17).

Unique Characteristics of Mark

Readers will find several things in Mark's Gospel that stand out stylistically. A first is that Mark's Gospel centers on Jesus as a person of action. Whereas the other three gospels focus to a large extent on His teaching, Mark is more interested in what Jesus did. He presents a fast moving narrative that more than 40 times uses the word *eutheōs* ("immediately") to link Jesus' rapid-fire actions to each other. Even when Mark tells his readers that Jesus taught, he often doesn't indicate what He said (2:13; 6:2, 6, 34; 10:1; 12:35).

A second unique characteristic of Mark is what scholars have come to know as sandwich stories. "This literary pattern," Tom Shepherd writes, "can be described as one story interrupting another, with a return to complete the first story after the conclusion of the interrupting story" (Shepherd, pp. 1, 2). Thus in Mark 5:21-43 the author embeds the healing of the woman with the issue of blood (5:25-34) between the two parts of the story of the raising of Jairus' daughter (5:21-24, 35-43). Other sandwich stories occur in Mark 3:20-35; 6:7-32; 11:12-25; 14:1-11; and 14:53-72.

A third aspect of the second Gospel that has startled readers across time is the so-called "messianic secret." The phrase gets its name from the fact that Jesus in Mark frequently commands persons to be silent regarding His true identity. Thus after certain unclean spirits referred to Jesus as the Son of God, "he strictly ordered them not to make him known" (3:11, 12, RSV). He made a similar statement to those who had witnessed the resurrection of Jairus' daughter (5:42, 43; see also 1:25, 34, 44; 7:36; 8:26, 30; 9:9).

Commentators have given three reasons for Jesus' emphasis on secrecy: (1) that He hoped to protect Himself from the false messianic expectations of those who would have liked to put Him forward as a military hero or a conquering king, (2) that Jesus knew that true faith must be based upon something deeper than a miraculous and/or sensational spectacle, and (3) that He employed the secrecy theme because it was impossible to fully understand who He was until after the crucifixion and resurrection (see Williamson, pp. 12, 13).

Structure of Mark

The structure of the second Gospel is quite straightforward. The book divides into two parts at Mark 8:27-30, in which Peter confesses that Jesus is the Christ. Up to that point the action largely takes place in Galilee and the focus is on the fact that Jesus is the Messiah. Once Peter's confession has settled that point for the disciples, the Gospel takes an entirely new direction. Immediately afterward Mark claims that "he began to teach them that the Son of man must suffer many things, and be rejected by the elders and the chief priests and the scribes, and be killed, and after three days rise again" (8:31, RSV).

The second half of the book progressively moves toward the cross. But it also falls into two parts. The first runs from Mark 8:31 through 10:52 and involves Jesus' journey to Jerusalem, centering on His three foretellings of His death and resurrection. The last part begins with the triumphal entry (11:1) and runs up through the resurrection narrative of chapter 16. Due to the clarity of the Gospel's major dividing points, R. T. France suggests that we can think of Mark's Gospel as "A Drama in Three Acts" (France, *Mark,* NIGTC, p. 11; see also Rhoads, p. 138).

Outline of Mark

I. Setting the scene (1:1-13) .
  A. Herald in the wilderness (1:1-8)
  B. Baptism in the wilderness (1:9-11)
  C. Temptation in the wilderness (1:12, 13)
II. Act I: Experiencing the blessings of God's rule—ministry in Galilee (1:14-8:30)
  A. Scene I: The beginning of preaching to the beginning of opposi-

tion (1:14-3:6)

    1. Jesus' essential message (1:14, 15)

    2. Calling the first disciples (1:16-20)

    3. Teaching and healing (1:21-45)

    4. Opposition arises (2:1-3:6)

B. Scene II: The struggle intensifies (3:7-6:6a)

    1. Teaching and healing (3:7-35)

    2. Parables of the kingdom (4:1-34)

    3. Teaching and healing (4:35-5:43)

    4. Rejection at Nazareth (6:1-6a)

C. Scene III: Moving beyond Galilee (6:6b-8:30)

    1. Teaching and miracles (6:6b-7:23)

    2. Journeying away from Jerusalem (7:24-8:21)

    3. Healing of the blind (8:22-26)

    4. Peter gains his sight (8:27-30)

III. Act II: Understanding and embracing the costs and expectations of God's rule—the road to Jerusalem (8:31-10:52)

A. Scene I: Jesus foretells His death and resurrection (8:31-9:29)

    1. The telling (8:31-9:1)

    2. The weaknesses and needs of the disciples (9:2-29)

B. Scene II: Jesus again foretells His death and resurrection (9:30-10:31)

    1. The telling (9:30-32)

    2. The weaknesses and needs of the disciples (9:33-10:31)

C. Scene III: Jesus a third time foretells His death and resurrection (10:32-52)

    1. The telling (10:32-34)

    2. The weaknesses and needs of the disciples (10:35-45)

    3. There is still hope for the blind (10:46-52)

IV. Act III: Facing persecution and death in the service of God—Jerusalem (11:1-15:47)

A. Scene I: Escalating conflict with the Jewish leaders (11:1-13:37)

    1. Challenging the establishment on its own ground (11:1-25)

    2. Jesus challenged (11:27-33)

    3. Teaching through a parable, questions, and an object lesson (12:1-44)

A Note on Authorship, Date, and Recipients

Although the Gospel itself does not claim Mark as the author, the early church unanimously agreed that it was his work. About 130 A.D. Papias, Bishop of Hierapolis, noted that "Mark, who had been Peter's interpreter, wrote down carefully, but not in order, all that he [Peter] remembered of the Lord's sayings and doings" (Papias, quoted in Eusebius, *History,* 3.39.15).

First Peter 5:13 supports the idea that Mark worked closely with Peter in Rome some time before the apostle's death. Thus we might think of Mark's Gospel as the memories of Peter as set forth by Mark under the guidance of the Holy Spirit.

The Mark under question is undoubtedly John Mark, a cousin of Barnabas (Col. 4:10) and one in whom Paul later came to depend upon (2 Tim. 4:11). The first Christians used John Mark's mother's home as a gathering place in Jerusalem (Acts 12:12). Some have conjectured that that home may have housed the upper room where Jesus ate the Passover with His disciples (Matt. 26:18; Mark 14:15). If so, Mark would have been in position to be the young man who followed Jesus with nothing "but a linen cloth about his body" on the night of His arrest (Mark 14:51, RSV).

That point cannot be proven, but the mention of a fact that is otherwise insignificant and private certainly adds force to the possibility.

Mark's Gospel was probably written between the time of Peter's death in A.D. 64 and the beginnings of hostilities between the Jews and Rome in A.D. 66.

The fact that the Gospel explains several Jewish customs and defines a few Aramaic words indicates that the book had Gentile Christians in mind. Since Mark and Peter were working together in Rome before Peter's death, many believe that Mark composed his Gospel there for the believers in the city. There are good reasons to believe that the great Roman fire of A.D. 64 may have provided the immediate setting for the writing of Mark. Rumor had fastened the blame on the Emperor Nero. "To scotch the rumour," the Roman historian Tacitus (c. A.D. 55–c. A.D. 120) tells us, "Nero substituted as culprits, and punished with the utmost refinements of cruelty, a class of men . . . whom the crowd styled Christians" (Tacitus, *Annals,* 15.44).

That passage sheds light on the situation that Mark was probably addressing if he wrote in A.D. 64-A.D. 66. The Roman church endured active persecution and martyrdom. Thus, Frederick C. Grant suggests, "Mark's purpose was . . . not historical or biographical, but it was intensely practical. He was writing a book for the guidance and support of his fellow Christians in a situation of intense crisis. The martyrdoms had fallen off, but there was no assurance—with Nero on the throne—when they might begin again; . . . every Christian's lamp must be trimmed, every Christian's loins girded for the struggle" (Grant, pp. 633, 634).

Mark's Relevance for the Twenty-first Century

Being a Christian in difficult times has never been easy. At the beginning of the twenty-first century most Christians may not face martyrdom, but they encounter threats of a more subtle type as they seek to navigate through what can easily and quickly become a hostile environment for people determined to stand for what they believe. One book points out that *"the story of Mark seeks to create ideal readers who will receive the rule of God with faith and have the courage to follow Jesus whatever the consequences"* (Rhoads, p. 138). That kind of faith is always of great value, especially when one realizes that it may be easier to stand firm on one's beliefs in a time of "war" than during a deceptively complacent "peace" when everyone is just kind of flowing with the current. Courage-developing faith is always relevant.

At the core of Mark's relevance is the theme of discipleship. He pictures the disciples as weak in faith because they were weak in understanding. That failure to understand ultimately resulted in personal failure. The disciples fell asleep when they should have been praying with Jesus (14:32-42), Peter denied his Lord in spite of his protestations (14:66-72), and all the disciples abandoned Jesus and fled (14:50). They all failed Him. Not only were they thick-headed, they were weak willed. Their failures were repeated ones.

Lamar Williamson suggests that "the disciples in Mark reflect the enthusiasms, misunderstandings, and failures characteristic" of the community that Mark was writing to "and of each succeeding generation of Christians" (Williamson, p. 16). In short, Mark's Gospel is relevant because we stand where the disciples did in being thick-headed and somewhat less than what we should be in upholding the right.

But the core of Mark's gospel (good news) message is that God didn't give up on those first disciples. To the contrary, the theme of Mark is one or repentance (1:4), believing (1:15), and receiving the kingdom of God as a child (10:15). For all who are willing to follow Jesus' first failed disciples in that process there is hope. Chapter 16 restores the failed disciples to their relationship with Him (16:7). The final note is one of grace—a grace that should empower disciples in the twenty-first century, since its lesson is that all is not lost if they fail.

The Ending of Mark

The final chapter of Mark's Gospel is problematic. The oldest and best manuscripts end abruptly at Mark 16:8. But a significant number of Greek manuscripts add verses 9-20, while other manuscripts supply a third ending to Mark.

No one knows exactly what happened to the final chapter in Mark's Gospel or how the book originally concluded (see Guthrie, pp. 89-93). The present commentary will run up through Mark 16:8, with an added section to cover verses 9-20.

List of Works Cited

Anderson, Hugh. *The Gospel of Mark*. New Century Bible Commentary. Grand Rapids: Eerdmans, 1976.

Apostolic Fathers, 2d ed. J. B. Lightfoot and J. R. Harmer, trans. Michael W. Holmes, ed. Grand Rapids: Baker, 1989.

Barclay, William. *The Gospel of Mark,* 2d ed. The Daily Study Bible. Edinburgh: Saint Andrew Press, 1956.

————. *The Gospel of Matthew,* 2 vols., 2d ed. The Daily Study Bible. Edinburgh: Saint Andrew Press, 1958.

Barrett, C. K. *The Gospel According to St John*. London: S.P.C.K., 1965.

Barth, Karl. *Church Dogmatics,* vol. 4, part 1, *The Doctrine of Reconciliation*. G. W. Bromiley, trans. Edinburgh: T. & T. Clark, 1956.

Barton, Bruce B. et al. *Mark*. Life Application Commentary. Wheaton, Ill.: Tyndale House, 1994.

Blunt, A. W. F. *The Gospel According to Saint Mark*. The Clarendon Bible. Oxford: Clarendon Press, 1947.

Bonhoeffer, Dietrich. *The Cost of Discipleship,* rev. ed. New York: Collier, 1963.

Branscomb, B. Harvie. *The Gospel of Mark*. The Moffatt New Testament Commentary. London: Hodder and Stoughton, 1937.

Bratcher, Robert G. and Eugene A. Nida. *The Gospel of Mark*. UBS Handbook Series. New York: United Bible Societies, 1961.

Brooks, James A. *Mark*. The New American Commentary. Nashville: Broadman, 1991.

Bromiley, Geoffrey W., ed. *The International Standard Bible Encyclopedia,* rev. ed., 4 vols. Grand Rapids: Eerdmans, 1979-1988.

Brown, Raymond E. *The Gospel According to John (i-xii),* 2d ed. Anchor Bible. New York: Doubleday, 1966.

Bruce, Alexander Balmain. *"To Kata Mapkon."* In *The Expositor's Greek Testament*. W. Robertson Nicoll, ed. Grand Rapids: Eerdmans, 1988, I: 341-457.

————. *The Parabolic Teaching of Christ,* 6th ed. London: Hodder and Stoughton, 1895.

Bruce, F. F. *New Testament History*. New York: Doubleday, 1980.

Chadwick, G. A. *The Gospel According to St. Mark*. The Expositor's Bible. New York: A. C. Armstrong and Son, 1905.

Charlesworth, James H., ed. *The Old Testament Pseudepigrapha,* 2 vols. New York: Doubleday, 1983, 1985.

Cole, R. Alan. *The Gospel According to Mark,* rev. ed. Tyndale New Testament Commentaries. Grand Rapids: Eerdmans, 1989.

Cranfield, C.E.B. *The Gospel According to Saint Mark.* Cambridge Greek Testament Commentary. Cambridge: Cambridge University Press, 1977.

Cullmann, Oscar. *Christ and Time: The Primitive Christian Conception of Time and History.* Floyd V. Filson, trans. Philadelphia: Westminster, 1950.

Danker, Frederick William, ed. *A Greek-English Lexicon of the New Testament and Other Early Christian Literature,* 3rd ed. Chicago: University of Chicago, 2000.

Denney, James. *The Christian Doctrine of Reconciliation.* London: James Clarke, 1959.

————. *Jesus and the Gospel: Christianity Justified in the Mind of Christ.* London: Hodder and Stoughton, 1908.

Dodd, C. H. *The Founder of Christianity.* London: Collier-Macmillan, 1970.

Dowd, Sharyn. *Reading Mark: A Literary and Theological Commentary on the Second Gospel.* Reading the New Testament Series. Macon, Ga.: Smyth and Helwys, 2000.

Edwards, James R. *The Gospel According to Mark.* The Pillar New Testament Commentary. Grand Rapids: Eerdmans, 2002.

English, Donald. *The Message of Mark: The Mystery of Faith.* The Bible Speaks Today. Downers Grove, Ill.: InterVarsity, 1992.

Erdman, Charles R. *The Gospel of Mark.* Grand Rapids: Baker, 1966.

Eusebius. *The History of the Church From Christ to Constantine.* G. A. Williamson, trans. New York: Penguin, 1965.

Evans, Craig A. *Mark 8:27-16:20.* Word Biblical Commentary. Nashville: Thomas Nelson, 2001.

Filson, Floyd V. *A Commentary on the Gospel According to St. Matthew.* Black's New Testament Commentaries. London: Adam & Charles Black, 1960.

Foerster, Werner. *From the Exile to Christ: A Historical Introduction to Palestinian Judaism.* Gordon E. Harris, trans. Philadelphia:

Fortress, 1964.

Foreman, Dale. *Crucify Him: A Lawyer Looks at the Trial of Jesus.* Grand Rapids: Zondervan, 1990.

France, R. T. *The Gospel of Mark.* Doubleday Bible Commentary. New York: Doubleday, 1998.

————. *The Gospel of Mark: A Commentary on the Greek Text.* The New International Greek Testament Commentary. Grand Rapids: Eerdmans, 2002.

Freedman, David Noel, et al. *The Anchor Bible Dictionary,* 6 vols. New York: Doubleday, 1992.

Garland, David E. *Mark.* The NIV Application Commentary. Grand Rapids: Zondervan, 1996.

Grant, Frederick C. "The Gospel According to St. Mark: Introduction and Exegesis." In *The Interpreter's Bible,* George Arthur Buttrick, ed. New York: Abingdon-Cokesbury, 1951, VII: 627-917.

Green, Joel B., Scott McKnight, and I. Howard Marshall. *Dictionary of Jesus and the Gospels.* Downers Grove, Ill.: InterVarsity, 1992.

Guelich, Robert A. *Mark 1-8:26.* Word Biblical Commentary. Dallas: Word Books, 1989.

Gundry, Robert H. *Mark: A Commentary on His Apology for the Cross.* Grand Rapids: Eerdmans, 1993.

Guthrie, Donald. *New Testament Introduction,* rev. ed. Downers Grove, Ill.: InterVarsity, 1990.

Hare, Douglas R. A. *Mark.* Westminster Bible Companion. Louisville: Westminster John Knox, 1996.

Haynes, Carlyle B. *Righteousness in Christ.* Takoma Park, Md.: Ministerial Association of Seventh-day Adventists, [1926].

Hengel, Martin. *Crucifixion in the Ancient World and the Folly of the Message of the Cross.* Philadelphia: Fortress, 1977.

Hooker, Morna D. *The Gospel According to Saint Mark.* Black's New Testament Commentaries. Peabody, Mass.: Hendrickson, 1991.

Hurtado, Larry W. *Mark.* New International Biblical Commentary. Peabody, Mass.: Hendrickson, 1989.

Johnson, Sherman E. *A Commentary on the Gospel According to St. Mark.* Harper's New Testament Commentaries. Peabody, Mass.: Hendrickson, 1988.

Jones, J. D. *The Gospel According to St Mark: A Devotional Commentary,* 4 vols. London: Religious Tract Society, 1919.

Josephus. *Complete Works.* William Whiston, trans. Grand Rapids: Kregal, 1960.

Juel, Donald H. *Mark.* Augsburg Commentary on the New Testament. Minneapolis: Augsburg, 1990.

Keener, Craig S. *The IVP Bible Background Commentary: New Testament.* Downers Grove, Ill.: InterVarsity, 1993.

Knight, George R. *Walking With Paul Through the Book of Romans.* Hagerstown, Md.: Review and Herald, 2002.

Lane, William L. *The Gospel According to Mark.* New International Commentary on the New Testament. Grand Rapids: Eerdmans, 1974.

Lenski, R.C.H. *The Interpretation of St. Mark's Gospel.* Minneapolis: Augsburg, 1961.

———. *The Interpretation of St. Matthew's Gospel.* Minneapolis: Augsburg, 1961.

Lewis, C. S. *Mere Christianity.* New York: Macmillan, 1960.

Luccock, Halford E. "The Gospel According to St. Mark: Exposition." In *The Interpreter's Bible,* George Arthur Buttrick, ed. New York: Abingdon–Cokesbury, 1951, VII: 627-917.

MacLaren, Alexander. *St. Mark, Chaps. I to VIII.* Expositions of Holy Scripture. Grand Rapids: Eerdmans, 1938.

———. *St. Mark, Chaps. IX to XVI.* Expositions of Holy Scripture. Grand Rapids: Eerdmans, 1938.

Malina, Bruce J. and Richard L. Rohrbaugh. *Social-Science Commentary on the Synoptic Gospels,* 2d ed. Minneapolis: Fortress, 2003.

Mann, C. S. *Mark: A New Translation With Introduction and Commentary.* The Anchor Bible. New York: Doubleday, 1986.

Marcus, Joel. *Mark 1-8: A New Translation With Introduction and Commentary.* Anchor Bible. New York: Doubleday, 2000.

Marshall, I. H. *St. Mark.* Scripture Union Bible Study Books. Grand Rapids: Eerdmans, 1968.

Martin, Ralph. *Mark: Evangelist and Theologian.* Grand Rapids: Zondervan, 1972.

———. *Where the Action Is: A Bible Commentary for Laymen, Mark.*

Glendale, Calif.: Regal Books, 1977.

McKenna, David L. *Mark*. The Communicator's Commentary. Waco, Tex.: Word, 1982.

Minear, Paul S. *The Gospel According to Mark*. The Layman's Bible Commentary. Richmond, Va.: John Knox, 1962.

Mishnah: A New Translation. Jacob Neusner, trans. New Haven, Conn.: Yale, 1988.

Moltmann, Jürgen. *The Crucified God: The Cross of Christ as the Foundation and Criticism of Christian Theology*. R. A. Wilson and John Bowden, trans. New York: Harper & Row, 1974.

Morgan, G. Campbell. *The Gospel According to Mark*. Old Tappan, N.J.: Fleming H. Revell, 1927.

Moloney, Francis J. *The Gospel of Mark*. Peabody, Mass.: Hendrickson, 2002.

Moule, C.F.D. *The Gospel According to Mark*. The Cambridge Bible Commentary on the New English Bible. Cambridge: Cambridge University Press, 1965.

Myers, Ched. *Binding the Strong Man: A Political Reading of Mark's Story of Jesus*. Maryknoll, N.Y.: Orbis, 1988.

Nichol, Francis D., ed. *The Seventh-day Adventist Bible Commentary,* 7 vols. Washington, D.C.: Review and Herald, 1953-1957, V: 561-660.

Nineham, D. E. *The Gospel of St Mark*. The Pelican Gospel Commentaries. Baltimore: Penguin Books, 1963.

Perkins, Pheme. "The Gospel of Mark." In *The New Interpreter's Bible,* Leander E. Keck, ed. Nashville: Abingdon, 1995, VIII: 507-733.

Philo. *The Works of Philo,* new and updated ed. C. D. Yonge, trans. Peabody, Mass.: Hendrickson, 1993.

Plummer, Alfred. *The Gospel According to St. Mark*. Grand Rapids: Baker, 1982.

Rawlinson, A.E.J. *St Mark,* 3d ed. Westminster Commentaries. London: Methuen, 1931.

Rhoads, David, Joanna Dewey, and Donald Michie. *Mark as Story: An Introduction to the Narrative of a Gospel,* 2d ed. Minneapolis: Fortress, 1999.

Ridderbos, H.N. *Matthew*. Bible Student's Commentary. Roy Togtman, trans. Grand Rapids: Zondervan, 1987.

Rogers, Cleon L., Jr. and Cleon L. Rogers III. *The New Linguistic and Exegetical Key to the Greek New Testament*. Grand Rapids: Zondervan, 1998.

Russell, D. S. *Between the Testaments*. Philadelphia: Fortress, 1960.

Ryle, J. C. *Mark*. Expository Thoughts on the Gospels. Edinburgh: Banner of Truth Trust, 1985.

Schneemelcher, Wilhelm, ed. *New Testament Apocrypha*, 2 vols., rev. ed. R. McL. Wilson, trans. Louisville: Westminster/John Knox, 1991, 1992.

Schürer, Emil. *A History of the Jewish People in the Time of Jesus Christ*, 5 vols. John MacPherson, trans. Peabody, Mass.: Hendrickson, 1998.

Schweizer, Eduard. *The Good News According to Mark*. Donald H. Madvig, trans. Atlanta: John Knox, 1970.

Shepherd, Tom. *Markan Sandwich Stories: Narration, Definition, and Function*. Berrien Springs, Mich.: Andrews University Press, 1993.

Stedman, Ray. *The Servant Who Rules: Exploring the Gospel of Mark,* vol. 1, Mark 1-8. Grand Rapids: Discovery House, 2002.

———. *The Ruler Who Serves: Exploring the Gospel of Mark,* vol. 2, Mark 8-16. Grand Rapids: Discovery House, 2002.

Stott, John R.W. *The Cross of Christ*. Downers Grove, Ill.: InterVarsity, 1986.

Tacitus. *The Annals,* books XIII-XVI. John Jackson, trans. Loeb Classical Library. Cambridge, Mass.: Harvard University Press, 1937.

Taylor, Vincent. *The Gospel According to Mark*. London: Macmillan, 1957.

Vincent, Marvin R. *Word Studies in the New Testament,* 4 vols. McLean, Va.: Macdonald, n.d.

Wessel, Walter W. "Mark." In *The Expositor's Bible Commentary*. Frank E. Gaebelein, ed. Grand Rapids: Zondervan, 1984, VIII: 601-793.

White, Ellen G. *Christ's Object Lessons*. Washington, D.C.: Review and Herald Pub. Assn., 1941.

———. *The Desire of Ages*. Mountain View, Calif.: Pacific Press Pub. Assn., 1940.

———. *Education*. Mountain View, Calif.: Pacific Press Pub. Assn., 1952.

———. *The Great Controversy Between Christ and Satan*. Mountain View, Calif.: Pacific Press Pub. Assn., 1950.

————. *Steps to Christ*. Mountain View, Calif.: Pacific Press Pub. Assn., n.d.

Williamson, Lamar, Jr. *Mark*. Interpretation: A Bible Commentary for Teaching and Preaching. Louisville: John Knox, 1983.

Witherington, Ben, III. *The Gospel of Mark: A Socio-Rhetorical Commentary*. Grand Rapids: Eerdmans, 2001.

Wuest, Kenneth S. *Wuest's Word Studies From the Greek New Testament*, 4 vols. Grand Rapids: Eerdmans, 1998.

Part I

Setting the Scene

Mark 1:1-13

1. And What Is the Gospel?

Mark 1:1
¹The beginning of the gospel of Jesus Christ, [the Son of God].

What kind of a book would you write to a group of believers facing the atrocities of Nero? The Roman historian Tacitus tells us that after Rome burned Christians "were covered with wild beasts' skins and torn to death by dogs" as public entertainment. Others were fastened to crosses and "when daylight failed were burned to serve as lamps by night" (Tacitus, *Annals,* 15.44). If you were Mark and perhaps a short time before had witnessed the martyrdom of Peter, what would you say to comfort and empower those fearing the renewal of persecution and maybe a brutal death?

Mark's answer to that question was an entirely new type of book that eventually came to be known as a gospel. Matthew, Luke, John, and others would follow Mark's lead, but he was probably the first person to develop such a document.

The word "gospel" did not signify a type of book that set forth the life and death of Jesus when Mark wrote. Rather, the word *evanggelion* had come to mean "good news." Thus in Mark's first verse *evanggelion* pointed to the content of his message rather than to its literary form. Quite literally Mark had some *good news* to share in the story of Jesus. In fact, it wasn't merely good news, it was the best of news. Paul Minear points out that "the greater the change in human affairs, the more urgent the news." If such news "offers power for men's deliverance (Rom. 1:16, ['the gospel . . . is the power of God for salvation to every one who has faith' (RSV)]), then its excellence beggars comparison" (Minear, p. 46). It is in that sense that Mark sets forth his good news. That meaning would have been obvious to anyone familiar with the Jewish Bible of Mark's day. The prophet Isaiah, for example, portrays God's servant as the anointed one who brings the gospel or good news of salvation to the afflicted (see Isa. 61:1-4).

Before leaving the word "gospel" we need to recognize that our author refers to his book's content as "the gospel of Jesus Christ" rather than as "the gospel of Mark." But even the "good news of Jesus Christ" has more than one possible meaning. It can be either the good news proclaimed *by* Jesus or the good news *about* Jesus. Both senses are true in Mark's book. Jesus is always at the center. He is both the speaker and the one spoken about.

"But," we might ask, "what did Mark see as the essential content of his 'good news'?" Much of his answer appears in his first verse, whose every word is filled with significance.

Take the word "Jesus," for example. Jesus was one of the most common first-century Jewish names. Being the Greek form of the Hebrew Joshua, it meant "Yahweh is salvation." For obvious reasons parents had selected that name ever since the Old Testament Joshua had brought his people into the Promised Land.

Thus both the meaning of the name and its historical background made it one of special significance. After all, God had sent Joshua to His people in their time of need. As R. Allan Cole points out, "What Moses could not do, Joshua would accomplish" as the ancient Israelites stood on the borders of Canaan. That made the "name 'Jesus' even more appropriate for the coming saviour" (Cole, p. 105).

A second word highlighting the essential content of Mark's good news is "Christ." We should keep in mind that people didn't consider Christ as a name when Mark wrote his book about Jesus. The person we think of as Jesus Christ was identified in His own lifetime as Jesus of Nazareth (1:9) to differentiate Him from the many others who bore the same name. Christ is equivalent to the Hebrew "Messiah," and means the "anointed one." In every other usage in Mark (8:29; 9:41; 12:35; 13:6, 21; 14:61; 15:32) Christ refers to an office, focusing on Jesus' role as the promised Messiah. It would take time for Christians to think of Jesus the *Christ* (His office) as being Jesus Christ (the person).

But the title itself had great significance to Jewish minds. They saw the Christ as the anointed person that God would send to save His people from their enemies. As you may have noticed in our discussion of the word "gospel," the word "anointed" has the significance of Savior in Isaiah 61: "The Spirit of the Lord God is upon me, because the Lord has *anointed* [the verbal form of Christ, literally christed] me to bring *good tidings* [gospel] to the afflicted; . . . to proclaim liberty to the captives, and the opening of the prison to those who are bound" (verse 1, RSV). With that perspective in mind, it is not difficult to see deep significance in Mark's words when he announces "the gospel of Jesus Christ," literally the good news of Jesus the one who would save God's people (cf. Matt. 1:21).

The Good News Is

That Jesus of Nazareth is
1. the New Testament Joshua who can take His people into the Promised Land,
2. the anointed Messiah/Christ, whom the Jews have been waiting for,
3. the divine Son of God who has the power and authority of God Himself.

A third element in Mark's understanding of the good news about Jesus is that He is the "Son of God." We should note that while it is quite probable that these words belong to verse 1, it is not absolutely certain. That is the reason for my brackets around the words in my translation. While it is true that the phrase is missing from a few early New Testament manuscripts, Ned Stonehouse makes an excellent point when he asserts that "'if these words are a gloss [scribal addition], they represent the action of a scribe who enjoyed a measure of real insight into the distinctiveness of Mark's portrayal of Christ'" (see Lane, p. 41). After all, the phrase "the Son of God" or its equivalent shows up repeatedly throughout the second gospel in such places as Mark 1:11; 3:11; 5:7; 9:7; 12:6; 13:32; 14:36, 61; 15:39.

The juxtaposition of the title of Christ with the idea of Jesus as the Son of God is important in understanding Mark's Gospel. Whereas Jewish writings tended to view the anointed one in terms of a human warrior king

juxtaposition - the state of being close together or side by side - especially for comparison or contrast

37

in the line of David, this earliest of the gospel portrayals of Jesus sets forth God's anointed as a divine being—"the Son of God."

As a result, from the very first verse in Mark, the biblical author gives his readers privileged information. They know from the beginning who Jesus is. That information, however, is not immediately available to the participants in the story that follows. They will only gradually come to the conclusions that readers understand from the start. The first great climactic point in the book occurs when Peter recognizes that Jesus is the Christ (8:29), the second when the Roman centurion proclaims at the foot of the cross that "truly this man was the Son of God" (15:39, RSV).

Thus Mark's readers stand on vantage ground as they watch the story's characters struggle with the identity of Jesus and how they should relate to Him. But for the readers the issues should be clear. They need to devote their lives to Jesus because He is no less than the Messiah and God's own son.

A final expression that we need to examine before moving on into Mark's gospel is "the beginning." Minear appears to be correct when he notes that we should not restrict those words to Mark's introduction. To the contrary, "Mark considered the entire series of events" recorded in his gospel "as 'the beginning.'" The beginning was "everything which led up to the proclamation of the gospel by the Apostles. The point where he ended his story was the point where the Apostles began to shout their personal testimony that this crucified Man had now been revealed as the Messiah. In this sense Mark may have wished to remind his readers of that other Genesis: 'In the beginning God created the heavens and the earth.' God had begun" through Jesus "a new thing in creating a new humanity, yes, even a new heaven and a new earth (Rev. 21:1). Understood against this background," Mark's first verse "makes a tremendous assertion" (Minear, pp. 47, 48).

That verse is not only a "tremendous assertion," but it was one that would bring comfort to Mark's readers—not only those being persecuted by Nero but all those down through the ages who would read the second gospel's portrayal of the good news.

2. The King's Herald

Mark 1:2–8

²As it is written in Isaiah the prophet: "Behold, I send My messenger ahead of You, who will prepare Your way; ³a voice crying in the wilderness: 'Prepare the way of the Lord, make His paths straight.' "

⁴John came baptizing in the wilderness and proclaiming a baptism of repentance for forgiveness of sins. ⁵And all those of the Judean countryside and all those in Jerusalem went out to him and, confessing their sins, were baptized by him in the Jordan River. ⁶Now John was clothed with camel's hair, had a leather belt around his waist, and ate locusts and wild honey. ⁷And he preached, saying, "After me comes One stronger than I, the thong of whose sandals I am not worthy to loosen. ⁸I baptize you with water, but He will baptize you with the Holy Spirit."

The fact that Mark's second and third verses are a quotation from the Old Testament is significant in that it serves as a reminder that Christianity was not a new religion but a development from within Judaism. As one author puts it, "Jesus is not an afterthought of God, as though an earlier plan of salvation had gone awry. Rather, Jesus stands in continuity with the work of God in Israel, the fulfiller of the law and the prophets (Matt 5:17)" (Edwards, p. 28).

The quotation itself is actually a composite of three Old Testament texts—Exodus 23:20, Malachi 3:1, and Isaiah 40:3. All three passages center on preparing the way of the coming One.

Several things stand out about this composite passage. The first is that it is the only occasion (unlike Matthew) in which Mark himself speaks of the fulfillment of Old Testament prophecy. All other references occur in the sayings of Jesus (see Hooker, p. 34). Thus the quotation must have an especially important message for Mark's readers, since he gives it such a prominent position.

We miss the point of the composite passage if we merely see it as pointing to the ministry of John, who in turn directs us to the coming of the Christ. It does that, but it does something else of even greater importance. A careful reader of the Malachi and Isaiah passages, for example, will notice that the Lord of Isaiah is identified as none other than God and that the messenger of Malachi is preparing the way for God Himself. Those facts indicate that John is not simply preparing the way for a kinglike messiah but for God Himself, appearing as Jesus of Nazareth. Thus the quotation reinforces the claims of verse 1 from the Old Testament.

Of course, it also identified the messenger, since on the basis of Malachi 4:5 a widespread expectation had developed in Judaism that Elijah would return as a forerunner of God's coming kingdom. Thus it is no accident that the Baptist arrived on the scene wearing "a garment of haircloth, with a girdle of leather" as did the Elijah of the Old Testament (2 Kings 1:8, RSV).

The very description of John portrays him as a person in protest of the status quo. Avoiding the luxury of the city for the brutal desert near the Dead Sea, he had given up fine clothes and ate a restricted diet of locusts and wild honey. The word translated as locusts has two possible meanings. The first is a grasshopperlike insect that Leviticus 11:22, 23 declared clean, while the second was a kind of bean (carob) that served as food for the very poorest people.

It was such a man that, Mark tells us, "all those of the Judean countryside and all those in Jerusalem" went out to see (1:5). Now it is unlikely that "all" went out to see John in the sense of every last person in Judea and Jerusalem. Mark appears to be using hyperbole. Yet, suggests Morna Hooker, Mark's "exaggeration . . . should not be dismissed as mere hyperbole. The words indicate the accomplishment of John's task; sufficient representatives of the nation heard the message of John for it to be said that he had completed his work and prepared the people for the coming of God in judgement and salvation" (Hooker, p. 37). John's popularity, first-century Jewish historian Josephus tells us, was even felt by Herod, "who feared lest the great influence John had over the people might put it into his power and inclination to raise a rebellion" (Josephus, *Antiquities,* 18.5.2).

But a man like John wasn't after Herod's throne—he sought his soul. No one could see or hear John the Baptist and view him as anything but counter-cultural. He not only looked the part but he had a counter-cultural message—one just as needed in the twenty-first century as in the first. Central to that message was John's call to repent. Repentance is one of those religious words that is easy for people to throw around without their really coming to grips with its meaning. Most people confuse feeling sorry for their sins with repentance. As Ellen White points out, "multitudes sorrow that they have sinned and even make an outward reformation because they fear that their wrongdoing will bring suffering upon themselves. But this is not repentance in the Bible sense. They lament the suffering rather than the sin" (White, *Steps to Christ*, p. 23).

Halford Luccock has it right when he writes that "repentance, in John's preaching, was a thoroughgoing change, as is all true repentance. The word is a strong one—'a new mind.' It calls for a rightabout-face, a will turned in a new direction. Hence repentance is always more than penitence. It is not remorse; not admitting mistakes; not saying in self-condemnation, 'I have been a fool.' Who has not recited such dismal rituals? They are common and easy. This is more. It is more even than being 'sorry' for one's sins. It is a moral and spiritual revolution.

"For that reason to repent genuinely is one of the hardest things in the world; yet it is basic to all spiritual change and progress. It calls for the complete breakdown of pride, of self-assurance, of the prestige that comes from success, and of that inmost citadel which is self-will" (Luccock, p. 649).

With the call to repentance John hit at the root of the sin problem. He had a message for both the Pharisee and the outward sinner. It applied not only to first-century people, but also to Pharisees (nice church people) and/or blatant sinners living 20 centuries later.

The second element in John's message is confession. Once again we are dealing with a religious concept that calls for both heart searching and change.

True confession is not merely people saying that they are sorry to God. To the contrary, it begins with our individual selves. The first step in confession is for me to confess to myself. It is to be honest with myself and to admit that I really did do wrong, that what I did was serious, and that I need God's forgiving grace in my life. The initial step in true confession is to come to grips with myself. "Someone," writes William Barclay, "tells of a man's first step to grace. As he was shaving one morning he looked at his own face in the mirror, and suddenly said, 'You dirty, little rat!'" (Barclay, *Mark*, p. 4).

A second aspect of confession is to go to those whom we have wronged. All too many people assume that they can confess to God without making things right with other people. They need to wake up and listen to the message of John the Baptist. Of course, it is a humbling experience to tell another person that we are sorry. But that humility is just what we need.

A third aspect of confession is going before God. One of the great promises of the New Testament is that "if we confess our sins, he is faithful and just to forgive us our sins, and to cleanse us from all unrighteousness" (1 John 1:9, KJV).

The need to be baptized was also an important element in John's message. What was especially surprising to the Jews was that he suggested that they needed to be baptized. The Jews of Christ's day knew that Gentiles required baptism to become a part of God's people, but believed they had no such need, since they were already children of Abraham.

Wrong! says John. Even religious people must come to God and repent and confess their sins and then be washed clean symbolically in the waters of baptism. All need to be buried in the watery grave and be raised to a new life in Christ (see Rom. 6:1-4).

The explicitness of John's message may have shocked the first-century Jews, but he could draw a crowd because they sensed their own need. Beyond that, he practiced what he preached. He had given up worldly symbols for a counter-cultural set of values. And he didn't merely speak about humbling himself before God, but, unlike those who were proud of their position or their possessions or their religion, he claimed that he wasn't even worthy to perform the duty of a slave—the task of loosening the laces of the Master's sandal (Mark 1:7).

John's message, if people take it seriously, is not one of comfort. We don't like to hear the kind of things the Baptist proclaimed. But it is a message that we need to take to our hearts. And it will be one that Jesus picks up as He supercedes His forerunner in the rest of Mark's Gospel.

3. The King's Anointing and Testing

Mark 1:9-13

⁹*In those days Jesus came from Nazareth of Galilee and was baptized in the Jordan by John. ¹⁰And immediately coming up out of the water He saw the heavens being opened and the Spirit like a dove descending into Him; ¹¹and a voice out of the heavens declared, "You are My beloved Son, in You I am well pleased." ¹²And the Spirit immediately drove Him into the wilderness. ¹³And He was in the wilderness forty days being tempted by*

Satan; and He was with the wild beasts, and the angels ministered to Him.

That passage is vintage Mark. It is short, crisp, clean, and to the point. Unlike Matthew or Luke, Mark has no genealogy of Jesus, no wise men traveling from afar, no angels rejoicing, no stories of young Jesus in the Temple. In Mark Jesus appears like a bolt of lightening out of the blue. That conciseness is an outstanding characteristic of Mark throughout his book.

I suppose that if you or I were writing the gospel story we would be quite precise and accurate in dating the event that changed the world. But not Mark. He merely says, "in those days" (1:9). His main concern is not to tell us the day or the year in which Jesus began His ministry, but rather to show the all-important connection between Him and the ministry of John the forerunner. Mark was following the earlier preaching of Peter to Cornelius, in which he began with "the baptism which John preached" and then moved on to "how God anointed Jesus of Nazareth with the Holy Spirit and with power" (Acts 10:37, 38, RSV).

Unlike Matthew, Mark seems to have no difficulty with Jesus undergoing John's baptism of repentance even though Jesus had no need to repent. We don't find John saying that he needs to be baptized by Jesus or Jesus even giving a reason for His baptism (see Matt. 3:14, 15). Rather, Mark in rapid strokes wants to get his readers to the important thing—the events surrounding the baptism of Jesus.

He lists three such events: (1) the opening of the heavens and the descent of the Holy Spirit, (2) the voice coming from heaven affirming Jesus as the Son of God, and (3) the Spirit driving Jesus into the wilderness to do battle with Satan.

The opening of the heavens is very important in the context of first-century Judaism, because people believed that after the last of the Old Testament prophets some 400 years before God had ceased speaking directly to His people (see 1 Macc. 4:46; 9:27; 14:41). Thus the opening of the heavens at the baptism of Jesus symbolized the long-awaited return of God's Spirit. The Testament of Levi had foreshadowed the entire sequence some 250 years earlier, in which we read of "a new priest to whom all the words of the Lord will be revealed. . . . The heavens will be opened, and from the temple of glory sanctification will come upon him, with a fatherly voice, as from Abraham to Isaac. And the glory of the Most High shall burst forth upon him. And the spirit of understanding and sanctification shall rest upon him" (Test. of Lev. 18:2, 6, 7).

In short, the Jews of the first century were ripe for the message unfolded in Mark 1:9–11. Mark's description is rich in biblical symbolism. The heavens (plural) were more than the sky. Paul in 2 Corinthians 12:2 speaks of ascending in vision to the third heaven. "Heavens" in Mark 1:10 not only implies the descent of the Spirit through the sky but that God had sent Him from the divine throne room in the heavenly temple. It implies that communication is being reopened between heaven and earth, between God and His people.

The imagery of the dove was also meaningful to those familiar with the Jewish Scriptures. Most immediately, perhaps, is the recollection of Genesis 8, in which the dove brings glad tidings to Noah after the flood. The Jews of the first century had come to believe that the Holy Spirit's descent would inaugurate the Messianic Age.

The Old Testament describes the Spirit as resting on prophets, kings, and other leaders to give them power to accomplish their various tasks. Thus it was in the cases of Gideon (Judges 6:34), Samson (Judges 15:14), and Saul (1 Sam. 10:6). Time after time in the Old Testament individuals began their work for God after the Spirit rested upon them. The Psalms of Solomon (a Jewish writing probably written in the first century before Christ) applies the empowerment of the Spirit to the coming Messiah. In describing the future king the author says that "God made him powerful in the holy spirit and wise in the counsel of understanding, with strength and righteousness" (Ps. of Sol. 17:37). From that perspective the coming of the Holy Spirit to the Messiah would be to equip Him and empower Him for His mission. So it was in the life of Jesus.

The "voice out of the heavens" declaring Jesus to be God's Son with whom He was well pleased (Mark 1:11) also raised specific ideas from the Old Testament in the minds of first-century Jewish readers. The quotation regarding Jesus was a fusion of two Old Testament verses—Psalm 2:7 and Isaiah 42:1. All Jews, except the Sadducees, accepted Psalm 2 with its declaration "You are my son, today I have begotten you" (RSV) as a description of the coming Messiah. The quotation from Isaiah 42 ("in you I am well pleased") begins a passage on the Servant of Yahweh, whose destiny is to suffer abuse and opposition, climaxing in the great Messianic chapter

53. With those facts in mind, William Barclay concludes that "in the baptism there came to Jesus two certainties—the certainty that He was indeed the chosen One of God, and the certainty that the way in front of Him was the way of the Cross. In that moment He knew that He was chosen to be King, but He also knew that His throne must be a Cross" (Barclay, *Matthew,* vol. I, p. 53).

> ## The Voice From Heaven
> ## Revealed Two Things to Jesus
>
> 1. That He was the Son of God
> 2. That His throne would be a cross

"To no prophet," writes James Edwards, "had words been spoken such as the words to Jesus at the baptism. Abraham was a friend of God (Isa 41:8), Moses a servant of God (Deut 34:5), Aaron a chosen one of God (Ps 105:26), David a man after God's own heart (1 Sam 13:14), and Paul an apostle (Rom 1:1)." But "only Israel (Exod 4:23)—and the king as Israel's leader (Ps 2:7)—had been called God's Son before. But where Israel failed, Jesus takes its place" (Edwards, p. 38).

Jesus' baptism was a pivotal event in His life, empowering Him to meet Satan on his own ground, not only in the wilderness temptation, but throughout His ministry. It is no accident that when the Sanhedrin later asks Jesus by what authority He acted, He referred His questioners back to John's baptism (Mark 11:27-33).

Immediately after the baptism, Mark tells us, the Holy Spirit compelled Jesus to go into the wilderness. He proceeds with two thoughts in His mind: (1) that He is God's Son, and (2) that His life will be one of conflict. That struggle not only begins right away but it takes place on Satan's turf—the wilderness, a region filled with wild beasts.

From the beginning the newly anointed Jesus will have to do combat with the devil. And throughout His life the conflict would be a lonely one. In every one of the crisis points in His life Jesus had to face the evil one alone, even though He wanted His disciples to stand firmly behind Him.

Unlike Matthew and Luke, Mark doesn't describe Satan's three temptations. The major lesson we should derive from Mark's brief description of the temptation is that Jesus was totally triumphant over the devil. And

His victory was strategic since "that victory assured triumph in temptations and battles which were to follow." The wilderness battle as Mark describes it was an extended one (40 days), but "after this victory Jesus was qualified to wrest other men from Satan's grasp. He could now command the demons and they would recognize his authority. The descent of power from God had thus precipitated a challenge to the only other ultimate power-center in human affairs and had accomplished a victory" which would extend throughout the second Gospel (Minear, p. 52).

The conflict theme that begins with the temptation of Mark 1:12, 13 consistently depicts Jesus as being victorious. That is true even when it looked as if Satan had gotten the upper hand at the cross. But the gospel story ends with a resurrection not a death. Thus the One who conquered Satan in the wilderness would eventually be able to say, "I am he that liveth, and was dead; and behold, I am alive for evermore, Amen; and have the keys of hell and of death" (Rev. 1:18, KJV).

The story of Jesus' anointing and temptation was pregnant with meaning for the fearful believers of Mark's day. After all, they had been baptized with the same Spirit as Jesus, they belonged to the family of God's Son, they were struggling with the same tempter as Jesus, and they could look forward to the same victory if they remained united to Him. That same scenario remains true for those of us who follow Him 2,000 years later.

Before moving away from the temptation, we should look at one phrase in Mark that is absent in Matthew's and Luke's accounts of the temptation: "He was with the wild beasts, and the angels ministered to Him" (Mark 1:13). The author may have had Nero's brutal persecutions in mind in choosing that illustration. If that was the case, Mark may have included "the unusual phrase 'with the wild beasts' in order to remind his Roman readers that Christ, too, was thrown to wild beasts, and as the angels ministered to him, so, too, will they minister to Roman readers facing martyrdom" (Edwards, p. 41).

That same logic has strengthened believers down through history as they have faced such beasts as those portrayed in Daniel 7 and Revelation 13. God's people may go through difficult times, but He does not abandon them. As Ray Stedman so nicely puts it, "Jesus had no human companionship or help. The only voice He heard in the wilderness was the voice of the enemy. Yet He was not alone" (Stedman, *Servant Who Rules,* p. 39).

Part II

Act One

Experiencing the
Blessings of God's Rule

Mark 1:14–8:30

4. The Essence of the Gospel

Mark 1:14, 15
¹⁴Now after John was imprisoned, Jesus came into Galilee preaching the gospel of God, ¹⁵saying, "The time has been fulfilled and the kingdom of God has drawn near; repent and believe in the gospel."

It is easy for the casual reader of the gospels to overlook the fact that Mark has left out more than a full year of Jesus' ministry between verses 13 and 14. That year included the miracle at the wedding at Cana (John 2:1-2), His encounter with Nicodemus (3:1-15), Jesus' conversation with the woman at the well (4:7-42), and other events recorded in the fourth gospel. As with Jesus' genealogy and His birth narrative, on which Mark is silent, the second Gospel has not one word about Jesus' first year of ministry, part of which took place in Judea. The Gospel of John tells us Jesus departed for Galilee after people began to see Him and John the Baptist as rivals (4:1-3). Subsequent to that time the local authorities arrested John the Baptist. Mark picks up the story of Jesus at that point (Mark 1:14).

The summary of Jesus' message as recorded in verse 15 lists four elements. The first two are statements of fact while the last two are commands.

    A. Statements of fact
        1. the time has been fulfilled
        2. the kingdom of God has drawn near
    B. Commands
        1. repent
        2. believe in the gospel or good news

Regarding the phrase "the time has been fulfilled," the Greek word used for time indicates a definite point of time. Oscar Cullmann tells us that *"kairos* in secular usage is the moment in time which is especially favorable for an undertaking; it is the point of time of which one has long before spoken without knowing its actual date; it is the fixed day, which in modern jargon, for example, is called D day" (Cullmann, p. 39).

"Of what 'time' did Jesus speak as being 'fulfilled'?" asks Paul Minear. "The time of sin and sorrow, the time of patient waiting and penitent preparation, the time of crucial decision and risk, the time which God had determined and promised, the time when he would bring final judgment and mercy to the earth" (Minear, p. 53).

To the Jewish mind that special time was the dawning of the Messianic Age. Or, as Raymond Cottrell put it, the people understood Jesus' announcement that "the time has been fulfilled" "as a declaration that the Messianic kingdom was about to be set up" (Nichol, vol. 5, p. 568).

The time prophecies of Daniel 9:24-27 had stimulated some of the excitement regarding the time element. Discussing the 70 weeks of years, the passage indicated the time for the coming of "the Messiah the Prince," who would "make reconciliation for iniquity" and "bring in everlasting righteousness" (KJV). The Babylonian Talmud (see b. Sanhedrin, 97a, b) has preserved some discussion on the topic. And Paul appears to be alluding to the same type of thinking when he wrote that "when the time had fully come, God sent forth his Son" (Gal. 4:4, RSV).

Jesus' second statement of fact in Mark 1:15, "the kingdom of God has drawn near," harmonized with the messianic understanding of Daniel 9. Most Jews of the day would have had no problems with those concepts and their relationships. But they would have had a great deal of difficulty with Jesus' understanding of the kingdom. They expected a Messiah-King who would sit on David's throne and act as a military conqueror who would vanquish Israel's enemies. The intertestamental Psalms of Solomon spoke to them of such a king, who would not only be endowed with supernatural gifts, but "with an iron rod" he shall "shatter all their substance" and "destroy the unlawful nations with the word of his mouth" (Ps. of Sol. 17:24, 25).

With such expectations in their minds, it is little wonder that the first century Jewish leaders had such a difficult time accepting Jesus as the Messiah. After all, His command was not to gird on their swords but to repent and believe. The working out of the nature of Christ's kingdom and Jewish understandings and misunderstandings of His message will be central to the rest of the Gospel of Mark.

But before we explore that we need to examine the two commands that stand at the heart of Jesus' gospel message. The first is "repent."

The word "repentance" translates the Greek word *metanoia*. It stands for a change of mind. But the human heart can be very deceptive. As William Barclay notes, "we are very apt to confuse two things—sorrow for the consequences of sin, and sorrow for sin. There is many a man who is desperately sorry because of the mess that sin has got him into, but that man very well knows that, if he could be reasonably sure that he could escape the consequences, he would do the same thing again. It is not the sin that he hates; it is the consequences of the sin. But real repentance means that a man has come, not only to be sorry for the consequences of his sin, but to hate sin itself. . . . Repentance means that the man who was in love with sin comes to hate sin because of its exceeding sinfulness" (Barclay, *Mark*, p. 17).

Christian Essentials

"Let us ask ourselves what we know of this repentance and faith. Have we felt our sins, and forsaken them? . . . We may reach heaven without learning, or riches, or health, or worldly greatness. But we shall never reach heaven, if we die impenitent and unbelieving" (Ryle, p. 8).

True repentance stood at the center of the messages of both John the Baptist and of Jesus. Unfortunately, their generation didn't like the idea any better than ours. Both men would eventually be put to death for their insistence that men and women needed to turn away from those sins that were destroying them—whether sins of the spirit, as in Jesus' clashes with the Jewish leaders, or sins of the flesh, such as in John's conflict with Herodias over her irregular marriage.

We humans hate nothing so much as a call to genuine repentance, a summons to give up those sins that we love so much. We are much happier with the superficial attitude satirized in a rewriting of the "'Prayer of General Confession' from the *Old Book of Common Prayer:* 'Benevolent and easy-going Father: we have occasionally been guilty of errors of judgment. We have lived under the deprivations of heredity and the disadvantages of environment. We have sometimes failed to act in accordance with common sense. We have done the best we could in the circumstances; and have been careful not to ignore the common standards of decency; and we are glad to think that we are fairly normal. Do thou, O Lord, deal lightly with our infrequent lapses. Be thy own sweet Self with those who admit they are not perfect; According to the unlimited tolerances which we have a right to expect from thee. And grant us as indulgent Parent that we may hereafter continue to live a harmless and happy life and keep our self-respect" (David Head in *Garland,* p. 65).

Now that is what most people would like to hear. But it wasn't the message of Jesus and John. For them sin was serious, it was deadly, and it needed to be renounced.

That is exactly where the second command of Mark 1:15 comes in. Jesus not only warned about the very real dangers of sin, but He pointed beyond sin and repentance to the solution to the problem. If Christ's first command in Mark 1:15 is to *turn away from sin* in repentance, His second command is to *turn to* belief in the gospel.

In His second command Jesus moved beyond John. The Baptist presented repentance, but Jesus preached repentance as a step toward belief in the all-important good news. And what is that good news? Mark will illustrate it throughout his gospel. At this point we will take but a peek at its content.

The good news is

- that the kingdom of God has come
- that God is with us in Jesus
- that God cares for us
- that Jesus can heal us both physically and spiritually
- that Jesus has gained the victory over sin and its results
- that in Jesus we have hope, peace of mind, and eternal life.

That is good news. It is that news that Mark's Gospel is all about. And it is that news that Jesus wants us to accept today.

5. A Glimpse of Discipleship

Mark 1:16-20

[16]And going along by the Sea of Galilee, He saw Simon and Andrew (Simon's brother) casting a net in the sea, for they were fishermen. [17]And Jesus said to them, "Follow Me, and I will make you become fishers of men." [18]Immediately, leaving their nets, they followed Him. [19]Going a little farther, He saw James the son of Zebedee and John his brother in their boat mending the nets. [20]Immediately He called them; and leaving their father Zebedee in the boat with the hired servants they followed after Him.

He saw."

Simple words, but full of meaning.

What did Jesus see?

I tell you what I see. I see nothing outstanding. Just four fishermen. Smelly, coarsely dressed, unlearned, rough men. I see one who has small ears and a big mouth. A mouth so big that Peter would be speaking when he should have been listening to the priceless words of Jesus. I see a man who would be forward to brag about his braveness and about his place in the world, but one who would be backward when Jesus needed him most.

And then I see James and John, men much the same as Peter, but ill tempered. So much so that they carried the nickname of Boanerges, meaning "sons of thunder" (Mark 3:17). They were so incensed on one occasion that they were willing to destroy a whole village of Samaritans merely because its inhabitants were inhospitable to Jesus (Luke 9:54). And when it came to worldly ambition they were not a wit behind Peter in seeking the most prestigious places in Christ's kingdom, even getting their mother (Jesus' aunt [cf. Mark 15:40; Matt. 27:56; John 19:25]) to plead for the two most important positions (Matt. 20:20, 21). As for being supportive of Jesus, though, they along with Peter would sleep in Gethsemane and would later leave Him to His lonely fate after the Romans took Him captive (Mark 14:50).

What do I see of encouragement and quality? Not much.

But what did Jesus see? He observed four men who could be molded and shaped to be mighty preachers of His gospel. He perceived Peter transformed into a pillar of strength and John becoming the most loving and most caring of people. Jesus saw what we cannot see. Ellen White put it nicely when she wrote that "in every human being He discerned infinite possibilities. He saw men as they might be, transfigured by His grace" (White, *Education,* p. 80).

The words "He saw" contain a hidden lesson. Jesus saw what other people did, but He saw more. While He noticed men at work in fishing boats, He also saw what such men could become.

The good news is that He still sees. He sees you and I with all our disabilities and problems and insufficiencies. But that is not all that He observes. He sees us fully transformed by His grace into powerful and skillful participants in His cause. He doesn't see us as we are but as we can be through His transforming and empowering grace as it acts upon our lives.

We can be thankful that "He saw." But we can also be thankful that He still sees. Even the words "He saw" have gospel in them.

But Jesus didn't merely see Peter, Andrew, John, and James. He also summoned them to follow Him.

A careless reading of the gospel stories might give us the impression that the calling came about from a chance meeting as Jesus just happened to be strolling by the seashore. But that is not the case. A process of knowing, growing, and maturing had taken place before the call. We get a glimpse of that earlier experience in John's Gospel. Some of these men had been John the Baptist's disciples. They had heard the Baptist declare that Jesus was the "Lamb of God" (John 1:29). At that point they had followed Him for a time. One of those men was Andrew and the other was undoubtedly John the son of Zebedee. Soon after Andrew told his brother (Simon Peter) that he had found the Messiah (verses 35-42). Beyond that, prior to their official call, these men had witnessed such miracles as Jesus turning the water into wine in Cana (2:1, 2).

They had known Jesus and He had known them. Their call was part of a developing relationship—a relationship that will continue to mature throughout Mark's Gospel.

The invitation of Jesus, our text points out, was not a summons to privilege and ease, but to service. He called them to perform a task that would occupy them for the rest of their lives. At least two of them (James and Peter) would suffer an early death for His sake and one of them (John), tradition tells us, was dipped into a pot of boiling oil before being exiled to Patmos. There would be a cost to their discipleship—and that price would not be light.

The purpose of their calling was to make them fishers of men. Note that Jesus did not summon them merely to sit in church, read their Bibles, or only to organize and administrate. Rather, He called them to catch men and women—an evangelistic responsibility. That is the calling of every disciple—even of those of us who follow 2,000 years later. It is "strange," Halford Luccock points out, "that such a clear, commanding invitation should ever be obscured! But it has been, time and again. The evangelistic purpose of the Christian fellowship, the priority of the fishing business, can easily go into low visibility. When that great 'first' becomes a second or a third" to even good churchly causes "a benumbing sterility strikes the church" (Luccock, p. 658).

Our short passage has still another lesson hidden away in it. Jesus called fishers of fish to become fishers of people. Here we have a truth that needs to be remembered. When a person comes to Jesus, He uses our natural and acquired talents. Our past skills and talents will not be discarded when we become disciples of Christ. Just as He employed fishermen to fish for people, so He can use the skills of writers, physicians, teachers, and carpenters in His service. While Christ's followers may have different skills, one thing is certain, and that is that every disciple has something in them that God can use to build up the kingdom evangelistically. J. D. Jones points out that when Jesus summons a person He "dignifies and exalts" their calling. "Notice, Christ does not destroy, He converts. He does not destroy the qualities of watchfulness and alertness these men had gained by their business as fishermen. He turns them to higher uses, 'Henceforth ye shall catch *men*'" (Jones, vol. 1, p. 33).

Verse 20 tells us that James and John abandoned "their father Zebedee in the boat" and "they followed after Him." All four of the disciples in Mark 1:16-20 left something behind. For Peter, Andrew, and the Zebedees it was their boats, their livelihood, and, in one sense, their families. They did not join up with Jesus with the attitude that "we will try this for a while to see if it works out." To the contrary, their discipleship had a finality about it. They left all to follow Him.

Discipleship is still a series of leavings. For some of us it is jobs, for others it is friends, and for yet others it may be prejudices. There can be no real following without a real leaving.

We need to examine yet one more aspect of discipleship. Jesus told His first disciples that if they would follow Him, He would "make" them "fishers of men" (1:17). The good news is that as disciples we are never really alone. The Master who calls also equips His disciples. Jesus would spend several years teaching His first followers so that they might be prepared for the task that He set before them. A careful reading of Mark's gospel reveals that in one sense it is the story of the development of the disciples as they progress from inadequacy to adequacy. The large proportion of the results of all Jesus' labor, of course, would come after Pentecost. We can see Mark's gospel as an illustration of discipling in action as Jesus prepares His followers to do His work. And that discipling didn't stop with the end of the gospel story. It goes on to the end of time and includes every person that has ever responded to the call of Christ.

"He saw."

He still sees.

Part of the good news is that if Jesus could work through those four fishermen, then He can just as certainly use you and me. In them He saw infinite potential. That, it seems, is not so difficult for us to grasp. But that He recognizes the same potential in us tends to stretch our imaginations to the breaking point. But it is true. He still sees. And it is us that He sees. It is us whom He is calling this very day. We are left with the nagging question as to how we will respond. And there exist only two answers—yes or no!

6. A Show of Authority

Mark 1:21-28

²¹And they went into Capernaum, and immediately on the Sabbath He entered into the synagogue and began to teach. ²²They were astounded at His teaching; for He taught them as one having authority and not as the scribes. ²³And at once there was in their synagogue a man with an unclean spirit, and he cried out, ²⁴saying, "What do You want with us, Jesus of Nazareth? Have You come to destroy us? I know who You are, the Holy One of God." ²⁵Jesus rebuked him, saying, "Be quiet and come out of him." ²⁶And the un-

clean spirit, convulsing him and shouting with a loud voice, came out of him. [27]And all were amazed, so that they discussed with one another, saying, "What is this? A new teaching with authority! He commands the unclean spirits and they obey Him." [28]And at once the report of Him went out everywhere into all the surrounding countryside of Galilee.

According to Matthew 4:13 and 9:1, Capernaum became Jesus' residence after His leaving Nazareth. Located on the northwestern shore of the Sea of Galilee (see map on p. 14), Capernaum was the largest of the fishing villages surrounding the lake. A village of some importance, it had both a customhouse (Matt. 9:9) and a Roman garrison. The garrison's captain was especially friendly to the Jews, even going so far as to build a synagogue for them (Matt. 8:5-13; Luke 7:1-10). Not only was Capernaum the home of Simon Peter and Andrew (Mark 1:29; Luke 4:38), but it was the place where Matthew received his call as he served as a tax collector (Matt. 9:9-13; Mark 2:14-17; Luke 5:27-32). Jesus would perform many miracles in Capernaum and do a great deal of teaching there, but He made little impression on its people (Matt. 11:23, 24; Luke 10:15).

The Bible does not tell us why Jesus made His headquarters in Capernaum. Perhaps it was because some of His earliest disciples lived there. Then again, Capernaum was fairly well isolated from the centers of power in both Judea and in Galilee. Herod Antipas' arrest of John the Baptist (Mark 1:14; 6:14-29) made that last consideration a significant one.

Mark 1:21 tells us that Jesus went to the Jewish synagogue on the Sabbath and began to teach. The synagogue was the center of Judaism in the local community. One was to be established where there were at least 10 adult Jewish males to form its board of rulers or elders.

We should not confuse the synagogue with the Temple in Jerusalem. The priests offered sacrifices in the Temple, and all Jewish males were to attend the Temple services for several of the major feasts during the year, Passover being the most well known.

By way of contrast, the Jews offered no sacrifices in the synagogue. Rather, they were places of teaching and instruction. Many scholars believe that the first synagogues originated during the Babylonian exile, when the Jerusalem Temple lay in ruins. They became a permanent fixture among the Jews after the return from captivity (see F. F. Bruce, pp. 143-148).

One of the interesting things about the synagogues is that they had no professional clergy. While the Temple and its ritual services were under the supervision of the Aaronic priests, no clerical control existed in the local synagogues. As Werner Foerster points out, "there were no professional readers and preachers. Anyone could read and address a word to the congregation. The ruler of the synagogue was responsible both for appointing the reader and for outward order (Acts 13:15)" (Foerster, p. 145).

That circumstance made the synagogue a natural place for persons with a message from God to begin their proclamation. Not only were God's people assembled there, but the very purpose of the institution was the reading and explanation of the Jewish Scripture. Jesus, even at this early stage in His ministry, had acquired a reputation for being a man with a message. It was only natural, in the period before opposition to Him hardened, that He would receive invitations to read the Scripture lesson and present His message.

But when Jesus taught, His hearers soon discovered that He was not like the usual teachers. Rather, "they were astounded. . . ; for He taught them as one having authority and not as the scribes" (Mark 1:22).

Please note that Mark tells us on this occasion that Jesus taught but that he doesn't indicate what He said. As C.E.B. Cranfield points out, "compared with the other evangelists, Mark does not give much of the actual teaching of Jesus" even though, like them, he lays "very great stress on Jesus' teaching ministry" (Cranfield, p. 72). Mark uses the verb "to teach" 16 times and the noun "teacher" 11 times.

In Mark 1:22 the author is not so concerned with reporting what Jesus presented but that He did so with such authority that it amazed the people. Mark goes on to indicate that one reason they were astounded is that He did not teach like the scribes. Perhaps the best insight into the meaning here is to go to the Sermon on the Mount as reported by Matthew. There we find a similar saying: "And when Jesus finished these sayings, the crowds were astonished at his teaching, for he taught them as one who had authority, and not as their scribes" (Matt. 7:28, 29, RSV). The difference between Mark and Matthew's reporting of the same idea is that Matthew demonstrates how Jesus' teaching was different. Whereas the scribes taught by relying on the authority of others ("Rabbi so and so has said. . . ."), Jesus was His own authority. "You have heard that it was said . . . , but I say to you" was His oft repeated phrase in Matthew 5 (see verses 21, 27, 33, 38, 43, RSV) as He explained the true principles of the law as opposed to scribal tradition.

No wonder His teaching repeatedly startled them. After all, who was He to contradict the nation's great minds and its hallowed traditions? He had no office, He had not been to the seminary, He was nothing but a carpenter. Yet it was that nobody who taught with authority.

But it was at that point that Mark differed with his fellow Jews. Jesus was not a nonentity. Rather, He was the Son of God. His authority was that of God Himself. And the people recognized it. Upon hearing Him they knew they were in the presence of a Holy Person, one who taught with authority (Mark 1:22).

But, some may have been thinking, *words are cheap. A good con artist can fool most of the people most of the time. Perhaps the charismatic young man is merely another shyster with a glib tongue and a forceful personality.*

That is where Mark 1:23-28 comes into the picture. Jesus not only amazed people because He spoke with authority, but He astounded them because He acted with authority. We see that fact demonstrated in the healing of a man with an unclean spirit in the same synagogue in which He had been teaching.

Once again, Mark tells us, "all were amazed, so that they discussed with one another, saying, 'What is this? A new teaching with authority! He commands the unclean spirits and they obey Him'" (verse 27).

The combining of verses 21 and 22 with verses 23-28 is no accident. To the contrary, Mark could make his point in no other way. He demonstrates that Jesus is authoritative in both word and deed. More than that, his juxtapositioning highlights the fact that Jesus' words are authoritative not only because of the manner of His teaching, but also because His deeds show that He has the power to successfully challenge the forces of evil in the "real world" of everyday experience, that He has power even over the supernatural. In short, Mark presents Jesus as an authoritative Person in every way. He reveals Him as one that we should listen to and obey.

After Jesus' teaching, Mark tells us that the people were astounded, and after the healing he reveals that they were amazed. How is it with us? Are we astonished at Jesus' teaching? Or has it become so familiar to us that it no longer makes a ripple in our brain waves? Have we come to the place where we have taken what He taught for granted, so much so that we are beyond being amazed when we read His words and view His actions?

The People Were Amazed:

1. at Jesus' authoritative teaching (verse 22)
2. at Jesus' authoritative actions (verse 27)

Without the authoritative actions, His teaching would have had no lasting impact. And without authoritative teaching, His actions would have been little more than sensationalism. Taken together, they demonstrated that He was who He claimed to be.

Is it not astounding that we are dealing with a person who declared Himself to be God? Is it not amazing that He claimed that He was going to die for the sins of the whole world? As C. S. Lewis argues, a person who makes those kinds of claims is either what he claims to be or is a "lunatic" of the "Devil of Hell" (Lewis, p. 56).

Perhaps our problem is that Jesus no longer astounds us. One student of Mark has suggested that "the reason we do not astonish the world more as Christians may be that we are not sufficiently astonished ourselves. . . . If we were more astonished, we would do more astonishing things" (Luccock, p. 660).

7. An Action-Packed Ministry

Mark 1:29-45

²⁹*And immediately after they came out of the synagogue they went into the house of Simon and Andrew, with James and John. ³⁰Now Simon's mother-in-law was lying sick with a fever, and right away they told Jesus about her. ³¹And He came to her, took her hand, and raised her up; and the fever left her and she served them.*

³²*And when evening came at the setting of the sun, they brought to Him all those who were ill and those possessed by demons. ³³And all the city gathered at the door. ³⁴And He healed many who were ill with various diseases, and He cast out many demons, but He did not allow the demons to speak because they knew Him.*

³⁵*Very early in the morning, while it was still dark, He rose up and*

went out to a deserted place and was praying. ³⁶And Simon and those with him searched for Him. ³⁷They found Him and said to Him, "Everyone is looking for You." ³⁸He said to them, "Let us go somewhere else—to the neighboring towns—so that I can preach there also. That is why I came." ³⁹And He went throughout all Galilee, preaching in their synagogues and casting out demons.

⁴⁰And a leper came to Him, pleading with Him and falling on his knees before Him, saying, "If You are willing, You are able to cleanse me." ⁴¹Being filled with tenderness, Jesus stretched out His hand, touched him, and said to him, "I am willing, be clean." ⁴²At once the leprosy left him and he was cleansed. ⁴³And Jesus sternly charged him and sent him away at once, ⁴⁴saying to him, "See that you tell no one anything, but go show yourself to the priest and offer for your cleansing that which Moses commanded, for a testimony to them." ⁴⁵But he went out and began to proclaim many things and to spread the news around, so that Jesus was no longer able to enter openly into a city, but stayed outside in lonely places. Yet the people came to Him from everywhere.

Beginning with the healing of the man with an unclean spirit in verse 23, Mark moves into his first cycle of Jesus' teaching and healing. Jesus had met and defeated Satan in the wilderness (Mark 1:12, 13). Now He is ready to meet the evil one in the world of men and women. Jesus aggressively enters into a contest that will take up the rest of Mark's Gospel.

Meanwhile, Jesus' four disciples and others watch what happens, all the time asking the question of "Who is this Jesus? What kind of authority does He possess?" (see 1:27). The onlookers aren't sure about the answer at the beginning. But point by point Mark will demonstrate how the story's participants came to see Jesus' true identity.

The readers of Mark's Gospel, of course, don't suffer from the same lack of knowledge. Mark told them right up front that Jesus was the Christ, the Son of God (1:1). But the readers aren't the only ones who have that knowledge. The unclean spirits who populate the pages of Mark's Gospel are also quite aware of the divine nature of their Adversary (verse 24).

We should regard Mark 1:21-45 as the public unveiling of God's power working through Jesus. The presence of power is undeniable as Mark pictures Jesus performing miracle after miracle in rapid succession. By verse 45 the eyes of the crowd have been opened along with those of Jesus' early disciples.

Verses 29 through 45 quickly lead Mark's readers through four snap-shots of Jesus in action. Each one tells us something about Him and His followers.

The first (verses 29-31) takes us from the synagogue where Jesus had healed the man with an unclean spirit to Peter's home, where we find the disciple's ailing mother-in-law. Jesus, even though it was apparently still the Sabbath, takes her by the hand and heals her. Wherever He encountered a human need He was ready to meet it. That was an important bit of information to Mark's first readers in Rome. They had very definite needs and they required all the encouragement they could get.

Tucked away in the final words of verse 31 is a side lesson on discipleship that Mark will emphasize throughout his book: "She served them." It is easy to overlook those words or to see them as a function of Peter's mother-in-law's character. But they initiate one of Mark's themes. Not only does he portray Jesus' life as one of service, but He quotes Jesus as saying that "if any one would be first, he must be last of all and servant of all" (9:35, RSV).

One author has written that the true function of education is to prepare "the student for the joy of service in this world and for the higher joy of wider service in the world to come" (White, *Education*, p. 13). It is that message that Mark will pound home beginning with his illustration of Peter's mother-in-law. One of the great lessons of the gospel is that those who are redeemed are saved to serve.

The second snapshot (verses 32-34) finds Jesus healing not merely individuals, such as the man with an unclean spirit (1:23-27) or Peter's mother-in-law (1:30, 31), but a large number who had spiritual and physical ailments.

Apparently the rumor internet of the neighborhood had transmitted the message of the day's earlier two healings. The population could hardly wait for the Sabbath to end so that they could take their needy ones to Jesus. As soon as the sun went down they brought their sick as "all the city" gathered at the door of Peter's house (1:33). There Jesus demonstrated to all that He had unlimited healing power.

Meanwhile, we find in verse 34 another of the recurring themes in Mark: Jesus' command not to speak. This time it involved evil spirits, as in verses 24 and 25, "because they knew Him." Here we discover one of the most interesting dynamics in Mark. Whereas, James Edwards points out, "the questions about Jesus' identity come from the human side (1:27; 2:7; 4:41; 6:2; 6:14-16), . . . the answers come, in part, from the demonic side (1:24; 1:34; 3:11; 5:7). The effect of the interplay between human questions and demonic answers reveals that the human participants do not yet understand Jesus' identity, whereas the demons do, for they, as he, belong to the spiritual world" (Edwards, p. 61).

The third snapshot (verses 35-39) moves away from the strictly healing ministry of verses 29-34 and back to the teaching and healing combination of verses 21-28. Verses 35 to 39 highlight important lessons about both Jesus and the disciples. Concerning Jesus, they help us see the centrality of prayer in His life. "In a life wholly devoted to the good of others," Ellen White penned, "the Saviour found it necessary to withdraw from the thoroughfares of travel and from the throng that followed Him day after day. . . . As one with us, a sharer in our needs and weaknesses, He was wholly dependent upon God, and in the secret place of prayer He sought divine strength, that He might go forth braced for duty and trial. In a world of sin Jesus endured struggles and torture of soul. In communion with God He could unburden the sorrows that were crushing Him. Here He found comfort and joy" (White, *Desire of Ages,* pp. 362, 363).

Prayer for Jesus, however, was not an end in itself. Rather, it involved preparation for the task ahead. After He prayed He arose to preach and heal throughout Galilee (verse 39). "Prayer," writes William Barclay, "will never do our work for us; what it will do is to strengthen us for tasks which must be done" (Barclay, *Mark,* p. 34).

Verses 35 to 39 also tell us something about the disciples. "For the first time," Eduard Schweizer points out, "the disciples' lack of understanding becomes evident" (Schweizer, p. 56). "Apparently," notes Vincent Taylor, "they thought that Jesus was losing a great opportunity afforded by the healings and exorcisms at Capernaum" (Taylor, p. 183). From their perspective it was time to capitalize on His newfound fame as a miracle worker.

Their enthusiasm, however, was the furtherest thing from Jesus' mind. The last thing He wanted was to be seen as a wonder-working Messiah— one who could presumably use His extraordinary powers to run the Romans out of Palestine. His, as the disciples would slowly learn, was a different kind of messiahship. But at this juncture Jesus doesn't show all of

His hand. He merely takes control of the situation and tells His followers that it is time for all of them to move on to places where He is less well known (Mark 1:38, 39). Even though the text doesn't say so, Peter and his friends must have been disappointed. Didn't Jesus understand the opportunity that He was letting slip away? He did, but from His perspective it looked more like a temptation than an opportunity.

The final snapshot (verses 40-45) finds Jesus doing the unthinkable— touching a leper. Leprosy was the most dreaded disease of the ancient world. Beyond the physical deterioration was the social ostracism that put such persons away from the comfort of home and community. Immediately upon diagnosis, the leper had to completely abandon normal human society. Moses wrote: "As long as he has the infection he remains unclean. He must live alone; he must live outside the camp" (Lev. 13:46, NIV). In the time of Jesus the authorities barred lepers from walled cities. Thus they were obviously excluded from the Temple worship. According to the Levitical regulations, those infected with leprosy had to wear torn clothes, avoid combing their hair, cover the lower part of their face, and cry, "Unclean! Unclean!" (Lev. 13:45, NIV) so that no healthy humans would ever jeopardize their own health by coming into contact with them.

Yet Jesus, being "filled with tenderness," healed a leper! He not only cured him, but He "stretched out His hand" and "touched him" (verse 41) before he was healed.

The incident reveals two scandals. The first is that the leper had the audacity to approach Jesus. The second was that Jesus touched him rather than rebuking him. The lesson is clear. Jesus put human need above His own safety or even the Levitical hygienic law. But we find a still deeper lesson: that Jesus has authority over even the most dreaded of diseases.

After the cleansing, Jesus did two things. He swore the healed leper to silence about the miracle. And he commanded the man to follow the Levitical regulations by going to a priest who could certify that he was clean (see Lev. 14:1-32). Unfortunately, the healed man couldn't keep his mouth shut and protect Jesus from becoming regarded as a miracle worker. But then who could remain silent in such a situation? And even if one did the whole community would know about it anyway once the healed person showed up back at home. Even Jesus knew the healing would be a testimony to the priest or priests who confirmed it (Mark 1:44).

Thus Jesus finds Himself caught in a paradoxical tension. He wants to remain anonymous, but the very things He does and teaches spread His reputation. That dynamic will push events throughout Mark's Gospel as they move toward their climax at the cross.

8. Jesus Has Authority Even Over Sin

Mark 2:1-12

¹After some days, when He returned to Capernaum, people heard that He was at home. ²And many assembled, so that there was no room, not even near the door, and He was speaking the word to them. ³And some people came to Him, four of them carrying a paralyzed man. ⁴And not being able to bring him to Jesus because of the crowd, they made an opening in the roof above Him, and, after tearing through it, they lowered the mattress on which the paralyzed man was lying. ⁵And Jesus, seeing their faith, said to the paralyzed man, "Child, your sins are forgiven." ⁶But there were some scribes sitting there, thinking in their hearts, ⁷"Why does this man speak like that? He is blaspheming. Who can forgive sins except God alone?" ⁸And immediately Jesus, knowing in His spirit that they were questioning among themselves, said to them, "Why do you question these things in your hearts? ⁹What is easier, to say to the paralyzed man, 'Your sins are forgiven,' or to say, 'Rise and take your mattress and walk?' ¹⁰But that you may know that the Son of Man has authority on the earth to forgive sins"—He said to the paralyzed man—¹¹"I say to you, rise up, take your mattress, and go to your house." ¹²And immediately he arose, took up the mattress, and went out before all of them, so that they were all astonished and glorified God, saying, "We have never seen anything like this."

Mark's plot thickens in chapter 2. Mark 1 closed with the fact that Jesus, even though He sought to keep the power of His ministry quiet, couldn't do so.

That problem flashed forth in technicolor in the opening verses of chapter 2. The first people we meet in that chapter are what we might term "the crowd." They had heard that Jesus was back in town and they not only flooded the house He was in but also the area around it, so much so, that it was difficult to get near the door, let alone near Jesus who was besieged on the inside.

The crowd plays a crucial role in the second Gospel. In his first nine chapters Mark refers to crowds nearly 40 times. They not only provided Jesus with an audience but His heart goes out to them. Yet crowds in Mark never respond to Jesus' message in repentance and belief. "The single most common attribute of crowds in Mark," James Edwards points out, "is that they obstruct access to Jesus. Thus, despite Jesus' popularity, crowds are not a measure of success" (Edwards, p. 74). Mark eventually pictures a crowd as turning against Jesus with the cry that He be crucified (15:13, 14).

Early in Mark Jesus' miraculous powers undoubtedly drew the crowd to Him. But the people also came because of His teaching. Yet "being part of the crowd around Jesus is not the same as being a disciple of Jesus. The crowd stands and observes; disciples must commit themselves to action, as illustrated by the plucky squad of four" who bring the paralyzed man to Jesus (Edwards, p. 75).

Those four men would stand out in any crowd. They are nameless. But even though we don't know who they were, it is impossible not to admire them for both their determination and their devotion to their helpless friend. Together they form the vanguard of a host of people who down through the ages have brought others to Jesus so that He might restore them physically, emotionally, and spiritually. Standing over against the crowd they are individuals with a mission. Rather than being merely passive listeners, they exhibit the active faith of the true disciple. If the crowd blocks access to Jesus, the highest goal of a true friend is to bring others to Him in spite of the difficulties involved.

One thing that we can say for those unknown men is that they utilized both ingenuity and persistence in getting their paralyzed friend to Jesus. It is one thing to try to push through a crowd to accomplish the task and quite another to create a spectacle by tearing through the roof.

Palestinian roofs of the day were flat and often served as a place for rest and to get away from the heat of the house. As a result, they had an outside stairway that went to the roof. The roof itself consisted of beams going from wall to wall about a yard apart. In between the beams were branches and rushes, all covered with dried mud. Thus the roof could have a hole torn through it without doing any permanent damage.

Just as we don't know much about the four faithful men, we have little information about the paralytic. We do know, however, that he must
have been a poor man, because the word used to describe his bed or mattress "implies a poor man's pallet" (Rawlinson, p. 26). Beyond that fact, it
appears that he was deeply troubled about his past life, which had been far
from perfect. After all, it is more than strange that Jesus' first words to Him
were ones of forgiveness for his sins. Who had said anything about sins?
No one! But the perceptive Jesus knew the individual's greatest fears and
misgivings. Jesus saw not merely a helpless paralytic, but a person with a
burdened conscience that was causing him even more anguish than his
physical disability.

Verse 6 introduces another group of people who will become central
to Mark's story as it builds toward its climax—the scribes. The scribes in
Jewish society were a learned class who were experts in the study of the
law of Moses. The New Testament sometimes refers to them as "teachers
of the law." They will later play a leading role in the arrest and trial of Jesus
(Mark 14:43, 53).

The Cast in the Drama of Mark 2:1-12

1. The crowd, who blocked access to Jesus
2. The friends, who vigorously created access to Jesus
3. The paralytic, who received total healing
4. The scribes, who sought to find fault
5. Jesus, who both met the scribes on their own ground and gave
   the most precious of all gifts

As I imagine the reaction in the crowded room as the four friends lowered the paralytic from the roof, I can picture a smile on Jesus' face as He
witnesses the act of faith taking place. But that is not the expression on the
faces of the scribes. Rather, it is closer to a scowl of contempt as they look
upon what they regard as a most irregular religious experience.

In contrast to the faith of the four friends, the scribes exude doubt.
Verse 8 aptly describes them as "questioning." Their attitude itself blinds
them to what really was taking place in that crowded room. They appear
to have missed altogether the significance of the amazing miracle. Obsessed
with orthodoxy, they had no heart for a human being in need. Their focus

on their traditions blinded them to the spiritual realities being enacted before their very eyes. All they saw and heard was that Jesus forgave the paralytic. That was enough for them. They now had a charge against Jesus that they would not let loose of in the days and months to come. "In the accusation 'It is blasphemy!'" writes Douglas Hare, "we have the first foreshadowing of the passion; it will be on the charge of blasphemy that Jesus will be condemned to death by the high priest's council (14:64)" (Hare, p. 37).

Of course, we shouldn't expect an attitude of faith on the part of the scribes. They hadn't come with the hope of believers. Rather, the religious leaders had undoubtedly sent them to check up on this self-proclaimed rabbi who was causing such a sensation in Galilee. From the first their minds were tilted toward criticism rather than faith. Unfortunately, their disposition is still alive and well in the church 2,000 years later. Every congregation has an element that is more than happy to pounce on any fresh ideas that transgress their traditions and usual way of doing things. Such people remind me of a bumper sticker I saw not long ago: "Jesus save me—from your people."

The final participant in the drama of Mark 2:1-12 is Jesus. He knew why the scribes, so to speak, were sitting on the front row watching His every move. Although He realized what their response would be to His pronouncement of forgiveness of sins on the paralytic, He did it anyway. Thus we should view His statement as an open challenge to the scribes.

But it wasn't a mindless confrontation. Jesus understood their theology. He knew that they considered illness a result of personal sin and that they had a saying that no sick persons could be healed until all their sins had been forgiven them. And He was also aware that they believed that only God could forgive sins.

As a result, His forgiveness of sins was both a claim and a challenge. And the scribes responded with the expected counter-challenge. To which Jesus replied: "What is easier, to say to the paralyzed man, 'Your sins are forgiven,' or to say, 'Rise and take your mattress and walk?'" (verse 9). The question put the scribes on the spot. After all, any trickster could claim to forgive sins. No one could ever confirm such a claim. But for a paralytic to be healed was both verifiable and, in the context of Mark 2, a claim to divinity. Jesus, of course, was more than able to produce the healing that proved His point. But in doing so, William Barclay asserts, "Jesus had signed His own death warrant—and He knew it" (Barclay, *Mark,* p. 43). And thus Mark places another piece in the unfolding drama as Jesus moves toward His cross.

We should highlight one final point before moving on—that Jesus still has the power to forgive sins.

- "If we confess our sins, he is faithful and just to forgive us our sins, and to cleanse us from all unrighteousness" (1 John 1:9, KJV).
- "If any man sin, we have an advocate with the Father, Jesus Christ the righteous" (1 John 2:1, KJV).
- "Wherefore he is able also to save them to the uttermost that come unto God by him, seeing he ever liveth to make intercession for them" (Heb. 7:25, KJV).

That, my friend, is the good news about Jesus.

9. You Don't Have to Be Good to Be a Disciple

Mark 2:13-17

[13]He went out again by the sea, and all the crowd came to Him, and He taught them. [14]As He passed by He saw Levi the son of Alphaeus sitting at the custom house, and He said to him, "Follow Me." And rising up he followed Him.

[15]And as He reclined at dinner in his house, many tax collectors and sinners reclined with Jesus and His disciples, for there were many of them, and they followed Him. [16]The scribes of the Pharisees, seeing that He ate with sinners and tax collectors, said to His disciples, "Why does He eat with tax collectors and sinners?" [17]Hearing them, Jesus said to them, "Those who are strong do not need a physician, but those who are ill. I did not come to call the righteous, but sinners."

No one is too bad for Christ to call" is the lesson that J. C. Ryle draws from the above passage (Ryle, p. 32). If there was anything worse than a leper in Jewish eyes it was a tax collector or publican (KJV). In Jewish literature "tax-gatherers . . . are placed in the same category as robbers" and other disreputable characters (Schürer, div. 1, vol. 2, p. 71). According to the Jewish Mishnah, if a tax collector even touched a house it was unclean (m. Hagigah 3:6). The Mishnah not only classes tax collectors with murderers and robbers, but it presents a ruling that a person could lie to a tax collector with impunity (m. Nedarim 3:4).

Levi Matthew was one of those untouchables. A person passing through Capernaum from Decapolis or from the territory of Herod Philip to the northeast of the Sea of Galilee would have been taxed by an agent such as Levi Matthew.

One of the biggest problems travelers faced from such men is that the tax rates were not standardized. Tax collectors leased the customs collection rights of a particular district for a fixed annual sum. The profits from the business came from charging people as much as the tax agents thought they could get. The excess, of course, went to line the pockets of these not so honest men (see Schürer, div. 1, vol. 2, pp. 68, 69). The fact that they worked for a foreign power and had its soldiers to back them up in cases of disagreement didn't help people's attitudes toward such individuals as Levi. The local population viewed them not only as robbers and extortioners but also as traitors.

That Jesus called such a person in Mark 2 is surprising if not shocking. But perhaps it is equally startling that Levi followed Him. After all, he was giving up a lucrative business for a job without a salary. And if we argue that Peter and John could have possibly returned to the fishing trade if things didn't go well with Jesus, the same would not apply to Matthew. Once he gave up his position he could not get it back. His was a step in faith—a faith based on a need in his heart and the conviction that what Jesus had to offer was better than the material goods of his past life.

The call of Levi Matthew has an important lesson for each of us. "We ought never to despair entirely of any one's salvation," writes Ryle, "when we read this passage of Scripture. He who called Levi, still lives and still works. The age of miracles is not yet past. The love of money is a powerful principle, but the call of Christ is more powerful" (Ryle, p. 32). Christ's summons still goes out not only to the rich and powerful, but to the destitute and even to the crooked and the perverted. No one is beyond the possibilities of God's saving and transforming grace.

Levi Matthew the tax collector must have been overjoyed that he had become Levi Matthew the disciple of Jesus, because he decided to throw a big party. His only problem was whom to invite. His choices were rather limited because respectable Jews would not let themselves be seen in the home of a publican. So Levi did the only thing he could do. He invited a bunch of people just like himself—"tax collectors and sinners," other disreputable characters (Mark 2:15).

"Sinners" is an interesting term. It could refer to one of two different groups. The word could apply to those who lived an immoral lifestyle (such as murderers, robbers, adulterers, and so on) or who had a dishonorable profession (such as tax collectors). But it could also indicate those who, from the Pharisees' perspective, failed to live up to the ritual law as spelled out in their tradition—the common people, the so called "people of the land." Robert Guelich argues that "since Jesus and his disciples fell in the latter category and thus would hardly have been faulted for eating with similar people, 'sinners' here refers more specifically to people of illrepute" (Guelich, p. 102).

The scribes of the Pharisaic party, as we might expect, were incensed and disgusted that Jesus had consented to attend such a party. That is not surprising. Neither is it extraordinary that Jesus, who claimed that He had come "to seek and to save that which was lost" (Luke 19:10, KJV), went to the feast. After all, for Him they represented a target audience. But what is surprising is that so many tax collectors and sinners came to a dinner given in honor of a religious leader. A. B. Bruce writes that it is a point of interest that such a "large number" of such people "in the neighbourhood, were beginning to show an interest in Jesus, and to follow Him about" (A. B. Bruce, *"Kata Mapkon,"* p. 353).

But perhaps that is not so strange as it first appears. The paradox of those who are ethically "good" people is that they tend to rely on their own merits and feel no need of a Savior. They correctly see themselves as better than other people. But a large portion of pride colors their condescending attitude to those not so good. The New Testament indicates that in actuality the most deadly sin of all is that of "goodness." "Of all sins," we read in *Christ's Object Lessons,* that of "pride and self-sufficiency . . . is the most hopeless, the most incurable." That is because goodness feels no need (White, *Christ's Object Lessons,* p. 154). By way of contrast, the tax collectors, sinners, and prostitutes recognized their true condition. Desiring to be near Jesus, they listened to Him gladly because they felt their great need of the cleansing that He had come to offer.

One of the real tragedies of Christian history is that many church members have not learned anything from Mark 2:13-17. They still look down their sanctified noses at those who are not quite as good as they are. I met one of them who was so spiritually obnoxious that I finally told him that if God was like him I didn't want to be in heaven. The good news, however, is that God is not like the rigid, holier-than-thou, ever-so-proper church member. No! The *wonderful* news is that He is like Jesus, the Jesus who fellowshipped with tax collectors and sinners, the Jesus who was more concerned with human need than with the rigidities of traditional orthodoxy.

It is at this point in our discussion that we need a bit of caution. Jesus, we must emphasize, did not become a sinner. Rather, His accepting manner let Him reach out to sinners in such a way that they felt comfortable around Him and desirous of accepting His saving message.

It was so with Matthew. Please note that Levi Matthew did not remain a tax collector. To the contrary, Jesus called him away from that occupation. Levi's commitment to follow Him transformed every aspect of his life. Whereas once he would have done anything, as the young people say, to rip people off to line his own pockets, afterward he would do anything to freely give people the gospel message. The disciple became a prime example of the transformed life (Rom. 12:2), an illustration of what Jesus wants to do in each of our lives.

But that understanding was beyond the comprehension of the Pharisees. All they could do was ask "Why does He eat with tax collectors and sinners?" (Mark 2:16). Jesus, never at a loss for words, replied to them that "those who are strong do not need a physician, but those who are ill. I did not come to call the righteous, but sinners" (verse 17).

In His answer we have what we might describe as a bit of sanctified sarcasm. Jesus would use the same approach in Luke 15:7 when He claimed that "there will be more joy in heaven over one sinner who repents than over ninety-nine righteous persons who need no repentance" (RSV). In that passage He was also speaking against the Pharisees and scribes who were murmuring and complaining that "this man receives sinners and eats with them" (verses 1, 2, RSV).

The plain fact is that there are no righteous people, no people who do not need to repent. The Pharisees knew that, because the Old Testament repeatedly taught that all are "corrupt; there is none that does good, no, not one" (Ps. 14:3, RSV). Paul, the ex-Pharisee, cites that passage and five others in Romans 3:10-18 to drive home the point that the Jewish Scriptures teach beyond a shadow of a doubt that "all [both Jew and Gentile] have sinned and fall short of the glory of God" (Rom. 3:23, RSV; see Knight, pp. 71-74, 83).

To put it bluntly, if one reads with a mind steeped in the Old Testament, Jesus is telling the Pharisees that all people are really sick. All need His healing and His call—even them. For such teachings He will eventually pay the ultimate price. Part of the message of Mark's Gospel is that there is nothing meaner than a self-righteous church person. It is that type who will eventually crucify the very Lord who came to save them.

And what is the bottom line in Mark 2:13-17? It's simple. You don't have to be good to be a disciple, but you do need to listen to the call of Christ, respond to Him, and let Him transform your life in the same way He did Matthew's.

10. Knowing the End From the Beginning

Mark 2:18-22
 [18]And John's disciples and the Pharisees practiced fasting. They came and said to Him, "Why do John's disciples and the Pharisees' disciples fast, but Your disciples do not fast?" [19]And Jesus said to them, "Can the wedding guests fast while the bridegroom is with them? While the bridegroom is with them they cannot fast. [20]But the days will come when the bridegroom will be taken away from them, and then they will fast in that day. [21]No one sews a patch of unshrunk cloth on an old garment; otherwise the patch tears away from it, the new from the old, and a worse tear results. [22]And no one puts new wine into old wineskins; otherwise the wine will burst the wineskins, and both the wine and the wineskins will perish. But new wine is put into fresh wineskins."

One word occurs repeatedly throughout Mark 2—"Why." It first shows up in verse 7 in the context of the forgiveness of sin. Then it reappears in verse 16 related to the issue of eating with disreputable people. The next occurrence in verse 18 involves fasting. And verse 24 has the final usage in the context of the Sabbath.

The first of those whys was something Jesus' adversaries were thinking in their heads, the second they addressed to the disciples about Jesus' actions, while the third and fourth they asked of Jesus regarding His disciples. Despite their different audiences, the four whys had certain things in common. For one, they were all critical of Jesus. A second is that the last three sought to create a division between Him and His disciples. And a third is that all of them dealt with religious practices or interpretations that Jesus had challenged.

The Four Whys

1. "Why does this man speak thus? It is blasphemy! Who can forgive sins but God alone?" (verse 7, RSV).
2. "Why does he eat with tax collectors and sinners?" (verse 16, RSV).
3. "Why do John's disciples and the disciples of the Pharisees fast, but your disciples do not?" (verse 18, RSV).
4. "Why are they [your disciples] doing what is not lawful on the sabbath?" (verse 24, RSV).

It is no accident that we find the four whys in the same chapter. We are not looking at a chronological selection of material, but rather a thematic selection that Mark made to demonstrate the growing tension between Jesus and the religious leaders. Mark knows where he is going in his writing. The series will climax with Mark 3:6: "The Pharisees went out, and immediately held counsel with the Herodians against him, how to destroy him" (RSV).

At that point Mark will have completed his first cycle of teaching. In chapters 1 and 2 he introduced Jesus (1:1-20), presented Him as a teacher and healer with amazing authority (1:21-45), and showed the developing opposition that will eventually lead to His sacrificial death (2:1-3:6). At that point Mark will present a second series with Jesus teaching and healing (3:7-5:43) that will climax in another rejection scene (6:1-6a).

Mark, through the Spirit's guidance, is an excellent writer. He knows what he is doing. And step by step he is opening the eyes of his readers to the gospel story in both its victories and its tensions. In the process he undoubtedly enabled his first readers in Rome to see that their own lives had many of the same victories and tensions. But they were also beginning to learn ever more thoroughly that the One they were following had the authority, desire, and ability to help them through every circumstance they might find themselves in. Mark's Gospel is more than just a story. It is also a teaching document, one meant not only for those struggling disciples in Rome but also a book with profound meaning in the lives of Christians till the end of time.

Verses 18 to 22 help us see that we serve a Christ who had a grasp of the course of events in His own life from the very beginning. The verses begin with the question of why Jesus' disciples didn't fast like those of the Pharisees and the Baptist.

Fasting had become an important topic in first-century Judaism. Even though the Old Testament only commanded one annual fast (the Day of Atonement), by the postexilic period the people observed at least 4 (Zech. 8:19). The Pharisees, however, had gone far beyond the Old Testament requirements, some of them fasting on Monday and Thursday of every week (Luke 18:12).

John the Baptist's remaining disciples had to some extent at least kept to his rigorous dietary regime (see Mark 1:6), which apparently involved some sort of fasting. We should point out that after Jesus began His ministry division had crept in among John's disciples. Some, such as Andrew and John the son of Zebedee, went over to Jesus (John 1:35-42), while others continued to follow John's teaching even after Herod had him put in prison (Mark 6:29; Matt. 11:2, 3). According to the book of Acts, they remained a distinct religious group for some years (see Acts 18:25; 19:1-7). Had they listened closely to John they would have all followed Jesus. But human nature being what it is, it is not only difficult to hear beyond our prejudices, but it is hard to give up old ways.

At any rate, it is clear from the New Testament that Jesus' teachings went far beyond those of the Baptist. The latter may have preached repentance, but Jesus preached beyond repentance to the outlining of the shape of His kingdom. And, as we have begun to see in our reading of Mark, His ideas would challenge many of the time-honored Jewish traditions.

But if fasting was the issue for the Jews in their encounter with Jesus in Mark 2:18-22, it wasn't for Him. He took their question as an opportunity to make several important statements. The first is tucked away in His counter question related to fasting: "Can the wedding guests fast while the bridegroom is with them?" (verse 19). Obviously He claimed to be the bridegroom Himself. That assertion, we should note, is not a messianic claim. No Old Testament passages connect the Messiah with the bridegroom imagery.

Jesus' claim to be the bridegroom is actually a much more significant claim, because the Old Testament repeatedly identified God as the bridegroom of Israel. Speaking of the restoration of Israel, God says to His people, "you will call me, 'My husband,' . . . for I will betroth you to me for ever" (Hosea 2:16, 19, RSV; cf. Isa. 61:10; 62:4, 5). Thus the careful listener to Jesus' bridegroom allusion would have realized that He was claiming to be no less than Yahweh, the God of the Old Testament.

But the reader of Mark's gospel finds nothing new in such a claim. Mark had announced Jesus' identity in his first verse, the Isaiah passage about the forerunner in Mark 1:2, 3 had alluded to it, the Father had declared it from heaven in verse 11, a demon had revealed it in verse 24, and Jesus had in essence asserted to be God in His claiming the divine right to forgive sin (2:1-12). So we find nothing new in the bridegroom allusion, just a reinforcing of a well-worked theme.

And that last point is the one we need to remember. Mark has been pounding home a crucial teaching—that Jesus of Nazareth is God in the flesh. That point is clear to the reader. But it was not so to the disciples, who won't recognize it until Mark 8:29. Nor did the religious leaders accept it. They will deny it to the end of Mark's Gospel, eventually sending Jesus to the cross on the charge of blasphemy.

But while Jesus' claim to be God is not a new idea in Mark, the bridegroom exchange does have a hidden teaching in it. The new element is that "the bridegroom will be taken away" (2:20). Here we find Jesus for the first time hinting at His own future. At this point in Mark He isn't very explicit about the meaning of His being "taken away," but it will later provide a recurring theme of the first magnitude as He tells His disciples that He will be crucified (8:31; 9:31; 10:33).

Thus Jesus not only knows who He is, but He understands His future. He is conscious of what at that point none of the other participants in the drama of His life have as yet grasped. But the reader is beginning to understand, and Mark is carefully crafting his presentation of the developing confrontation between Jesus and the religious leaders that will provide the dynamic that leads to their final conflict.

The two brief parables of Mark 2:21, 22 highlight part of that interaction. Those two parables illustrate that Jesus was well aware of the fact that much of what He had to teach was both new to the traditional Jewish mind and offensive to it.

He also realized that His new concepts would not fit into the traditional Jewish way of thinking. His dynamic ideas would be like the ferment of fresh wine, whose action would split the rigid traditions of the Jews. His teachings would not and could not fit into the "usual way of doing things" or the traditional thought frames. They were incompatible. The combining of the two would result in a ripping or tearing of the old. What was needed was not a rigid maintenance of religious tradition, but new ways of acting and thinking, which He represented as new wine skins.

When Jesus comes into our lives it must not be like sewing a new patch on an old garment or pouring new wine into old skins (2:21, 22). That will never work. Rather, becoming His disciple demands a total change in our way of thinking and believing. Jesus' philosophy of life, His way of life, is not a partial change but a total transformation. It is exactly such a change that the Pharisees of every age find impossible to accept.

When it comes right down to it, Jesus in Mark's Gospel is battling against those rigidities that eventually manage to capture each and every religious movement until it becomes more of a museum of things past than a relevant force for the present and the future.

Ray Stedman caught that concept when he cautioned his readers to "beware" of "the trap of tradition. The attitude that says, 'This is how we've always done it,' is deadly to vibrant, exciting relationships with God and with others. Jesus fought rigid, confining tradition in His day, and we, as His followers, must fight it in our day, in our lives, and our churches. We must become gentle [or not so gentle] subversives, always at war against those traditions that would stifle the reality of a living relationship with God and with one another" (Stedman, *Servant Who Rules,* p. 88).

11. Authority Over the Sabbath

Mark 2:23–3:6

²³And it happened as He passed through the grainfields on the Sabbath, as they made their way along, His disciples began picking the heads of grain. ²⁴The Pharisees said to Him, "Look, why are they doing what is not lawful on the Sabbath?" ²⁵And He said to them, "Have you never read what David did when he had need and was hungry, he and those with him? ²⁶How he entered into the house of God in the days of Abiathar the high priest and ate the consecrated loaves of the presence, which it is not lawful to eat (except for the priests), and also gave it to those with him?" ²⁷And He said to them, "The Sabbath was made for people and not people for the Sabbath. ²⁸So the Son of Man is Lord even of the Sabbath."

¹He entered again into a synagogue, and a man was there having a withered hand. ²They carefully watched Him to see if He would heal on the Sabbath, that they might accuse Him. ³He said to the man having the withered hand, "Stand up in the front." ⁴And He said to them, "Is it lawful on the Sabbath to do good or to do evil, to save life or to kill?" But they were silent. ⁵And looking around on them with anger, being utterly distressed at the hardness of their heart, He said to the man, "Stretch out the hand." And he stretched it out, and his hand was restored. ⁶And the Pharisees went out and immediately plotted with the Herodians against Him, so that they might destroy Him.

Beginning in Mark 1:40 the author of the Gospel has presented a selection of events in which Jesus repeatedly challenged certain interpretations of the law. In 1:41 He touched a leper, in 2:1-12 He claimed the divine prerogative to forgive sin in His own person, in 2:15, 16 He ate and fellowshipped with tax collectors and sinners, and in 2:18-20 He questioned Pharisaic approaches to fasting. Three of those four challenges had to do directly with the importance of human need over that of tradition and ritual regulations and observances. The two stories regarding the Sabbath in Mark 2:23-3:6 continue the stories of conflict and challenge and bring them to a climax in 3:6, in which the Pharisees link up with the Herodians in their decision to kill Jesus. And once again the two Sabbath stories uplift human need above religious ritual.

In the first story Jesus and the disciples walked through a grainfield, with the disciples not only picking some of the grain but rubbing it between their palms so as to separate the kernels from the chaff. The ever present Pharisees challenged Jesus on the legality of such action.

In our day we might think that they were upset because the disciples were taking grain that did not belong to them, that they were stealing. But that was not the problem. In fact, in gathering and eating the grain as they passed through a field they were doing what the law of Moses explicitly allowed. Deuteronomy 23:25 tells us that it was permissible to pick a neighbor's grain with the hand but not with a sickle.

It wasn't picking the grain that was the problem, but doing it on the Sabbath. Such an act was harvesting, and harvesting on the Sabbath was defined as work, and work on the Sabbath, of course, was sin. But they were not only harvesting, they were also, as they rubbed the grain between their hands, threshing. And threshing also represented a forbidden Sabbath activity. Then, of course, the Pharisees could also have been accusing the disciples of traveling. Tradition considered walking more than 1,999 paces to be taking a journey and thus a breach of the Sabbath. It appears, however, that the Pharisees were probably alluding to the reaping and the threshing, since the accusation was against the disciples who had eaten the grain and did not include Jesus, who was obviously traveling with them.

The Pharisees may have expected Jesus immediately to put a stop to such unlawful activity, although they undoubtedly had a sneaking suspicion that He wouldn't do so. Rather, to their surprise, He met them on their own ground by retelling a story found in 1 Samuel 21:1-6. David, fleeing for his life, came to the tabernacle at Nob and demanded food from Ahimalech (not Abiathar, Ahimelech's son [1 Sam. 22:20], as Mark has it). But Ahimelech had nothing, except the recently changed holy bread that had for a week been before the Lord in the holy place of the tabernacle. God through Moses had specifically stipulated that only the priests could eat the holy bread consecrated to God. Yet David took and ate that bread. In the process he broke the law.

R. T. France correctly states that it is "not immediately obvious" why Jesus told that particular story (France, *Mark,* NIGTC, p. 145). The most obvious reason why Jesus may have selected that illustration is that it demonstrates that the Bible itself presents an example in which human need took precedence over the law of Moses. But, as France points out, "a previous breach of the law . . . is hardly in itself justification for a further infringement!" *(ibid.)*. Beyond that problem, David had broken the law at a time when his men were starving. That comparison hardly holds up with the disciples who were merely hungry.

The real issue for Jesus, France argues, is not the justification of any particular action by the disciples. "It was rather, as vv. 27, 28 will make clear, whether Jesus" as Lord of the Sabbath "had the right to override" the traditional understandings. The use of the Davidic illustration, therefore, was not so much for what David did "as on the fact that it was David who did it, and that Scripture records his act, illegal as it was, with apparent approval. The logic of Jesus' argument therefore implies a covert claim to a personal authority at least as great as that of David" *(ibid.)*.

Following the illustration about David comes the twofold claim of Jesus that

- "The Sabbath was made for people and not people for the Sabbath"
- And that Jesus Himself is the Lord of the Sabbath (Mark 2:27, 28).

In the first of those claims Jesus states a basic truth that lies at the foundation of all true religion. That is, that the focus of religion is upon human need rather than tradition or ritual as an end in itself. As far as the Sabbath is concerned, Jesus asserts that when correctly understood, it is an institution established to meet the needs of men and women. As William Barclay puts it, "Man was created before . . . the . . . Sabbath law came into existence. Man was not created to be the victim and the slave of Sabbath rules and regulations; the Sabbath rules and regulations were in the beginning created to make life fuller and better for man" (Barclay, *Mark,* p. 58). The Lord created human beings on the sixth day. The God who knew all of their needs instituted the Sabbath on the seventh. The Sabbath exists to make human life a better life.

Speaking to Mark 2:27, 28, G. A. Chadwick writes that "the text . . . says nothing about the abolition of a Day of Rest. On the contrary, it declares that this day is not a Jewish but a universal ordinance, it is made for man" and not just for one sector of humanity—the Jews. "Let those who deny the Divine authority of this great institution ponder well the phrase which asserts its universal range, and which finds it a large assertion of the mastery of Christ that He is Lord 'even of the Sabbath'" (Chadwick, p. 69).

Also helpful are the comments by J. D. Jones, who argues that the meaning of Mark 2:23-28 is not that Jesus was a "Sabbath-breaker," but that "He was the true Sabbath-keeper. There is no hint or suggestion in any of these stories of His conflicts with the Pharisees of any repudiation of the Sabbath law, of any intention to interfere with the day of rest. The hallowing of the Sabbath was one of those Divine commandments which our Lord bade others observe, and one which He observed Himself. What our Lord did protest against and fight against was the debasement of the Sabbath, that perversion of the commandment which had changed what God meant for a gracious boon into a most grievous burden" (Jones, vol. 1, p. 76).

Jesus' claim to be Lord of the Sabbath is another of His confrontational proclamations. The Jews were well aware that God had instituted the Sabbath (Gen. 2:3). In describing Himself as the Lord of the Sabbath, Jesus once again makes a claim to divinity, a fact not lost on His listeners.

Mark 3:1-6 will follow that challenge with still another. In that passage Jesus enters the synagogue on the Sabbath and soon discovers a man with a withered hand. The Pharisees, as had become their practice, waited to see if Jesus would heal the man and thus, from their perspective, break the law. Jesus didn't skirt the issue. Nor could He avoid seeing His detractors. After all, synagogues reserved their front seats for such dignitaries. Now Jesus knew that the Pharisees were not against medical care or healing on the Sabbath, so long as it involved a matter of life and death for the sick person. But the man with the crippled hand obviously didn't fit into that category. He had had the disability for some time and his healing could have easily waited a day or two.

But for Jesus it was a test case. He called the man up front where everybody could see and asked the watching Pharisees whether it was lawful to do good or evil on the Sabbath (verse 4). That put them in a dilemma. No one could answer that it was permissible to do evil. Thus they had no choice but to answer that it was lawful to do good. And wasn't healing a person to do good?

That first question put the Pharisees on the spot. Why Jesus asked it is quite obvious. But the second question at first leaves us baffled. "Is it lawful . . . to save life or to kill?" After all, who was killing anybody? All that was in question was the healing of a man's hand. But here Jesus once again indicates that He understood the human heart (see John 2:25). At that very moment the Pharisees were beginning to concoct a plan to kill Him. Thus Jesus who at the very worst was going to break their Sabbath tradition was on far better ground than those who were contemplating His murder. No wonder they remained silent to His questions.

Such a perversion of religion, Mark tells us, made Jesus angry. In the presence of everyone He healed the man.

But the Pharisees went out and began negotiations with the Herodians on how they might destroy Jesus. Here we have the ultimate irony. Those Pharisees who were so careful in maintaining their traditions, so strict that they were eager to put Jesus to death for breaking them, at the same time were willing to transgress their own tradition by working with the Herodians whom they despised for their religious laxness and for their collaboration with the Romans. But a common enemy can make strange bedfellows. For Mark the uniting of the religious Pharisees with the secular Herodians represents "the comprehensiveness of the opposition . . . ranged against [Jesus] and his authority" (Anderson, p. 114). In the end either His authority or theirs would win out. Jesus was on a collision course with the authorities of His day.

12. Attracting a Multitude/Choosing a Few

Mark 3:7-19

   [7]*Jesus departed with His disciples to the sea. A great multitude from Galilee followed, and also from Judea, [8]from Jerusalem, from Idumea, beyond the Jordan, and the vicinity of Tyre and Sidon, a great multitude, hearing what things He did, came to Him. [9]And He told His disciples that a boat should remain near Him because of the crowd, lest they should crush Him. [10]For He healed many, so that as many as had diseases pressed upon Him that they might touch Him. [11]Whenever the unclean spirits saw Him, they fell before Him and cried out, saying, "You are the Son of God." [12]And He sternly charged them that they should not make His identity known.*

   [13]*And He went up on the mountain and called to Him those whom He wanted, and they came to Him. [14]He appointed twelve that they might be with Him and that He might send them out to preach [15]and to have authority to cast out demons. [16]And He appointed the twelve: Simon (to*

whom He gave the name Peter), [17]*and James the son of Zebedee and John his brother (to whom He gave the name Boanerges, which means sons of thunder),* [18]*and Andrew, and Philip, and Bartholomew, and Matthew, and Thomas, and James the son of Alphaeus, and Thaddaeus, and Simon the Cananaean [Zealot],* [19]*and Judas Iscariot, who betrayed Him.*

Jesus' labors have reached a crisis point. Unless He desired to become involved in a deadly collision with the religious authorities He had better steer clear of the synagogues for a while.

And that is exactly what He did. Mark tells us that "He departed with His disciples to the sea" (3:7), undoubtedly the sea of Galilee. Jesus did not withdraw because of fear. He had already demonstrated His fearlessness in several confrontations. Rather, He retreated as an act of prudence. Unless He wanted to precipitate a crisis before He and His followers were ready for it, caution was the better part of wisdom. As John so aptly put it, "his hour was not yet come" (John 7:30, KJV).

It is unfortunate that some of Christ's followers haven't learned the lesson of prudence. They act as if every hill is one to die on and create nothing but dissension in the church and often in their families. We as Christians need to learn from every aspect of Christ's life, even from His passive side. Some of us have yet to grasp the fact that there is a time to retreat as well as a time to advance.

Even though Jesus could escape the cities and the synagogue, He couldn't avoid the crowd (Mark 3:7, 8). Curious and hopeful people mobbed Him from all over. Those who came were truly a mixed multitude. Galilee, Judea, and Jerusalem were overwhelmingly Jewish territories, while Tyre and Sidon were almost entirely Gentile regions. In between were those from Idumea and beyond the Jordan with their mixed populations of Jews and Gentiles. Jesus truly had become a more famous preacher than John the Baptist, whose followers, according to Mark 1:5, came from the rather limited area of Jerusalem and Judea. The crowd pressed Jesus so hard that He had to order a boat to stand by as a way of escape, lest the mass of people crush Him. Verse 10 tells us that Jesus' work as a healer brought Him into special danger, "for the sick people did not even wait for Him to touch them," but "rushed to touch Him" (Barclay, *Mark,* pp. 65, 66).

And the unclean spirits, as they did in Mark 1:24 and desired to do in 1:34, announced Jesus as the Son of God (3:11). Up to this point in Mark the unclean spirits have been the only ones to make such an identification except for God the Father in Mark 1:11. Seeing Jesus as the Son is obviously one of the main points of Mark's Gospel. Yet Jesus repeatedly forbids the spirits to proclaim that all-important truth (3:12). Why? Because, as we noted earlier, His time had not yet come. He needed opportunity to teach His followers, and others if possible, that His Messiahship was one of suffering and service—an idea totally at variance with the popular messianic understandings of the day, which expected a conquering king at the head of a mighty army. It was essential that He have time to educate His followers, lest rumors create a drive to crown Him as king, which would lead to disaster. Such a movement almost got underway in John 6:15, and one such crusade, under the sons of Judas the Galilean, would eventually lead to the destruction of Jerusalem in A.D. 66-70. Caesar was no more likely to overlook what appeared to be a rebellion in Jesus' time than he was a few decades later. It was therefore imperative for the unclean spirits to hold their peace.

But not everyone would be silent forever. Mark 3:13-19 finds Jesus appointing 12 who will eventually speak for Him. As we know, they were not the first disciples whom He called. We saw the four fishermen (Simon, Andrew, James, and John) answer the summons of Jesus in Mark 1:16-20 and Levi Matthew the tax collector do the same in Mark 2:14. But Jesus has come to the point in His ministry when He must formalize the arrangement. He needs to choose several from among His immediate followers whom he can train to guide His movement after He is no longer with them.

We don't know how large His immediate group of followers was at this time in His ministry. But the Bible has preserved the names of Joseph called Barsabbas and Matthias, who had followed Jesus from the time of His baptism to His resurrection, but who did not belong to the formally-commissioned disciples (see Acts 1:22, 23).

The selection of 12 rather than 10 or 13 disciples was important to Jesus because that was the number of the tribes of Israel. In the selection of 12 Jesus announced that in His understanding His New Israel of God would be a continuation of the blessings bestowed upon Abraham for all nations in Genesis 22:17, 18 and 26:4.

It is of interest to note that Jesus called His disciples to Him. That was not the usual way that Jewish teachers operated. Rabbis did not invite others to be their disciples, but were chosen by them, somewhat like the way a modern graduate student selects a certain program at a particular university due to the presence of a specific professor whom he or she wants to study under. But Jesus takes the initiative. And just as He called His first disciples, He is still in the business of inviting men and women to participate in His work today.

And why did Jesus call His 12 disciples? Mark 3:14, 15 supply three reasons:

1. "that they might be with Him,"
2. "that He might send them out to preach,"
3. and that they might "have authority to cast out demons."

Those verses highlight the difference between a disciple and an apostle. The Greek word for disciple *(mathētēs)* means "one who engages in learning through instruction from another," a *"pupil,"* or *"apprentice"* (Danker, p. 609), while the word for apostle *(apostolos)* stands for one who is sent out. The Twelve needed to be near Jesus so that He could instruct them. Much of the book of Mark focuses on that training. Most specifically, Mark concentrates on the Twelve from Mark 8:31 to the end of his Gospel. Jesus had only begun to "send them out" *(apostellein)* to preach and have authority over unclean spirits after He had had time to sufficiently instruct them for their first formal assignment without Him (see Mark 6:7-13). Their experiences and failures during that mission provided the framework for further instruction in discipleship.

That process is still the one God uses 2,000 years after Jesus. First, God calls persons into ministry. Then He utilizes the educational agencies He has established through His people to prepare (disciple) men and women so that they might go out with His authority to preach and bring healing to people in the far corners of the earth.

The Twelve called to an apprenticeship with Jesus were an unlikely bunch for the future leaders of a world church. They didn't have what we would call social or church connections, they didn't have a proper pre-seminary education, and some of them, such as Peter, James, and John, were quite rough and uncultured—more the type that we would think of as construction workers than preachers. But, as we noted earlier, Jesus saw promise in them, He recognized latent talents that He could develop.

First Comes Discipleship/Then Apostleship

"Jesus appointed the Twelve to be with him, and then he sent them out with his authority to proclaim the Good News. Many people want the authority of a Peter or John without first going through the school of discipleship. Those twelve needed instruction, coaching, practice, and above all, time to mature. We must be willing to spend time learning from the Master before we go forward to do his public work" (Barton, p. 81).

The list by itself is quite interesting. Of some of them, such as Bartholomew, James the son of Alphaeus, Thaddeus, and Simon the Zealot, we know nothing further. Jesus went out of His way to assign at least three of them nicknames. To Peter He gave the title of "rock" (*Petros* in Greek and *Cephas* in the Aramaic of Palestine). Peter, interestingly enough, was anything but a solid rock for the rest of the Gospel of Mark. But he would certainly demonstrate rocklike characteristics after Pentecost in the early chapters of Acts. To John and James Jesus assigned the name "sons of thunder" (Mark 3:17), probably meaning that they had hot tempers. It is one of the marks of the efficiency of Jesus' discipling program that John went from being a son of thunder to the disciple of love and that the spongy Peter of the gospel story became solid like a rock.

We also find some strange combinations among the disciples. It is hard to imagine Simon the Zealot and Matthew the tax collector getting along in the same small group. After all, the Zealots "believed that they were called by God to engage in a Holy War against 'the powers of darkness'" (Russel, p. 38). As such, a Zealot like Simon was more likely to stick a knife into a turncoat tax collector than to fellowship with him. But such is the transforming power of Christ that He could even include so unlikely a combination in His small group of apprentices.

Then there is Judas Iscariot, an indication that the cross is never far away in the mind of Mark. But the mention of the name of "Judas Iscariot, who betrayed Him" (Mark 3:19) should also remind us that the church of Jesus has never been perfect. It has always had its Judases, even in the ministry. But God doesn't forsake it. Rather, He works with it in spite of itself.

13. The Unforgivable Sin

Mark 3:20-30

   ²⁰He entered into a house, and the crowd came together again so that they were not able to eat a meal. ²¹His family, hearing of this, went to take custody of Him, for they said, "He is beside Himself." ²²And the scribes who came down from Jerusalem were saying, "He is possessed by Beelzebul! He casts out demons by the prince of the demons." ²³So Jesus called to them and spoke to them in parables. "How can Satan cast out Satan? ²⁴If a kingdom is divided against itself, that kingdom cannot stand. ²⁵And if a house is divided against itself, that house will not be able to stand. ²⁶And if Satan has risen up against himself and is divided, he cannot stand, but his end has come. ²⁷But no one can enter into the house of the strong man and ransack his goods unless he first binds the strong man, and then he can ransack his house.

   ²⁸"Truly I say to you, that all sins and blasphemes shall be forgiven the sons of men, whatever they shall blaspheme, ²⁹but whoever blasphemes against the Holy Spirit never has forgiveness, but is guilty of an eternal sin"—³⁰for they were continually saying "He has an unclean spirit."

It must be getting pretty bad when even your family thinks you are crazy. How is it, we may be wondering, that *Jesus' family could come to such a conclusion.* If we think about it, possible reasons aren't too difficult to discover (see Barclay, *Mark,* pp. 71, 72).

For one, Jesus had left what was apparently a prosperous carpenter's business at Nazareth. And for what? To become a wandering teacher with no visible means of support. Normal, sensible people just don't do those kinds of things. They don't throw away security, eventually coming to the point where they have no place to lay their head (Matt. 8:20).

Second, Jesus wasn't coming across as politically astute. In fact, He was obviously on a collision course with both the religious and secular leaders of the nation. Didn't He realize that opposing the powers that be is dangerous? No person in his right mind throws safety to the wind.

Third, Jesus had formed a religious society of His own. And it was a strange little one at that. What a crowd—fishermen, a reformed tax collector, a fanatical nationalist—riffraff. Those are not the kind of people that you gather around you if you want to make an impact on society. In fact, prudent people did not even want it known that they associated with such types.

The family could come to only one conclusion: Jesus, for all His good qualities, was losing touch with reality. Beyond that, His course of action not only endangered Himself, but might eventually put the entire family at risk. Thus their attempt to take custody of Him so that they could keep Him away from trouble. From Jesus' perspective, we can only wonder if such experiences lie behind His saying that "a man's foes will be those of his own household" (Matt. 10:36, RSV).

What meaning, we might ask, does that episode have for us? Much in every way. Madness is the verdict of the secular and even the religious world for all those who enthusiastically give their entire lives to a religious or philanthropic cause. "The world honours the man who for the sake of fame risks his life in battle; but if a man risks his life for souls for whom Christ died, it counts him a fool. The only kind of religion the world tolerates is religion of the tepid, Laodicean sort. But religion that breaks through the bonds of respectability and convention, religion that is earnest, red-hot, and means business, it calls mad" (Jones, vol. 1, p. 93).

"Has anyone ever called us 'mad'?" asks Halford Luccock. "If not, we may wonder whether we have really counted, whether we have cut sharply and deeply enough to make any lasting impression. . . . 'He is mad' has always been an ultimate tribute in Christian history to those who served, not two masters, but One. Paul won that distinguished service decoration. Festus cried, 'Paul, you are mad' (Acts 26:24)" (Luccock, p. 691).

How is it with me? Am I mad or just a plain old normal church member?

Jesus' family were not the only ones concerned with His "aberrant" behavior. The scribes who had come from Jerusalem also found Him to be both out of line and threatening. Their accusation didn't exactly charge Him with insanity (even if they may have thought it in their minds), but rather that He was linked up to Beelzebul, the prince of demons. "The logic of the scribes," Ched Myers points out, "was simple: because they believed themselves to be God's representatives, Jesus' 'secession' necessarily put him in allegiance with Satan" (Myers, p. 165).

Jesus' response was a series of short parabolic sayings about the self-defeating nature of civil war (Mark 3:23-26). He then pointed out in His parable of the strong man (verse 27) that being in league with the devil wasn't the only way to overthrow his kingdom. One could also invade it. "Jesus explains [that] he is the one who binds the strong man and thereafter plunders his possessions, in this case his captives. This is meant to indicate that Jesus is the adversary, not the ally, of Satan" (Witherington, pp. 157, 158) and that the goal of His ministry is to tie up Satan and destroy his power. That binding had begun with the temptation in the wilderness (1:12, 13) and had continued through Jesus' teaching and healing ministry. It would not be completed until the strong man was completely restrained.

The second part of Jesus' answer to the Jerusalem scribes is His statement about the unpardonable sin. What most people miss in that statement is its positive side. After all, He plainly taught that *"all* sins and blasphemes shall be forgiven the sons of men" (Mark 3:28). "We ought to notice," writes J. C. Ryle, *"what a glorious declaration our Lord makes in these verses about the forgiveness of sins. He says 'all sins shall be forgiven to the sons of men. . . .'*

"These words fall lightly on the ears of many persons. They see no particular beauty in them. But to the man who is alive to his own sinfulness and deeply sensible of his need of mercy, these words are sweet and precious. 'All sins shall be forgiven.' The sins of youth and age,—the sins of head, and hand, and tongue, and imagination,—the sins against all God's commandments,—the sins of persecutors, like Saul,—the sins of idolaters, like Manasseh,—the sins of open enemies of Christ, like the Jews who crucified Him,—the sins of backsliders from Christ, like Peter,—all, all may be forgiven. The blood of Christ can cleanse all away. The righteousness of Christ can cover all. . . .

"The doctrine here laid down is the crown and glory of the gospel. The very first thing it proposes to man is free pardon, full forgiveness, complete remission, without money and without price. . . . Let us lay hold on this doctrine without delay, if we never received it before" (Ryle, p. 55).

There exists, however, one exception to the blanket offer of forgiveness set forth by Jesus. That involves he who "blasphemes against the Holy Spirit" (verse 29).

And what, you may be thinking, *is blaspheme against the Holy Spirit?* To understand what Jesus meant we need to go to the passage's context. Not only were the Jerusalem scribes claiming that Jesus' power came from the devil, but "they were *continually* saying 'He has an unclean spirit'" (verse 30).

Here we have a contrast between two spirits—the spirit of Satan and the Holy Spirit, who had descended upon Jesus at His baptism and had impelled Him into His earliest conflict with the evil one (Mark 1:10, 12).

The issue of which spirit stood behind Jesus' ministry was not a minor one. To claim that He operated on the basis of Satanic power, if it were true, not only explained away His miracles, but it invalidated His teachings, including the promise of forgiveness.

"But why," we need to ask, "is that sin unforgiveable?" The answer lies in the nature of the work of the Holy Spirit. Part of the role of the Spirit is to convict people regarding sin (John 16:8). Responding under that divine leading, they confess their sin, then are forgiven and cleansed (1 John 1:9).

But what if they don't confess? Beyond that, what if they reject the conviction of sin itself? What if they attribute their sense of guilt to the power of the devil? Such people would see no need of confession. Nor would they recognize the sinfulness of sin. They would be, in the words of Paul, like people whose consciences had been seared with a hot iron (1 Tim. 4:2). Eventually such people would become so insensitive that they would not even be able to hear the voice or feel the impulse of the Spirit. Without the acceptance of conviction, they would not confess. And without repentance and confession there would be no forgiveness.

The Unpardonable Sin

"We may lay it down as nearly certain, that those who are troubled with fears that they have sinned the unpardonable sin, are the very people who have not sinned it. The very fact that they are afraid and anxious about it, is the strongest possible evidence in their favour. . . . It is far more probable that the general marks of such a person will be utter hardness of conscience,—a seared heart,—an absence of any feeling,—a thorough insensitivity to spiritual concern" (Ryle, pp. 58, 59).

The results of such a course of action, Jesus tells us, are eternal (Mark 3:28). God is not in a position, nor does He have the disposition, to fill heaven with rebels who will continue the misery and death that have caused such anguish here on earth. The focus of the Bible is on the fact that God will eventually bring an end to the sin problem. Those who are safe to save will be those who through the conviction of the Spirit have come to hate sin and its results in their inmost being.

"But," says the sensitive person, "how do I know that I have not already committed the unpardonable sin?" The answer is short and simple. The very fact that a person worries about the topic is the surest indication that they have not committed that ultimate sin. Walter Wessel is right on when he writes that the unpardonable sin "is not an isolated act but a settled condition of the soul" (Wessel, p. 645). Those who are concerned about their standing with God are by that very anxiety indicating that they are still open to the promptings of the Holy Spirit.

14. Qualification for Belonging to the Family of God

Mark 3:31-35

[31]His mother and His brothers came, and standing outside they sent to Him and called Him. [32]A crowd sat around Him, and they said to Him, "Look, Your mother and Your brothers are looking for You." [33]Answering them, He said, "Who is My mother and brothers?" [34]And looking around at those sitting in a circle around Him, He said, "Look, My mother and My brothers. [35]Whoever does the will of God, that one is My brother and sister and mother."

Outside of Mary and Joseph (to a lesser extent) we don't find much about Jesus' family in the New Testament. Matthew names His brothers as James, Joseph, Simon, and Judas and mentions the sisters without naming them (Matt. 13:55, 56). Those siblings may have been Joseph's by an earlier marriage, may have been his and Mary's after the birth of Jesus, or may have been a combination of the two possibilities. Most assume that Joseph died before Jesus' ministry began, since outside of the birth narrative and Jesus' experience in the Temple when He was 12 years old, the New Testament never mentions Joseph.

John tells us that Jesus' "brothers did not believe in him" and that He couldn't be straightforward about His plans with them (John 7:5, 3, 10, RSV). On the other hand, the birth and early childhood narratives of

Matthew and Luke leave no doubt that Mary understood and believed in her Son's forthcoming mission.

The events of Mark 3:31-35, in which Jesus redefines His family, began in verse 21 when His brothers and mother show up to take custody of Him, fearing that He was losing His bearings. Thus the two family passages form a sandwich around the opposition of the Jerusalem scribes who believed He had a devil (verses 22-27). The sandwich finds unity in that both groups oppose Jesus and believe that He is under the control of an evil power. It is impossible to say if Mary shared that attitude, or if she was merely under the domineering influence of Jesus' brothers who had no doubts about His problems. On the other hand, Mary may have become discouraged. After all, things weren't turning out as she probably imagined they would. Instead of Jesus acting like the promised Messiah, as far as she could see He was merely making a mess out of His life and heading for a collision with both the political and the religious authorities. She also may have begun to doubt. The one thing we know for sure is that Mary was with Jesus' siblings when they came to take custody of the family's wandering star.

Before moving to the teaching of Mark 3:30-35 we should note that some, if not all, of Jesus' brothers eventually came to believe in Him, probably after His death and resurrection. After that event Jesus appeared to James before making Himself known to the eleven apostles (1 Cor. 15:7). James, described specifically as the Lord's brother, later became a leader and perhaps the head of the Jerusalem church (Gal. 1:19; 2:9, 12; Acts 12:17; 15:13; 21:18). He would also write the book that carries his name, while Jesus' brother Jude would write the letter that bears that title (James 1:1; Jude 1:1).

But those two brothers were a long way from their eventual apostleships in Mark 3 when they believed that if Jesus was not crazy, He was at least approaching the edges of insanity.

It was their attempt to control Jesus that called forth His redefinition of "family" in Mark 3:32-35. One basic underlying thought of that passage is that there are relationships that are closer than those of blood. It took such ties to bind together two such men as Matthew the tax collector and Simon the Zealot. In their previous existence they would have welcomed each other's death. But now they belonged to the brotherhood of Jesus' inner circle. Their shared faith, dedication, goals, and experiences had welded them together with the other disciples as a family for Jesus that was infinitely more intimate for Him than His birth family.

Two basic ideas flow out from Jesus' teaching in verses 32-35. The first is that those who follow God will eventually find themselves in conflict with those who live by the principles of the prince of this world.

That had certainly been the case with Jesus. In His desire to fulfill God's principles wholeheartedly He had not only run into conflict with the religious and secular authorities but also with His flesh-and-blood family. From what we understand of His nature, He did not enjoy such encounters any more than we do. The very basis of His teaching centered on love and the need to care for one another. He even defined His followers in those terms when He claimed that "all men will know that you are my disciples, if you have love for one another" (John 13:35, RSV).

Jesus' teaching must have meant a great deal to Mark's first readers. Because of their Christianity, they also had faced rejection by their families, persecution, and even brutal deaths. But "in place of broken family [and other] relationships, ostracism, and persecution," they now had a "close and intimate relation to the Son of God" himself (Grant, p. 694) and to those who were their brothers and sisters in the faith.

The dynamic of both family rejection and inclusion in the family of God is still with the church in the twenty-first century. "Again and again," Halford Luccock writes, "in most lives the natural possessiveness of family ties comes into tension, not only with one's possibilities of maturity and independent development, but also with one's service to the world. Family love so often tends persistently to build imprisoning walls, to put blinders on the eyes of the children and young people in the home. . . . Thousands who have gone to overseas mission fields [or dedicated their life to Christ in some other way] have had to face a conflict like that which Jesus" faced (Luccock, pp. 694, 695).

At its best, "true family affection should be an incentive and support of service in the larger realm, and not a substitute for it. A family should be a harbor from which the ship leaves to sail the seas, and not a dock where it ties up and rots" (ibid., p. 695). Such a supporting family, of course, can only result from shared faith and common values among its members. The lack of those commonalities is precisely the problem that

Jesus faced with His flesh-and-blood family. His situation and His teachings about a more important family have encouraged believers in like situations from His time to ours.

A second fundamental idea that emerges from Mark 3:32-35 is that the basis for building God's new family in Jesus is following God's will: "Whoever does the will of God, that one is My brother and sister and mother" (verse 35).

Alexander MacLaren points out that "the doing of the will of God was the very inmost secret of [Jesus] own being. He was conscious, only and always, of delighting to do the will of God. When, therefore, He found that delight in others, there He recognized a bond of union between Him and them" (MacLaren, *I to VIII,* p. 130).

MacLaren goes on to note that "we must carefully observe that these great words of our Lord" regarding the fulfillment of God's will "are not intended to describe the means by which men become [Jesus'] kinfolk, but the tokens that they are such. . . . In other words, He is not speaking about the means of originating this relationship, but about the signs of its reality." Thus Christ's teaching in Mark 3:35 "does not in the slightest degree contradict or interfere with the great teaching that the one way by which we become Christ's brethren is by trusting in Him" (*ibid.,* pp. 130, 131).

But once one is in a saving relationship with God through Christ, the Bible is consistently clear that obedience (doing God's will) is central. That truth concludes Jesus' teaching in the Sermon on the Mount ("Not every one who says to me, 'Lord, Lord,' shall enter the kingdom of heaven, but he who does the will of my Father who is in heaven" [Matt. 7:21, RSV]). It also provides the key idea of the bracket text that Paul uses in the book of Romans, in which he highlights that one of the major purposes of his book is "to bring about the obedience of faith" (Rom. 1:5; 16:26, RSV). That is, those who truly have a saving faith in Christ will be obedient. Christ, of course, asserts that it is that very obedience that indicates whether believers are His brothers and sisters and thus members of the family of God.

15. Thinking About Parables

Mark 4:1-12

> [1]*He began to teach again by the sea. Such a very large crowd assembled to Him that He got into a boat in the sea and sat down, and the whole crowd was on the shore.* [2]*And He taught them many things in parables. In His teaching He said to them,* [3]*"Listen! A farmer went out to sow.* [4]*As he sowed some seed fell beside the pathway, and the birds came and devoured it.* [5]*Other seed fell on rocky places where it did not have much soil, and it immediately sprang up because it had no depth of soil,* [6]*and when the sun rose it was scorched, and it withered because it had no root.* [7]*Yet other seed fell among thorns, and the thorns came up and choked it, and it gave no grain.* [8]*And still other seed fell into good soil, and grew up and produced grain, bearing thirtyfold, sixtyfold, and a hundredfold."* [9]*And He said, "He who has ears to hear, let him hear."*
>
> [10]*When He was alone, those around Him with the Twelve began to inquire of Him about the parables.* [11]*He told them, "To you has been given the secret of the kingdom of God, but to those on the outside everything is said in parables.* [12]*So that seeing they will not perceive, and hearing they will not understand, lest they turn and should be forgiven."*

A major transition has arrived in Jesus' ministry. His earlier teaching had largely taken place in the synagogue. That was understandable, because it was the place where the Jewish people expected to hear God's word expounded. But the opposition to Jesus' teaching made it prudent to avoid what for Jesus had become places of confrontation. Beyond that, Jesus' popularity with the people had become so great that no synagogue could hold the crowds. Thus Mark 4 finds Jesus again teaching by the lakeside.

He not only had a new venue for His teaching, but also a new methodology: "He taught them many things in parables" (Mark 4:2). It isn't that He hadn't ever used parables before, but as opposition increased He began to employ them more.

In a book that focuses on Jesus' actions rather than His teachings, Mark 4 is one of the longest teaching sections in the Gospel. It is certainly the chapter in Mark that most features parables. Mark, as we might expect, presents the reader with fewer parables than Matthew and Luke.

Jesus was not the first Jewish teacher to use parables, but, writes K. R.

Snodgrass, "there is no evidence of anyone prior to Jesus using parables as consistently, creatively and effectively as he did" (in Green, p. 594).

We might best define a parable as "an earthly story with a heavenly meaning" (Barclay, *Matthew,* vol. 2, p. 62). It employs an illustration of something familiar on earth to help people grasp a heavenly or spiritual reality.

As noted above, the context of Mark 4 provides us with one of the primary reasons that Jesus began to use more parables. The religious leadership had spurned Him, but that rejection did not mean that He had any intention to stop preaching. Rather, it signaled that He needed to become more careful. After all, as noted in Mark 3:6, the Pharisees and the secular Herodians were already "plotting" how they might destroy Him. Thus it behooved Him to teach in a manner that would not unduly alienate His enemies or provide them with concrete words that they could use against Him in an attempt to prove that He was a subversive. He still desired to reach the religious leaders, but how to do so was becoming a growing issue. Parables were a part of His answer to the problem. Because they used figurative language, parables could convey a message in a manner that was "safe."

Parables

- were a "safe" way for Jesus to speak
- were interest grabbers
- made truth concrete
- enabled the hearers to rethink the lessons as they went about their daily business
- helped individuals discover truth for themselves

Beyond being safe, parables also grabbed the hearer's interest. People love stories, and the Jews of old were no exception. Jesus, who proved Himself to be one of the greatest storytellers of world history, capitalized on a significant psychological factor through His use of parables. His parables, which begin with things familiar in the lives of His audience, helped keep their attention. Every preacher knows the power of a story in helping maintain the congregation's focus. If that is true inside a church sanctuary, it is even more crucial while preaching in the open air, where people are free to come and go as they please.

Another function of parables is to make truth concrete. Jesus was not speaking in abstractions, but about things familiar in the people's daily lives—such things as the sowing of seeds (Mark 4:3-9), the placement of a lamp (4:21, 22), and the growth of grain (4:26-29). Parables moved Jesus' hearers from the world around them to spiritual realities beyond their everyday affairs. But it was their world He was talking about. They could see that His stories not only had an everyday meaning but also had one beyond their earthly experience.

Yet another value of parables is their ongoing dynamic teaching function. Because Jesus' parables utilized concrete things from the daily lives of His hearers, every time they saw these things they remembered His lessons. Ellen White put it nicely when she wrote: "Afterward, as they looked upon the objects that illustrated His lessons, they recalled the words of the divine Teacher. To minds that were open to the Holy Spirit, the significance of the Saviour's teaching unfolded more and more. Mysteries grew clear, and that which had been hard to grasp became evident" (White, *Christ's Object Lessons,* p. 21).

A final merit of parables is that they compel individuals to discover truth for themselves. Reflection on what He had said led Jesus' hearers to flesh out truth for themselves as their interest in the subject matter of the parables caused them to think through the truth in the stories. Conversely, as William Barclay puts it, "the parable *conceals truth from those who are either too lazy to think or too blind through prejudice to see"* (Barclay, *Matthew,* vol. 2, p. 62). It is that dual emphasis that Jesus seems to be driving at in the rather difficult saying in Mark 4:10-12.

Before examining those verses we need to look briefly at the parable of the sower, which will be the topic of section number 16 below. At the present time, we will merely note that it offers an excellent illustration of the virtues of a parable. For example, it utilized an experience familiar to Jesus' hearers. In fact, one can imagine that as they took their eyes off Jesus they could see sowers at work on the surrounding hillsides. And since such scenes were part of their daily life, Jesus' teaching would often echo in their minds as they walked along. Furthermore, since they constantly encountered the imagery that He had used, they found themselves forced to think about the meaning of the various types of soil and how the sowing of the seed related to their own lives.

That thought brings us to the perplexing statement of verses 10-12, in which Jesus seemingly claims that He taught in parables to hide the truth rather than to make it clear to all His hearers. What did He mean when He told His disciples, "To you has been given the secret of the kingdom of God, but to those on the outside everything is said in parables. So that seeing they will not perceive, and hearing they will not understand, lest they turn and should be forgiven"?

Did Jesus speak in parables to make ideas clearer or to muddle truth in such a way that people wouldn't be able to understand His meaning? Beyond that, did He really want to keep some of His hearers in an unforgiven or lost state?

A Problematic Statement

Many find Mark 4:10-12 to be one of the most problematic passages in the Bible because (1) it suggests that Jesus used parables to block communication, and (2) it implies that Jesus desires some people to remain unforgiven.

The statement in verses 10-12 (based on Isaiah 6:9, 10) has troubled many people across time, since it seems to contradict the very reason that Jesus used parables. And if He wished outsiders not to understand certain teachings, Harvie Branscomb correctly points out, "the most obvious method would have been not to have dealt with those particular topics in public discourse" (Branscomb, p. 78).

But Jesus did present those topics, and He did make the problematic statement of verses 10-12. Why? One way of resolving the problem is to remember that Jesus was simultaneously speaking to at least four groups of people in the same audience:

1. the 12 disciples,
2. a believing but somewhat fluctuating larger group of followers,
3. the "crowd," which included many who were curious but did not necessarily believe, and
4. His adversaries, such as the Pharisees and the scribes from Jerusalem.

It is of more than passing interest that the parable of the sower forms a sandwich around verses 10-12, thus it literally surrounds the difficult passage. And, we should point out, the parable of the sower is about how people hear and respond to the word. Snodgrass notes that "in Mark 4:10-

12 the Evangelist shows what typically happened in Jesus' ministry. . . . Jesus taught the crowds, but his teaching called for response. When people responded, additional teaching was given" (in Green, p. 597). That was certainly the case for the disciples, who received additional instruction in verses 13-20. It also illustrated the soon to be made point that "to him who has will more be given; and from him who has not, even what he has will be taken away" (verse 25, RSV).

"This method of teaching by parables became," concludes J. D. Jones, "a kind of judgment. It sifted out the tares from the wheat, those who were generally spiritually minded from those whose thoughts were of the earth. . . . For these latter, while they heard the story, missed entirely its heavenly meaning; hearing they heard, but did not understand; seeing they saw, but did not perceive. It was foolishness to them, for these things are spiritually discerned" (Jones, vol. 1, p. 112). Or as Matthew Henry cryptically put it, "A parable is a shell that keeps good fruit for the diligent but keeps it from the slothful."

16. Thinking About Discipleship

Mark 4:13-20

¹³And He said to them, "Do you not understand this parable? How then will you understand any parables? ¹⁴The farmer sows the word. ¹⁵And these are the ones beside the pathway where the word is sown, and when they hear, Satan immediately comes and takes the word that had been sown in them. ¹⁶And these in like manner are the ones sown on the rocky places, who when they hear the word receive it immediately with joy, ¹⁷yet not having root in themselves, they are temporary. Afterwards, when affliction or persecution comes on account of the word, they are immediately offended. ¹⁸And the others are those sown among the thorns. These are the ones who hear the word, ¹⁹but the worries of the world, and the deceitfulness of riches, and the desires for other things come in and choke the word, and it is unfruitful. ²⁰And these are the ones sown on the good soil, who hear the word and welcome it and bear fruit—thirtyfold, sixtyfold, and a hundredfold."

Thus far in Mark the reception of Jesus has been a mixed bag. Some have accepted His message and become followers, others have listened but done nothing about it, and some have not only rejected His teachings but have done so aggressively. All of the gospel writers faced a dilemma as they wrote several decades after the death of Jesus: How was it that His own people could reject the Messiah? That repudiation seems to go against Jewish eschatological expectations. Why have some responded to Jesus while most have spurned Him?

Mark's response is to report Jesus' parable on the four types of soil. The parable itself has an autobiographical ring to it. After all, Jesus Himself had experienced the stony-ground minds of the scribes and Pharisees, and He had met the shallow and unstable enthusiasm of the crowd. Thus in a sense Jesus describes the results of His own sowing (preaching). But there is also an aspect in which He is depicting the results of all those who will follow Him in teaching and preaching God's message. It may be a beautiful message but the majority of soil types (hearers) will reject it. They did so in His case and the same has proved consistent down through history.

Before examining the parable itself, it is important to note that the main thrust of the parable focuses on soils, not sowing. That is, it is about different kinds of people and how they respond to the gospel message rather than about preaching that message.

Two constants continue throughout the parable. First, the sowing seems to be the same for all types of soils. They all get the same treatment, the same word. Second, all four types hear the message. Where they differ is not in hearing but in responding. One point the four types share is that they are all *potential* disciples in the sense of being followers of Christ's message. Whether potentiality advances to actuality is not in hearing the word but in responding to it.

David McKenna refers to the pathway hearers as the "no-growth people" (see McKenna, pp. 94-97). The fields in Palestine tended to consist of long, narrow strips divided by pathways. Anybody who has ever had a vegetable garden knows that such pathways soon come to be packed soil in which even weeds have a difficult time growing.

The farmer, needing to use time efficiently, can't help but sow seeds on the pathway. But it does no good. They can't penetrate the hardened soil and soon become a meal for some bird.

In a similar manner, the parable suggests, the paths of some hearers' hearts and minds have been hardened "from the constant tramp of life-long habits" (*ibid.,* p. 94). They have developed an impenetrable shell of emotional and intellectual defenses that will not easily permit the entrance of the gospel message. And, as Jesus points out, Satan is all too ready to snatch away the message before it has a chance.

McKenna refers to the rocky-ground hearers as the "shallow-growth" people. The reason the ground is rocky is not because it is full of stones, but because it consisted of a thin layer of soil covering a sheet of rock. Such hearers have some hope. They do have some good soil, but not very much of it. Such soil can make a good show at first. Because it is fertile it can support nice upward and outward growth. But the problem is that there is not adequate possibility for downward and inward growth because of the rock beneath the plant.

Some hearers, says Jesus, are shallow-soil people. They have potential, but they don't allow God's word to enter deeply into their emotions and intellect. It doesn't become the controlling force in their life. As a result, when trouble comes they fade away, just as does an inadequately rooted plant in the full glare of the summer sun. Mark's readers in Rome had undoubtedly seen many of this type wilt in the heat of Nero's persecution of Christians. But such people aren't limited to the first century. What Christian hasn't witnessed a promising new convert accept Christ with enthusiasm, only to fade away when the excitement is over.

"Stunted-growth" people is McKenna's description for the thorny-ground Christians. Like many people, I love vegetable gardening, but I don't like weeds. Weeds are aggressive and grow rapidly. They are also difficult to root out of the ground. It is easier to ignore them or to cut them off level with the ground. The latter approach has a major drawback. For a while it may look as if we have solved the problem, but the root soon sprouts a new top. And it is a law of life that weeds grow faster than vegetables. Weeds come up by themselves, but ever since Eden, vegetables grow only by "the sweat of thy face" (Gen. 3:19, KJV). The plain fact is that those without an efficient weed-control program cannot have a healthy garden.

Jesus compared that situation to those hearers who allow the "worries of the world, and the deceitfulness of riches, and the desire for other things" to "come in and choke the word" (Mark 4:19). Halford Luccock refers to such people as those who live the "strangled life." He goes on to tell of the schoolboy who, "in reading a list of the chief causes of death, discovered a new fatal disease unknown to him. When asked what it was, he spelled out the word 'miscellaneous.' It *is,*" reports Luccock, "a terrible disease! Millions have died from 'miscellaneous.' The life of the spirit sickens when it is buried under a landslide of miscellaneous things" (Luccock, pp. 697, 698).

People have never lacked "things" to divert them from spiritual concerns, but the twenty-first century certainly hasn't helped. Those in developed societies seem to be obsessed with things, while those in undeveloped places put things on the top of their agenda if they ever get the chance to obtain them. The sad fact, Jesus said, is that a love of things chokes out religious experience. Nothing is truer than the fact that "no man can serve two masters: for either he will hate the one, and love the other; or else he will hold to the one, and despise the other. Ye cannot serve God and mammon" (Matt. 6:24, KJV).

It is only after that rather dismal catalogue of potential Christians who remain in a state of potentiality that we come to the good news of what McKenna labels as "full-growth" people. Here is the good news. Those who keep on sowing the word will see results. They may not be as consistent or as plentiful as the sower may desire but they will come. Failure should not cause Christians to become discouraged. As Pheme Perkins points out, "this parable provides encouragement. . . . The word of the gospel is not too weak for the job. Loss has been part of the process from the beginning. Despite the vigorous opposition to the word, it still yields a rich harvest" (Perkins, p. 574). Jesus tells us that when the word finds root in responsive minds it will bear fruit—thirtyfold, sixtyfold, and even a hundredfold (Mark 4:20). Here we find something about true disciples. They not only hear the word, but they respond to it. And they not only respond to the word but they bear fruit. According to Jesus, there are no true disciples who are fruitless.

But Christian work is not easy. Rejections are ever present, and positive results often are not immediately visible. Remember that germination and early growth take place underground and generally invisibly to the sower.

A quotation that has encouraged me when my life doesn't seem to be making a difference in the world appears in a little book entitled *Education.* Speaking of resurrection day, the author writes, "All the perplexities of life's experience will then be made plain. Where to us have appeared only confusion and disappointment, broken promises and thwarted plans, will be seen a grand, overruling, victorious purpose, a divine harmony.

"There all who have wrought with unselfish spirit will behold the fruit of their labors. . . . Something of this we see here. But how little of the result of the world's noblest work is in this life manifest to the doer! How many toil unselfishly and unweariedly for those who pass beyond their reach and knowledge! Parents and teachers lie down in their last sleep, their lifework seeming to have been wrought in vain; they know not that their faithfulness has unsealed springs of blessing that can never cease to flow; only by faith they see the children they have trained become a benediction and an inspiration to their fellow men, and the influence repeat itself a thousandfold. . . . Men sow the seed from which, above their graves, others reap blessed harvests. They plant trees, that others may eat the fruit. They are content here to know that they have set in motion agencies for good. In the hereafter the action and reaction of all these will be seen" (White, *Education,* pp. 305, 306).

The word from Jesus to each of His disciples is "Keep on sowing."

> **Jesus pictures the true disciple as one**
> - who hears the word
> - responds to the word
> - bears fruit because of the word

17. The Necessity of Ears

Mark 4:21-25

> *[21]And He said to them, "Is a lamp brought so that it can be put under a measuring bowl, or so that it may be put under a bed, rather than being placed on a lampstand? [22]For there is nothing hidden, except that it may be revealed. Nor is anything covered, except that it may come into the open. [23]If anyone has ears to hear, let him hear." [24]And He said to them, "Pay attention to what you hear. In the same measure you measure to others it will be measured to you, and even more will be given to you. [25]For to him who has, more will be given; and to him who has not, even what he has will be taken from him."*

Exploring Mark

One of the most fascinating things about Mark 4:21-25 is that the passage consists of four sayings that also appear in Matthew and Luke. But whereas in Mark we find them in one place, they are scattered throughout the other two synoptic gospels. Thus Mark 4:21 is found in Matthew 5:15 and Luke 11:33, verse 22 is repeated in Matthew 10:26 and Luke 12:2, verse 24 is in Matthew 7:2 and Luke 6:38, and verse 25 in Matthew 13:12; 25:29 and Luke 19:26.

That difference in arrangement is a fact. But what does it mean? Some have argued that it "indicates that Mark assembled the material in this section from a pool of Jesus' sayings that had been gathered prior to his writing" (Edwards, p. 139) and arranged them accordingly. Others suggest that as Jesus went from place to place He undoubtedly said many things more than once in different contexts.

While we may not be able to discover the full reason for the variation of arrangements that we find in the synoptics, we do know that in Mark 4:21-25 we have a series of sayings that form a unit and build upon the parable of the sower in verses 1-20. Both sections emphasize the importance of adequate hearing. Beyond that, verses 21-25 deal with the responsibilities of the fruitful discipleship highlighted in verse 20. Thus we can argue that verses 21 to 25 are an application of the parabolic sermon of verses 1-20. From another perspective, Jesus might have intended verses 21 to 25 to straighten out possible misunderstandings that could have arisen from His saying in verses 11 and 12 on why He taught in parables.

Taking verse 21 in the context of verses 1-20, two things stand out. First, a direct connection exists between verse 20, which speaks of some bearing fruit up to a hundredfold, and verse 21, which commands those who have heard God's word to let their light shine so that others may see it.

A second connection is more subtle. The Twelve may have been feeling quite smug that they were privileged people, that they were the ones to whom Jesus had taken time to explain the secrets of the kingdom (verses 11, 33, 13-20). With the possibility of smugness in view, the command in verse 21 to let their light shine is in part a lesson to the Twelve and to all Christians that privilege brings responsibility with it.

That obligation is the sharing of God's truth with other people so that they also might hear. "Every gift conferred upon us by God is conferred upon us for use; not for our own enjoyment or enrichment, but for service. God never blesses a man for his own sake; He blesses him that he may become a blessing. He never saves a man for his own sake; He saves him that he may become a saviour. He never enriches a man for his own sake; He enriches him that he in his turn may become a source of enrichment to others" (Jones, vol. 1, p. 137).

That is true of all God's gifts. Take spiritual gifts, for example. In Ephesians 4, after listing the gifts, Paul states their purpose: "to equip the saints for the work of ministry, for building up the body of Christ" (verses 11, 12, RSV).

The same goes for the Word (a central theme of Mark 4:1-20). The Word of God is a gift from Him to help men and women find their way to His kingdom. "Thy word," said the Psalmist, "is a lamp unto my feet, and a light unto my path" (119:105, KJV). That being so, those who hope to produce a thirtyfold, sixtyfold, or a hundredfold increase will not be hiding their light.

Many in the church are experts at light hiding. A story tells of two men on a bus who were reading the obituary notice of a man they both knew well. "One exclaimed, 'Look—Smith was a member of the First Church. What do you know about that!'" Halford Luccock, in commenting on the incident, points out that the plain fact is that "we know a good deal about that." Here "was a man who managed to keep [hidden the fact] that he had any relationship to the church of Jesus Christ" (Luccock, p. 702). His lamp was under a bushel rather than on its stand.

Most Christians struggle with Smith's temptation. It is all too easy not to let people know what we believe in—that we are Christians. When that temptation arises we need to rediscover our ears and listen anew to Jesus in Mark 4.

"For there is nothing hidden, except that it may be revealed. Nor is anything covered, except that it may come into the open" (Mark 4:22). "For" is the key word in the verse, tying a person's light-handling style (i.e., hiding it or putting it on a lampstand) of verse 21 to the judgment scene of verse 22. The Bible is clear throughout that even though people may masquerade as one type of soil rather than another, everything that is hidden will ultimately be revealed. "Hypocrisy," Alfred Plummer notes in commenting on verse 22, "is not only wicked but futile, for one day there will be a merciless exposure" (Plummer, p. 129). "For," says Jesus later in

Mark, "whoever is ashamed of me and of my words in this adulterous and sinful generation, of him will the Son of man also be ashamed, when he comes in the glory of his Father with the holy angels" (Mark 8:38, RSV).

How we hear is important. And how we handle the light God gives us is significant to Him. We might be able to fool most people most of the time, but no one deceives God. In the end there will be a soil-testing time, a light-testing time, when even that which we have carefully hidden will be brought out into the open. Jesus pushed home that thought with His oft-repeated words in Mark 4, "If anyone has ears to hear, let him hear" (verse 23).

Hearing is also the topic of verse 24, in which Jesus cautions His followers to "pay attention to what you hear." As some have discovered, hearing is more complex than it first appears. After all, the rocky-soil and thorny-soil hearers of verses 1-20 heard. But what did they hear? They listened with their physical ears but not with the ears of their soul. As a result, they failed to truly understand and they neglected to accept the Word. Hearing in the biblical sense is much more than receiving sounds with one's ears. A matter of heart and soul, it is a spiritual experience.

The rest of verse 24 and all of verse 25 also need to be understood in the context of hearing. As R.C.H. Lenski points out, "He bade them to see well to what they were hearing. Let them bring a full measure of attention and eagerness to learn—Jesus would return to them even a fuller measure of precious and saving truth. To what they had far more would be given. But those who cared not to heed, who brought no need and no desire to Jesus, would naturally find the same measure measured out to them, and that most generously, even going them one better in niggardliness. And by keeping this up . . . the result would be loss of the little that these hearers had at the start" (Lenski, *St. Mark's Gospel,* p. 183).

According to Jesus in Mark 4, nothing is more important than how we hear. All four soils listened to the Word, but only one heard it spiritually, only one responded and let its light shine that it might produce a manifold increase.

And just as the disciples who heard with their heart got further instruction (as God measured it back to them they received more [verses 24, 25]), so it was that the pathside hearers, the rocky-ground hearers, and the thorny-ground hearers who didn't listen with their hearts and respond eventually lost what they had (verse 25). They saw but didn't perceive, they heard but did not understand.

According to Jesus, nothing is more important than the condition of a person's spiritual ears.

18. The Imperative of Growth

Mark 4:26–34

²⁶And He said, "The kingdom of God is like a man casting seed on the earth. ²⁷He sleeps and rises night and day, and the seed sprouts and grows, but how he knows not. ²⁸On its own the earth bears fruit, first a blade of grass, then a head, then the mature head of grain. ²⁹But when the grain is ready, he immediately puts in the sickle, because the harvest has come."

³⁰And He said, "To what should we compare the kingdom of God, or by what parable shall we present it? ³¹It is like a mustard seed, which, when it is sown upon the ground, is smaller than all the seeds on earth. ³²Yet when that which has been sown comes up it becomes larger than all the garden plants and produces great branches, so that the birds of the air are able to dwell under its shade."

³³With many such parables He spoke the word to them, as they were able to hear. ³⁴And He did not speak to them without a parable. But privately He explained everything to His disciples.

We should see the parable of the growing seed (Mark 4:26-29) as an extension of the parable of the sower (verses 1-20), especially the final verse, which deals with the fruitfulness of the good soil. All in all the parable of the sower was rather discouraging, since it predominantly spoke of failure for the person who sows the gospel seed, with only one fourth of the hearers truly accepting the word.

The parable of the growing seed is in one sense a correction provided for any ancient or modern disciples who might be feeling discouraged with the amount of fruitless labor they had extended toward those with "hearing" problems. The bottom line in the parable of the growing seed is that things are happening, even when it doesn't look that way.

Here is a parable for those impatient with what they see in the church around them, people who wish that everybody who claims to be a Christian would just "shape up" and become everything that they should be—now!

The main lesson of the parable is not that human effort is unimportant. After all, farmers must sow the seed and eventually harvest the crop. And they probably need to cultivate some in between. Jesus is not denigrating human effort.

On the other hand, He is definitely teaching that humans have limits to what they can do. The farmer sleeps, Jesus tells us, after he has planted a crop. But just because he is sleeping doesn't mean nothing is happening to the seeds. They are germinating and taking root underground, out of sight of the farmer. Things are taking place but the farmer has no part in them. In fact, there is nothing that he can do. Germination is not something that he is capable of causing. He can only do his part, while leaving the rest to the God of nature.

Jesus tells us that that is what the kingdom of God is like. Individual Christians can plant gospel seeds in the minds of family members, friends, or even total strangers, but they can't make the gospel germinate in a person's life. That is the work of the Holy Spirit. No human can change another person's heart or give an individual a new birth experience. All people can do is plant seeds and cultivate them. God alone performs the new birth experience of John 3:3-7. "The wind blows where it wills," Jesus said in explaining our inability to understand the process, "and you hear the sound of it, but you do not know whence it comes or whither it goes; so it is with every one who is born of the Spirit" (verse 8, RSV). We, like the farmer, can do our part and then rest, not comprehending how the Spirit works any more than the farmer of Jesus' day truly understood or could control germination. Humanity can accomplish only so much.

Some 35 years ago I went to Texas as a young pastor. I had determined that I would hold a full evangelistic series every year. My first "crusade" was hardly impressive. It took place in a little church of 12 members that had no pastor. Twelve at that point was not my favorite number, especially since 11 of them were female and 10 of the 12 were more than 70 years of age.

Now I had nothing against females. After all, my mother was one.

Likewise, I had nothing against "old" people. But as a 26-year-old evangelist I desperately desired to see some young people in my congregation— especially a young male.

Fortunately, there was one at hand who had grown up in my denomination. I went to visit him in his dormitory room at the local branch of the state university, full of confidence that if I exerted my persuasive powers (and perhaps applied a little guilt) he would attend some of my meetings.

In that positive attitude I met with him, prayed with him, prayed for him, pled with him, and did everything I could think of. But to no avail. He never attended one meeting. I concluded that I had failed with that young man.

That wasn't my only failure. Not understanding fully the gospel message myself, a couple of years after that experience I resigned from the ministry with a determination to eventually leave the church and Christianity and to return to the "happy hedonism" in which I had spent my first 19 years of life.

In that condition, the last thing I wanted was to be a Christian. Then one day I just happened to stop at a grocery store in the town where the church had a college. A young man was coming out as I entered. He stopped and inquired if I was George Knight. When I replied in the affirmative he asked me if I remembered him. At that point I generally try to fake it, but I was so discouraged that I just said no. Then he told me that years before I had visited him in his dormitory room and that it had been the turning point in his life, that he was studying to become a minister. I didn't tell him what I was doing.

> ### A Growing-Seed Prayer
>
> "Thank you, Lord, that your kingdom is established by your own power, not by our ability. Help us to cooperate in your sovereign work, and to have full confidence that in our day, as in the days of Jesus, you will produce the harvest" (France, *Mark*, Doubleday, p. 59).

That experience caught me off guard, because I "knew" at the time that I had failed. But that is where the parable of the growing seed comes in. I had planted the seed, but unlike the good farmer I didn't realize that God through His Holy Spirit was doing what I could not do. The message of the kingdom was growing in the young man's heart, but no one could see it. Fortunately, that same work took place in my own life, and a few years later I became a Christian—after I had been a church member for 14 years.

But the Spirit's work in the new birth experience isn't the only lesson in the parable of the growing seed. A second is that growth is gradual rather than immediate—"first a blade of grass, then a head, then the mature head of grain" (verse 28). Ellen White expands upon that point when she writes that "the germination of the seed represents the beginning of spiritual life, and the development of the plant is a beautiful figure of Christian growth. As in nature, so in grace; there can be no life without growth. The plant must either grow or die. As its growth is silent and imperceptible, but continuous, so is the development of the Christian life. At every stage of development our life may be perfect, yet if God's purpose for us is fulfilled, there will be continual advancement. Sanctification is the work of a lifetime" (White, *Christ's Object Lessons,* p. 65).

The third horticultural parable in Mark 4 is that of the mustard seed (verses 30-32). In actual fact the mustard seed is not the smallest one, even in Palestine. But Jesus wasn't providing us with scientific facts. His "point is that it was proverbially small and yet yielded a large shrub. Around the Sea of Galilee, it can reach a height of ten feet and has sometimes reached fifteen feet, although its usual height is about four feet" (Keener, p. 146). Readers of the Bible need to read to understand the concept it is seeking to demonstrate rather than to make Scripture into some kind of an encyclopedia of scientific and historical minutia. That latter course is fraught with pitfalls, since it is not the reason God gave us the Bible.

If the parable of the growing seed might best be thought of as the developing of the kingdom of God in the human heart, the parable of the mustard seed can be regarded as the advance of the Christian movement.

As such, it is a highly positive parable, one that the first disciples probably needed to hear. After all, their humble carpenter from Nazareth was a far cry from the conquering Messiah-king of Jewish dreams. D. E. Nineham highlights the parable's lesson when he writes that the "outwardly insignificant ministry of Jesus may not look [like] the sort of thing that can usher in the kingdom of God, but then, the parable says, the example of the mustard seed should prevent us from judging the significance of results by the size of the beginnings" (Nineham, p. 144).

Christian history provides the most impressive commentary on the parable of the mustard seed. The insignificant little movement begun by Jesus has spread to the ends of the earth and has indeed become "larger than all the garden plants" (Mark 4:32).

19. Authority Over Nature

Mark 4:35-41

35On that day, when evening had come, He said to them, "Let us go over to the other side." 36Leaving the crowd, they took Him, just as He was, in the boat. And other boats were with Him. 37And a hurricane-like storm with great gusts of wind came up, and waves beat into the boat, so that the boat was already filling up. 38He was in the stern, sleeping on a cushion. And they woke Him and said to Him, "Teacher, does it not matter to You that we are perishing?" 39Having awoken, He rebuked the wind, saying to the lake, "Quiet! Be still!" And the wind died down and there was a great calm. 40He said to them, "Why are you afraid? Have you no faith?" 41And they were very much afraid and said to one another, "Who then is this, that even the wind and the sea obey Him?"

The first 34 verses of Mark 4 presented parables about the kingdom of God. With verse 35 Mark's Gospel makes a radical change in direction. The four stories running from Mark 4:35 to 5:43 all highlight Jesus as a miracle worker, as one who has authority over nature (4:35-41), the supernatural (5:1-20), disease (5:21-34), and death (5:35-43). The accounts themselves are longer and more detailed than most of those in Mark. But most important, notes James Edwards, is the fact that "His mighty acts evoke a judgment from those who witness them. The disciples in the foundering boat must choose between faith and fear (4:35-41); the witnesses of the healed Gerasene demoniac must choose between acceptance and rejection of Jesus (5:1-20); [and] both Jairus and the hemorrhaging woman must choose between faith and despair (5:21-43)" (Edwards, p. 147). Following those four stories Mark presents a scene in Nazareth in which the participants must choose between belief and disbelief (6:1-6).

Running throughout the authority miracles is the underlying question:

"Who then is this?" (4:41). Moving beyond simple statements of amazement at Jesus' authority found earlier in Mark (see 1:22, 27), the identity of Jesus becomes a central theme as the gospel narrative pushes toward its first climax in Mark 8:29, in which Peter confesses that Jesus is the Christ.

The first story treats the calming of the storm on the Sea of Galilee (4:35-41). Few recorded miracles were as likely to impress the minds of the disciples as that one. At least four of them had been fishermen on that body of water and they knew the power of such tempests.

The Sea of Galilee was notorious for its storms. Lying nearly 700 feet below sea level, it is surrounded by hills and mountains that are especially steep on the east side. And just 30 miles to the northeast is the 9,200 foot Mount Herman. The interchange of the cold air from Mount Herman and the warm air of the lowlands and the Sea of Galilee at times produces fierce weather conditions as the wind races through the numerous ravines. Given the right conditions, a storm can arise unexpectedly on even what appears to be a clear day. It was the hurricanelike winds and waves of such a storm that caught Jesus and the disciples in Mark 4:35-41.

The event tells us a great deal about both Jesus and the disciples. The first thing that it reveals about Jesus is that He is truly human, that He is like us. Our first view of Him is "sleeping on a cushion" (verse 38). He had had a long and difficult day. Mark emphasizes the fact that it was "on that day" (verse 35) that they crossed the lake. "That day," given the emphasis in the flow of Mark's Gospel, was the day that He had poured out His soul in teaching the parables of the kingdom (4:1-34). He had taught in the open air and the crowd was extremely large (verse 1). Such teaching in the hot sun would be hard work even today, but before the advent of microphones it was even moreso.

One result of such a strenuous occasion was that it left Jesus exhausted. After a wearing day He saw only one way of escape from the pressing crowds, and that was to cross the lake. But even then a small fleet of boats followed the one containing Him and His disciples (verses 35, 36). Jesus soon fell into a sound sleep as the disciples worked the boat.

The tired Jesus was indeed like us. He was "God with us" in human flesh (Matt. 1:23), able to sympathize with our weaknesses (Heb. 4:15; 2:17).

A second thing the incident depicts about Jesus is that He could be seemingly heedless to the needs of the disciples. Ordinarily it should not have taken more than an hour and a half to cross the lake. But this was no ordinary day. Caught in the full fury of the storm, their boat was not only being buffeted by fierce winds and waves, but was filling with water.

The disciples were doing all they could to keep it afloat, but it was a losing battle. While they fought for their lives, Jesus took a nice nap, seemingly oblivious to the situation and their fears. But at last they awoke Him, uttering a reproach in the process: "Teacher, does it not matter to You that we are perishing?" (Mark 4:38). Don't You care?

It wasn't the only experience in the New Testament in which Jesus seemed not to care about His followers. Think of the death of Lazarus. Lazarus' sisters told Him about their brother's serious illness before he died. Mary and Martha undoubtedly expected Jesus to drop everything and to rush right over since Lazarus was one whom Jesus loved in a special way. But that's not what happened. Instead of coming to help His friend, Jesus "stayed two days longer in the place where he was" (John 11:6, RSV). During that time His friend Lazarus died. What must Mary and Martha have been thinking? Didn't Jesus even care?

But the story of the storm on the Sea of Galilee raises a third point about Jesus—that He is mighty in power, even having authority over the forces of nature. Upon being awakened, "He rebuked the wind, saying to the lake, 'Quiet! Be still!' And the wind died down and there was a great calm" (Mark 4:39). That display of power impressed the wearied and fearful disciples, who began to ask each other who Jesus was, since "even the wind and the sea obey Him" (verse 41).

Their question was not an idle one. In the Old Testament it is Yahweh (God) alone who has the power to quell natural storms (Ps. 65:7; 89:9; 104:6, 7; Isa. 51:9, 10). Especially impressive is Psalm 107:23-32, in which we read of individuals who, like the disciples, cry to God in their distress and are delivered. Only Yahweh could have "made the storm be still" (Ps. 107:29).

Thus Mark 4:35-41 not only pictures Jesus as a human being who gets weary and as one who doesn't seem to care, but it also presents Him in all His power—power that identifies Him with none other than Yahweh, the God of the Old Testament. Slowly but surely the disciples are learning Jesus' true identity.

The good news is that the Jesus who saved His disciples from the storm is still mighty. Christians have nothing to fear in the long run, because they serve a Lord who has authority. That authority, as Mark's miracle stories and his entire Gospel illustrate, is even over the power of death (5:35-43; 16:1-8). That message was especially important to Mark's readers in Rome, since, as Ralph Martin puts it, "they faced the demonic outrage of persecution" and the "'little ship of the church'" was being "rocked in the storm and is almost swamped" (Martin, *Where the Action Is,* pp. 34, 35). Or as Robert Guelich notes, "this story assures Mark's readers through the concluding question (4:41b) that in Jesus they have one in whom God was and is at work, one whom the 'wind and the waves' do obey, even when it appears the storms may overwhelm them" (Guelich, p. 271).

That lesson is still important today as we face life's trials. The good news is that we don't encounter them alone. We do so with the mighty Jesus by our side.

Another thing that it is vital for us to keep in mind is that "Jesus not only rebuked the storm; he also rebuked his disciples. Tenderly, lovingly, none the less truly, he censured their faithless fear, 'Why are ye fearful? Have ye not yet faith?' There is a searching message in those words, 'not yet.' After all they had seen and heard, the disciples should have trusted the Master and should have believed themselves safe in his company. How much more reason for faith have we, who now know, not only the miracles of the Man of Galilee, but the continued marvels of a risen Lord!" (Erdman, p. 86). Our faith as Christians is an anchor point of hope and assurance as we face the difficulties of life.

A final thing that we should note before leaving Mark 4:35-41 is that Jesus only appeared to be unconcerned with His followers' needs. That was true in the case of Lazarus, in which the delay glorified God by giving Jesus the opportunity to demonstrate that He had authority even over death (John 11:1-44). And it was also true during the storm on the Sea of Galilee. Jesus' seeming lack of response helped the disciples to see the depth of their lack of faith and their utter need of Him. When those lessons were evident the Jesus who seemed not to care became the saving Jesus of might and authority. Those aspects of His character are crucial for each of us to understand and remember because we also have times in our lives when God seems to be uncaring and silent. To each of us at such occasions the miracle on the Sea of Galilee still has meaning.

20. Authority Over the Supernatural

Mark 5:1-20

¹They came to the other side of the lake into the country of the Gerasenes. ²When He got out of the boat, immediately a man from the tombs with an unclean spirit met Him. ³He lived among the tombs and no one could bind him anymore, even with a chain. ⁴For he had often been bound with shackles and chains, but he shattered the chains and broke the shackles, and no one was able to subdue him. ⁵Constantly, night and day, among the tombs and in the hills, he was crying out and cutting himself with stones. ⁶Seeing Jesus from a distance, he ran and worshiped Him, ⁷and crying out with a loud voice, he said, "What do we have to do with each other, Jesus, Son of the Most High God? Swear by God that You will not torture me." ⁸For He was saying to him, "Unclean spirit, come out of the man." ⁹And He asked him, "What is your name?" He replied, "My name is Legion, because we are many." ¹⁰And he begged Him again and again that He would not send them outside the country. ¹¹Now there was a great herd of pigs feeding nearby on the hillside. ¹²And the demons begged Him, saying, "Send us into the pigs, so that we may enter them." ¹³He gave them permission. And the unclean spirits came out and entered into the pigs, and the herd rushed down the steep bank into the lake, and about 2,000 of them were drowned in the lake.

¹⁴And those herding the pigs fled and told it in the city and in the countryside, and they came to see the thing that had happened. ¹⁵They came to Jesus, and seeing the demon-possessed man—the man who had had the legion—sitting, clothed, and in his right mind, they were afraid. ¹⁶And those who had seen it related what had happened to the demon-possessed man and to the pigs. ¹⁷And they began to beg Him to depart from their territory. ¹⁸As He was getting into the boat, the demon-possessed man begged Him that he might be with Him. ¹⁹He refused him, but said to him, "Go to your house and to your people and report to them everything the Lord has done for you and that He had mercy on you." ²⁰And he left and began to preach in Decapolis everything Jesus did for him, and everyone was amazed.

In Mark 5:1-20 we have an extremely long story in a Gospel noted for its brevity. "That special importance attaches to the subject," G. Campbell Morgan writes, "is evidenced by the fact that Mark has given so much space to this particular story, relating it with much more . . . detail than either Matthew or Luke, who nevertheless both record the miracle" (Morgan, p. 110). Whereas Mark gives 20 verses to the story, Matthew allots 7 and Luke 14. Mark uses 330 words to tell the story, while Matthew's much longer gospel employs only 135.

With those statistics in mind, it is obvious that this particular story has a special significance for the biblical author. Part of that interest is that the story forcefully displays the authority of Jesus. But more than that, it presents the demons as providing the most striking christological title for Jesus to this point in Mark's Gospel: "Jesus, Son of the Most High God" (Mark 5:7). However, what is even more important in the context of the flow of his presentation is that all of these things took place in Gentile territory. Jesus is not only moving outside of Jewish territory to give His message, but the miracle demonstrates that He has power over the forces of evil even away from Jewish areas. Readers are getting a perspective that His message has universal import, rather than being only something for the Jews. Jesus highlights that theme with His command to the healed man to "go to your house and to your people and report to them everything the Lord has done for you and that He had mercy on you" (verse 19). R. T. France points out that "this recognition that the Jewish Messiah has a ministry which must ultimately extend outside Jewish circles will become more central to Mark's plot towards the end of Act One (7:24 onward)" (France, *Mark,* NIGTC, p. 226).

The exact location of the miracle is somewhat unclear today, but that it took place in the region known as Decapolis on the southeast shore of the Sea of Galilee is quite certain (see map on p. 14). The term "Decapolis" consists of two Greek words that mean 10 cities. Those cities had banded together for mutual protection. The fact that it was a Gentile region is indicated by the presence of a large herd of pigs, something that would not be found among a Jewish population.

"The awful picture of the demoniac," Alexander MacLaren suggests, "is either painted from life, or it is one of the most wonderful feats of the poetic imagination. Nothing more terrible, vivid, penetrating, and real was ever conceived by the greatest creative genius" (MacLaren, *I-VIII*, p. 177). The picture of him that Mark gives is bad enough, but Matthew adds that he was a terror to others (Matt. 8:28), while Luke tells us that he wore no clothes (Luke 8:27).

Thus the picture is of an uncontrollable, naked madman rushing at the somewhat startled disciples and Jesus. The rather complex event takes place in a context in which Jesus had already established His supremacy over Satan and his followers in the wilderness temptation (Mark 1:12, 13). The forces possessing the man in Mark 5 recognized that supremacy, since he fell down and worshiped Jesus and correctly identified Him as the Son of God (verses 6, 7). But a struggle still took place with the unclean spirits unwilling to leave upon Jesus' first request (verse 8). That led to a dialogue, with the demons asking to be sent into a nearby herd of swine and Jesus granting that request, after which the pigs ran down the hill into the lake and drowned (verses 9-13). Mark then pictures the demon-possessed man as "sitting, clothed, and in his right mind" (verse 15).

The change is a remarkable part of the story. But not the most extraordinary aspect. "The wild and naked madman," writes William Barclay, "had become a sane and sensible citizen. And then there comes the surprise, the paradox, the thing that no one would really expect. One would have thought that" the citizens of the region "would have regarded the whole matter with joy; but they regarded it with terror. And one would have thought that they would have besought Jesus to stay with them and to exercise still further His amazing power; but they besought Him to get out of their district as quickly as possible" (Barclay, *Mark*, p. 120).

And why? Because even though a man had been healed it also led to the destruction of their pigs. That was too much for them. "Jesus," Ray Stedman points out, "had just hit these people in the tenderest part of their anatomy: the pocketbook. Pigs, remember, were a ceremonially unclean animal to the Jews; the law of Moses forbade the eating of pork. Yet pigs were important to the economy of the region. Perhaps pigs were raised to be sold to the Romans who occupied the land. In any case, a huge profit drowned in the sea when Jesus sent the demons into that herd of pigs. That is why, instead of rejoicing that a man was healed and restored to his right mind, these people pleaded with Jesus to go away" (Stedman, *Servant Who Rules*, p. 162).

The Four Surprises of Mark 5:1-20

1. that the man was healed,
2. that the only wish of his neighbors was to get rid of Jesus,
3. that Jesus wouldn't let the healed man come with Him,
4. that Jesus never told the healed man to be quiet, but rather to go tell what He had done for him.

The next big surprise in the story is when the healed man begged to follow Jesus in His travels and Jesus forbade it (Mark 5:18, 19). It may be the only case recorded in the gospels in which Jesus turned a person away. And what a needy person he must have been. Here is an eager new convert who desperately wants to be with his Healer, yet Jesus sends him away.

And why did Jesus tell him to go away? Possibly because the healed demoniac was a Gentile, and, outside of Jesus, nobody was yet ready for Gentiles to be included in His evangelistic team. But there is another reason, a more important one. Jesus has a mission for him. That brings us to the next big shock of this story. Whereas Jesus had repeatedly in the book of Mark told people not to tell others what He had done for them, now He orders this man to do just the opposite. Vincent Taylor writes that "the command to tell his story stands out in contrast to the injunctions to silence in i.25, 44, iii.12, v.43, vii.36, etc., but is credibly explained by the fact that the district lay outside Galilee" (Taylor, p. 285). Outside of the sphere of Jewish influence Jesus faced no danger that people would precipitate a political crisis because of any preconception of the kingly side of the Messiah. In that context the powerful message of a man who had been totally transformed was safe to preach. In fact, France suggests, those who had known him before could hardly "ignore the dramatic change which [had] resulted from his encounter with Jesus" (France, *Mark,* NIGTC, p. 232). Thus the banishment of Jesus by the citizens of Decapolis did not rid them of Him. Instead, they had His message in the person of the man healed of a legion of unclean spirits.

Before moving away from this story of Jesus' authority over the supernatural, we should note one final thing. In verse 19 Mark provides his readers with another clue to Jesus' true identity when he reports Him as saying, "Go to your house and to your people and report to them everything the Lord has done for you." But according to Mark, the man went out and told "everything Jesus did for him" (verse 20). Thus he equated Jesus with the Lord. "In the Gospel of Mark," notes James Edwards, "the healed demoniac becomes the first missionary-preacher sent out by Jesus. Remarkably, he is a Gentile sent to Gentiles" (Edwards, p. 160).

21. Authority Over Disease

Mark 5:21-34

[21]And when Jesus had crossed over again in the boat to the other side, a large crowd gathered to Him, and He was beside the sea. [22]One of the synagogue leaders named Jairus came, and seeing Him, fell at His feet [23]and begged him again and again, saying, "My daughter is at the point of death. Come that You may lay Your hands on her, so that she will be healed and may live." [24]And He went with him.

And a great crowd followed Him and was pressing against Him. [25]And a woman having had a flow of blood for 12 years, [26]and having suffered many things by many physicians, and having spent everything that she had without having been helped at all, but rather having become worse; [27]that woman, hearing reports about Jesus came in the crowd from behind and touched His garment. [28]For she said to herself, "If I can even touch His garments, I shall be healed." [29]And immediately her fountain of blood was dried up, and she knew in her body that she was cured from the disease. [30]And at that very instant Jesus knew in Himself that power had gone forth from Him. Turning in the crowd, He said, "Who touched My garments?" [31]His disciples said to Him, "You see the crowd pressing against You, yet You say, 'Who touched Me?'" [32]And He looked around to see who did this. [33]Now the woman, fearing and trembling, knowing what had happened to her, came and fell down before Him and told Him the whole truth. [34]He said to her, "Daughter, your faith has healed you, go in peace and be healed of your disease."

With Mark 5:21-34 we discover another of Mark's key themes: the healing power of faith as it takes hold of Jesus. To gain the full significance of these stories we need to recognize that the Greek word for to heal *(sōzō)* also means to save. In these miracle stories the two are not separate. Those who are healed also come into saving contact with Jesus as

Lord. It is that healing faith that unites the story of Jairus with that of the hemorrhaging woman. In fact, Mark sandwiches the woman's case (verses 25-34) between the two parts of the story of Jairus (verses 21-24; 35-43) in such a way as to emphasize the efficacy of faith. That faith and its healing effects as it takes hold of Jesus is what unites the two stories.

The cases themselves are quite different. Jairus was a man of some stature in his community. As the leader or ruler of a synagogue he was, so to speak, the president of its board of elders and in charge of the synagogue's religious services.

But "even more important to the story than Jairus' position as a Jewish leader," suggests Joel Marcus, "is his position as a father" (Marcus, p. 365). He is the parent of a girl who has reached the age of 12—the very age in Jewish culture when a girl became a woman.

Mark not only pictures Jairus as a father, but as a loving and concerned father, one who was willing to cast aside his prejudices and perhaps even his leadership position in coming publicly to Jesus as he did. Remember, this story probably takes place in Capernaum, where Jesus has already faced difficulty with the scribes from Jerusalem and other Jewish leaders. The crowds, who had undoubtedly heard of the curing of the wild man with an unclean spirit in Decapolis (5:1-20), may have been excited to see Jesus return from the other side of the lake. But the religious leaders must have been of a different mind, believing perhaps that He should have stayed in that Gentile region.

It is in that context that Jairus openly went to Jesus. And why? Because he was desperate. Because his precious daughter was ill to the point of death. Because from what he had heard about Jesus, Jairus believed that He could heal his child. This man was a true father. His prejudices and position were nothing compared with the life of his daughter.

But Jairus not only cast aside his prejudices, he also abandoned his dignity and his pride. Mark tells us that he "fell at [Jesus'] feet, and begged Him again and again" that He might come to his house and lay His hands on her and heal her (verses 22, 23).

The fact that Jairus was a synagogue leader who had faith in Jesus must have been of special interest to Mark's first readers in Rome, who lived in a world some decades after the crucifixion of Jesus, years that had witnessed the growing gulf between Jews and Christians. Their own contacts with the Jews may not have always have been pleasant. That such an important person in the Jewish community could come to faith and cross over to Jesus would especially encourage them in their own difficult situation.

The woman, by way of contrast to Jairus, was nobody of importance. In fact, she had been a social outcast for the past 12 years. She apparently had had a vaginal hemorrhaging, a monthly period that just wouldn't stop. According to Levitical law, "if a woman has a discharge of blood for many days, not at the time of her impurity, or if she has a discharge beyond the time of her impurity, all the days of the discharge she shall continue in uncleanness; . . . she shall be unclean" and everything she touched was unclean (Lev. 15:25-27, RSV). Thus the woman with an issue of blood was in somewhat the same social position as a leper. Both were untouchable and social outcasts, cut off from normal fellowship with other people.

Mark pictures this particular sufferer as one who had tried everything before she came to Jesus. Not only does the biblical author tell us that she had exhausted all her funds on physicians to no avail, but she had also probably tried the kind of cures later recorded in the Talmud. Some of them were tonics and astringents, but others were just plain superstition, such as carrying the ashes of an ostrich egg in a linen rag or a barley corn discovered in the manure of a white female donkey (see Barclay, *Mark*, p. 128). In her desperation it is not hard to imagine that this woman had sampled every possible cure. After all, 12 years is a long time.

And then she heard about Jesus. But how to approach Him. That was the problem. Her condition was not the kind of thing that you just shout out in the crowd. No, it was an embarrassing disease, something private.

So she decided that she would handle it discreetly. She would just sneak up behind Jesus and touch the edge of His garment. In obedience to Numbers 15:38-41, devout Jews in Jesus' time wore an outer robe with a tassel at each of its four corners as a sign that they belonged to the God that had brought them out of the land of Egypt. It was apparently one of those tassels that the woman touched.

And when she did so, so to speak, lightning flashed, healing power surged between them. She knew that she had been healed and Jesus recognized it also. At that point Jesus did something that seems uncharacteristic of Him and, from one perspective, even cruel.

He did what the woman feared most. Pausing, He asked who it was that had touched Him. That was the last thing the woman wanted. She didn't want herself and her problem or even her healing to become a public spectacle. That is why she had been so secretive in the first place. And now Jesus, whom she had trusted in, was bringing the whole thing out in the open.

Why such "cruelty?" we need to ask. In actuality it wasn't cruelty but offered an opportunity to bestow a second and more important blessing upon the woman. David Smith points out that " 'had she been suffered to steal away, she would have lost the chief blessing of her life. She would have gained the healing of her body, but she would have missed the healing of her soul. She would have proved the power of Jesus, but she would have remained a stranger to His love. For look what He said to her, as she lay there fearing and trembling at His feet: "Daughter"—He had never addressed any woman by that gracious name before—"thy faith hath made thee whole; go in peace" (v. 34). If I know anything about human nature, I know this, that that woman would thank God all her days that she could not be hid. It was worthwhile to be put to shame in the eyes of the crowd, to hear that gracious word from the lips of Christ: "Thy faith hath made thee whole" ' " (quoted in Jones, vol. 1, p. 214). She could rejoice forevermore that she had met the Lord who could not only heal her physical malady but could save her from her spiritual disease.

The one thing that distinguished the woman from the crowd was her faith. They were all jostling and bumping into Jesus and pressing against Him as the somewhat skeptical disciples pointed out (verse 31). But when that one person touched Him, healing energy flashed forth. The difference was that she had faith.

Donald English writes that "as the Jewish leadership plots against him, some of his family doubt him, his disciples stumble along more or less perceiving in isolated flashes what is going on, and as a synagogue ruler is on his way to discovering what trust in Jesus can mean, this unnamed woman has cut through all the barriers, impelled by need, and by two steps has found the secret of faith—trusting Jesus and telling him all. What he accused the disciples of still not properly having (4:40) he now praises the woman for possessing (5:34). The crescendo of Jesus' miraculous deeds is rising still. It is also another response of faith to encourage Jesus Himself, and Mark's readers" (English, 115).

But it wasn't a mature faith—yet. It was what we might call a timid touch of the edge of the garment sort of faith, one not yet strong enough to bring her openly to Jesus. Also it was a superstitious faith in the sense that she believed that some kind of magical power resided in Jesus' garments.

But He honored that faith. And not only that, He enriched it and deepened it when He said, "Daughter, your faith has healed you, go in peace and be healed of your disease" (verse 34).

Her story teaches us that Jesus meets us where we are. As weak and defective as our faith may be, He recognizes it for what it is and enables that faith in Him to grow so that healing faith transforms into saving faith.

22. Authority Over Death

Mark 5:35–43
[35]While He was still speaking they came from the house of the synagogue leader, saying, "Your daughter has died, why trouble the Teacher further?" [36]But Jesus, overhearing the words being spoken, said to the synagogue leader, "Fear not, only believe." [37]And He did not allow anyone to accompany Him except Peter and James and John the brother of James. [38]They came into the house of the synagogue leader, and He saw a commotion and weeping and loud wailing. [39]Entering, He said to them, "Why are you making a commotion and weeping? The child did not die, but sleeps." [40]And they ridiculed Him. But, putting out everybody, He took the child's father and mother and His companions and went in where the child was. [41]Taking the child's hand, He said to her, "Talitha koum!" (which is translated as "Little girl, I say to you, arise.") [42]And immediately the little girl rose up and walked, for she was 12 years old. And at once they were overcome with astonishment. [43]He strictly ordered them that no one should know this, and He told them to give her something to eat.

Possibly Jairus had met Jesus before. In Luke 7:1-10 we read of the healing of the servant of the centurion in charge of the Roman garrison in Capernaum. His servant "was sick and at the point of death" (verse 2, RSV). Instead of approaching Jesus Himself the centurion sent the elders of the Jews to request Him to heal the servant. The Jews meeting Jesus verified that the centurion was a worthy man who had even built them a synagogue. The centurion, demonstrating extraordinary faith, witnessed the healing of his servant.

It is possible that Jairus, as the leader of a synagogue in that same city, may have been a part of that delegation. If not, he had certainly heard about the healing of a person at the very point of death.

And Jairus didn't forget. Soon his own daughter, as we noted in section number 21, found herself in the same condition. What Jesus had done for the centurion's servant, Jairus reasoned, He could do for his daughter. At that point, with hope in his heart and more than a glimmer of faith, he threw caution, pride, and dignity to the wind and went to Jesus, begging Him to help him in his need (Mark 5:22, 23).

How excited Jairus must have been when Jesus agreed to go with him. Hope welled up in his heart. He knew that this was his last chance. Also he realized that time was of the essence. His daughter was at death's doorstep. If ever there was a time for haste it was now.

But instead of haste there was delay as Jesus not only stopped to minister to the hemorrhaging woman (verses 25-34), but also to have a short conversation with her. Those few short minutes must have seemed like hours to Jairus as he impatiently waited for Jesus to solve the crisis of his life.

But the delay was fatal. Messengers soon arrived saying that it was too late, that the girl had died (verse 35).

Hope must have perished for Jairus also. He knew that Jesus could heal the sick, even the deathly ill. Jesus had done plenty of that in Capernaum and the surrounding area. But sickness was one thing and death another. The latter had a finality to it.

His daughter had not only died but so had his hope. Why had Jesus delayed? There might have been a chance. But now nothing could be done.

It was at that very point that Jesus uttered a short but absolutely essential sentence: "Fear not, only believe" (verse 36). Simple words but with a difficult lesson. After all, Jesus said "fear not" *after* events had already confirmed Jairus' worst fears. The girl was dead. And Jesus said "only believe" when there seemed no longer to be reason for faith or hope.

But here the ruler of the synagogue was wrong. What to Jairus had been a delay had to Jesus been an opportunity to give him an even greater blessing than he had at first asked for—a blessing that was not only for him but for the suffering Christian community in Rome to whom Mark wrote, and a blessing that will encourage God's people to the end of time. God's delay, God's silence, often has a purpose. It was so in the case of Jairus.

"Only believe." Easy to say and difficult to do—especially in the midst of crisis. It is easier to give up, to turn our backs upon Jesus and walk away.

"Fear not, only believe." That, writes James Edwards, "is the challenge before Jairus, and before everyone who meets Jesus: to believe only in what circumstances allow, or to believe in the God who makes all things possible? One thing only is necessary—to believe. The present tense of the Greek imperative means to keep believing, to hold onto faith rather than give in to despair. With respect to his daughter's circumstances, Jairus's future is closed; but with respect to Jesus it is still open. Faith is not something *Jairus has* but something that *has Jairus,* carrying him from despair to hope. Jesus' authoritative word to Jairus is not to fear but to believe" (Edwards, p. 166). And that is His authoritative word to me also, even when everything looks impossible.

"Of all the Christian graces," J. C. Ryle notes, "none is so frequently mentioned in the New Testament as faith, and none is so highly commended.—No grace brings such glory to Christ. Hope brings an eager expectation of good things to come. Love brings a warm and willing heart. *Faith brings an empty hand, receives everything, and can give nothing in return.*—No grace is so important to the Christian's own soul. By faith we begin. By faith we live. By faith we stand. We walk by faith and not by sight. By faith we overcome. By faith we have peace. By faith we enter into rest" (Ryle, p. 102, italics supplied).

Christ's authority as a basis for faith

1. Authority over nature (4:35-41)
2. Authority over the supernatural (5:1-20)
3. Authority over diseases (5:21-34)
4. And even authority over death (5:35-43)

The Bible's message is that God can do what He has promised in Jesus.

"Only believe." And Jairus did, following Jesus and His inner circle of disciples (Peter, James, and John) to his own home. There they came face to face with the "experts on death," hired professional mourners, who laughed with derision at Jesus' statement that "the child did not die, but sleeps" (verse 39). The mourners "know full well that the girl is dead and that dead people don't come back to life" (Marcus, p. 371).

But Jesus, practicing the "art of ignoring," takes His three disciples along with the girl's parents into the room where He does the impossible. Taking her hand and telling her to arise (Mark 5:41), He demonstrates that He has power over death itself.

That teaching is one of the most important in the New Testament. It will climax Mark's Gospel, when Jesus Himself gains victory over death and rises from the grave (16:1-8). Beyond that, it becomes a centerpiece for Paul. "We would not have you ignorant, brethren, concerning those who are asleep," he wrote, "that you may not grieve as others do who have no hope. For since we believe that Jesus died and rose again, even so, through Jesus, God will bring with him those who have fallen asleep. For this we declare to you by the word of the Lord, that we who are alive, who are left until the coming of the Lord, shall not precede those who have fallen asleep. For the Lord himself will descend from heaven with a cry of command, with the archangel's call, and with the sound of the trumpet of God. And the dead in Christ will rise first; then we who are alive, who are left, shall be caught up together with them in the clouds to meet the Lord in the air; and so shall we always be with the Lord. Therefore comfort one another with these words" (1 Thess. 4:13-18, RSV).

> "Lord, teach us what faith means when human possibilities are exhausted. May we not join the laughter of the crowd, but come into the little room in faith, even when we can have no idea what you are going to do" (France, Mark, Doubleday, p. 71).

And what comforting words they are, especially when contrasted with those who have "no hope" once death falls upon them or their loved ones (4:13). The healing of the synagogue ruler's daughter is Jesus' first demonstration in Mark that Christians indeed have nothing to fear, even in death, but have every reason to believe in Him (Mark 5:36). Why? Because what He did for Jairus' daughter He eventually will do for each and every one of His followers. Jesus demonstrated in Mark 5 what He will later verbalize in John 11: "I am the resurrection and the life; he who believes in me, though he die, yet shall he live, and whoever lives and believes in me shall never die" (verses 25, 26, RSV).

The miracle of raising Jairus' daughter was of crucial importance to Mark's Roman audience. They had already seen some of their relatives and fellow church members martyred in Nero's amphitheaters. And who knows, they themselves might be next. To such a people the message that Jesus had power over death was an important truth of the first order. It is still an anchor for Christians in the twenty-first century. We still, when the going gets tough, must choose faith over fear. In fact, we need to make that choice even when the going isn't so tough. "Fear not, only believe" is not a statement only for Jairus. It is a motto for every Christian.

Ralph Martin summed up the message of Mark 5:35-43 nicely when he wrote that "People laughed at Jesus (5:40). Now, because of Jesus and His victory, Christians laugh at death (1 Cor. 15:54-57)" (Martin, *Where the Action Is,* p. 45).

23. Rejection Versus Mission

Mark 6:1-13
¹He went away from there and came into His hometown, and His disciples followed Him. ²When the Sabbath came He began to teach in the synagogue and many listeners were astonished, saying, "Where did this man learn these things? And what is the wisdom given to Him so that miracles come through His hands? ³Is not this man the carpenter, the son of Mary and the brother of James and Joses and Judas and Simon? Are not His sisters here with us?" And they were offended at Him. ⁴Jesus said to them, "A prophet is not without honor except in his hometown and among his relatives and in his own house." ⁵And He could not do any miracles there, except that He laid His hands on a few sick people and healed them. ⁶He was amazed because of their unbelief.

He went around the villages in a circuit teaching. ⁷He called to Him the Twelve and began to send them out two by two, and He gave them authority over unclean spirits. ⁸And He commanded them that they should take nothing on the road except only a walking stick—not food, not a knapsack, not copper coins in their belt—⁹but to wear sandals and not to put on two tunics. ¹⁰He said to them, "Whenever you enter into a house, re-

main there until you leave that place. ¹¹And whatever place does not wel-
come you or listen to you, go from there shaking the dust from your feet as
a testimony to them." ¹²They went out and preached that people should re-
pent. ¹³And they expelled many demons and anointed many sick with oil
and healed them.

Jesus' hometown is an obvious reference to Nazareth. It was not an impressive place. Situated on a rocky hillside, it had a population of 500 at
the most (see Bromiley, vol. 3, pp. 500, 501). The village was not noted
for anything. Thus the quip of Nathanael, "Can anything good come out
of Nazareth?" (John 1:46, RSV). Probably not much did. And it appears
that even its citizens didn't expect much from it.

They certainly didn't want to see Jesus as an exception to that rule.
After all, they knew Him. Some of them had played with Him as boys.
Others had hired Him to do work for them as a carpenter. Not only had
they watched Him grow up, they even knew His mother and brothers and
sisters. The significant thing in the family history of Mark 6:3, contrary to
Jewish custom, is that it does not mention Joseph. He should have been
called the Son of Joseph rather than the Son of Mary. The wording may
reflect one of two realities. First, it might be a slur on Jesus' birth by the
townspeople, inferring that Mary had become pregnant before marriage,
or it might be a deliberate allusion by Mark to the virgin birth.

Whatever the case, Jesus to the citizens was nothing special. They
knew both Him and His family. He had spent 30 years in their community as one of them. Nazareth illustrates that familiarity breeds contempt.

Jesus was like them in His humanity, yet there was something different
about Him. Whether they wanted to or not, they had to admit that point.
They would have denied it if they could have. In spite of their prejudices
they had no choice but to acknowledge that He wasn't just like them.
Their problem came in trying to explain the contrast. As they expressed it,
His differences fell into two categories.

First, "Where did this man learn these things?" (Mark 6:2). Stories of
Jesus' teaching ministry had undoubtedly filtered back to Nazareth. They had
heard that He not only taught but did so with authority. But the Nazarenes
couldn't account for His learning or His authority. Although He hadn't stud-
ied with the scribes in Jerusalem, yet He successfully rebutted their challenges.

The citizens of Nazareth were dumbfounded at His knowledge.

Second, "What is the wisdom given to Him so that miracles come through His hands?" (verse 2). Prophets of old such as Elijah had performed miracles, but those were exceptions and relatively few. By way of contrast, Jesus' ministry provided a stream of powerful miracles. He healed lepers, cast out unclean spirits, and "as many as touched him were made whole" (Mark 6:56, KJV). Repeatedly the people had been "amazed and glorified God, saying, 'We never saw anything like this'" (2:12, RSV).

Here was a problem. How could Jesus come up with power that neither Moses nor Elijah could equal. Heredity was obviously not the answer. Just look at His brothers. They had nothing special about them. And it certainly couldn't be attributed to environment—at least not the environment of Nazareth. Since they couldn't figure out why He was different, they merely reacted emotionally and were "offended at Him" (6:3).

The Nazarenes faced a problem that all people who meet Jesus have to answer personally for themselves. He is either who He claims to be or He is inspired by the devil. There is no middle ground with Jesus of Nazareth. Meeting Jesus is to be forced to make a response. We can either be offended at Him or have faith. No other options exist.

Having said that, it is not all that difficult to see why the people of Nazareth felt the way they did. Let's transfer the situation to our times. Imagine a well-known, but "uneducated" working person from our town suddenly declaring himself the founder of a new kingdom. Some of us would undoubtedly shake our heads. But if we could see beyond our prejudices we would eventually have to evaluate his claims and make a decision. So it was in Nazareth. Their choice was doubt rather than faith.

And because of their decision the Bible tells us that "He could not do any miracles there" (verse 5). Jesus' miracles required two pre-conditions. The first was power, which Jesus seemed to have in plentiful supply. The second was faith, as recently taught by the miracles of the woman with an issue of blood and Jairus' daughter (5:21-43). It was faith that was in short supply among the citizens of Nazareth. "He was amazed because of their unbelief" (6:6).

But notice that word "except." Because of their unbelief He couldn't do any miracles there *"except* that He laid His hands on a few sick people and healed them" (verse 5). It is easy to look to a congregation or a group of people and see nothing but a sea of doubt. But, as in Nazareth, there always exist those hidden ones that truly believe in spite of the overwhelming prejudice of the larger population. It was so in the days of Elijah, when, even though he thought he was the only one, some 7,000 still remained faithful in Israel, many undoubtedly the fruit of his own ministry. And it was so in Nazareth. Jesus was able to do no miracle there except that He healed a few. Even when the crowd is against us, it is still a possibility to opt for faith rather than for doubt and offense. The choice is a personal one and is not dictated by majority vote of the community. I also have power and authority—the power and authority of choice.

Still, Jesus "was amazed because of their unbelief" (verse 6). Scripture tells us two things that always surprised Him: unbelief and belief. He truly was amazed at the faith of a Roman centurion: "He marveled, and said to those who followed him, 'Truly, I say to you, not even in Israel have I found such faith'" (Matt. 8:10, RSV). As J. D. Jones points out, "it was a mighty faith, discovered in an unexpected quarter." In a similar manner, "He marveled at the *unbelief* of Nazareth," because "it was unbelief in spite of knowledge. It was unbelief in spite of the recognition of His greatness" (Jones, vol. 1, p. 249).

Yet in spite of His rejection by His hometown and most of His family, Jesus did not give up. "We read of no abatement of His labours. He did not, like the fiery prophet, wander into the desert and make request that He might die. And it helps us to realize the elevation of our Lord, when we reflect how utterly the discouragement with which we sympathize in the great Elijah would ruin our conception of Jesus" (Chadwick, p. 167).

Rather than give in to disappointment, He changed His field of labor, going around teaching in the various villages (Mark 6:6). In that He followed the counsel that He would later give to His disciples: "When they persecute you in one town, flee to the next" (Matt. 10:23, RSV). But more than that, He moved to put the education of the Twelve into phase two. When He first called them, He did so that they could "be with him, and . . . be sent out to preach" (Mark 3:14, RSV).

By now He had introduced them to the first part of His curriculum. They had been with Him and heard Him teach, heal, and comfort. In addition, they had seen Him handle abuse and rejection. But they could learn only so much vicariously. They now required hands on experience, they needed to try their own skills at preaching and healing (6:7-13). After their return to Jesus, their successes and failures would provide the basis for more refined instruction as Jesus continued to prepare the Twelve for taking over the leadership of His church (see on Mark 6:30, 31 in section number 25). In the process He was slowly turning disciples into apostles, from followers into those sent out to do God's work.

Of course, Jesus knew that they would face opposition and rejection, but that is to be expected when people are made to face the choice between faith and doubt. I suppose that none of us like rejection any more than the disciples. But being a true follower of Jesus means risk. Our problem is that most of us would like to be disciples all our lives and never have to risk ourselves and our dignity by becoming apostles. We like the comforts of the cocoon rather than the uncertainties of the wider world. But Jesus, knowing human nature and the needs of His disciples, pushed them out of their comfort zone so that they could continue to develop.

Jesus thus began Christian mission. He sent His disciples out to do what He could not do. Unable to reach everyone personally, He commissioned them as extensions of Himself. Today Jesus is still dispatching those willing to follow Him. And once again each of His followers has the privilege and responsibility of making a choice. It may be more comfortable for us to be disciples, but Jesus wants to make us into apostles. And if we are willing He will equip us, authorize us, and guide us.

24. The Real Meaning of John the Baptist

Mark 6:14-29
[14]And King Herod heard of it, for His name had become well known. And some were saying, "John the Baptist has been raised from the dead, and that is why miraculous powers are working in Him." [15]But others were saying, "He is Elijah." And yet others were saying, "He is a prophet like one of the prophets of old."

[16]But hearing of it, Herod said, "John, whom I beheaded, has risen." [17]For Herod had sent and arrested John and bound him in prison because of Herodias the wife of Philip his brother (whom he had married), [18]because John had said to Herod, "It is not lawful for you to have your

brother's wife.'' [19]Now Herodias had it in for him and wished to kill him, yet she couldn't [20]because Herod feared John. Knowing him to be a righteous and holy man, he kept him safe. And when he heard him he was greatly disturbed, yet he gladly listened to him. [21]But an opportunity came when Herod gave a festive supper on his birthday for the court nobles and military commanders and leading men of Galilee. [22]When the daughter of Herodias entered and danced, she pleased Herod and those reclining at table with him. And the king said to the girl, "Ask me whatever you wish and I will give it to you." [23]And he swore to her, "Whatever you request I will give to you, up to half of my kingdom." [24]After leaving she said to her mother, "What should I request?" And she said, "The head of John the Baptist." [25]And immediately, entering with haste to the king she requested, saying, "I wish that you would give me at once the head of John the Baptist on a serving platter." [26]And the king became very sorrowful, but because of his oaths and his dinner guests, he did not want to refuse her. [27]Immediately, the king, sending for an executioner, gave an order to bring his head. And he went and beheaded him in the prison [28]and brought his head on a serving platter and gave it to the girl, and the girl gave it to her mother. [29]Hearing about this, his disciples went and took his body and put it in a tomb.

Not a pretty story!

Why is it even in the Bible? Probably for at least two specific reasons, one having to do with the comparison between John the Baptist and the disciples, and the second dealing with the lives and deaths of John and Jesus.

Concerning the disciples, Mark introduces the passage with the words "and King Herod heard of it" (verse 14). Heard of what? If we go by the context of Mark 6:7-13, it was the preaching and ministry of the disciples. The mission of the Twelve and the excitement it caused had brought the Jesus movement to the attention of Herod Antipas, the ruler in Galilee.

Now what is of interest about the placement of the story of Herod and John is that Mark set it between (sandwiched) Jesus' sending out of the Twelve (6:7-13) and their return to report back to Him (6:30). That particular placement seems a bit odd. It is difficult to agree with Morna Hooker who sees the positioning as a literary device to create "an interlude for the disciples to complete their mission" (Hooker, p. 158). More to the point is James Edwards' suggestion that it "exemplifies the consequences of following Jesus in a world of greed, decadence, power, and wealth. Mark sandwiches the brutal and moving account of the martyrdom of the Baptist between the sending of the Twelve (6:7-13) and their return (6:30) in order to impress upon his readers the cost of discipleship" (Edwards, p. 183). Jesus Himself reinforces that interpretation in Mark 8:34, in which He tells the disciples that "if any man would come after me, let him deny himself and take up his cross and follow me" (RSV).

Now the preaching and healings of Jesus and the Twelve must have been good news to the common people of Galilee, but they disturbed Herod. For him they created a crisis of the first order, stirring up a guilty conscience to the point of paranoia. In particular, Herod feared that Jesus might be John raised from the dead (6:16).

At that point Mark flashes back to the relationship between Herod and John and the occasion of the latter's death. The problem, it appears, all started as a case of lust. The plain fact is that Herod was infatuated with Herodias. The big problem was that she happened to be married to his brother Philip (verse 17). No problem! Herod would override his brother's wishes and take his wife as his own.

But that created more difficulties. Her union with Herod was against the law of Moses, which clearly prohibited marriage to a brother's wife while the brother was still alive (Lev. 18:16; 20:21; see also Josephus, *Antiquities,* 18.5.4). John met the situation head-on, condemning Herod and his new wife for their unlawful marriage (Mark 6:18).

While the Baptist's reaction created complications for Herod, it enraged Herodias, who wanted to kill John (verse 19). It is at that very point that a good side of Herod surfaces. He protected John from his vicious wife. Why? Because Herod knew that John was a "righteous and holy man" who he "gladly listened" to, even though John's message "disturbed" him greatly (verse 20).

The good news is that at this stage of his experience Herod was not beyond help. He was open to goodness. We may think of Herod Antipas as an incorrigibly wicked man, but that is not the Bible picture of him. Still open to John's appeals, he had not hardened his heart to the place where the Baptist couldn't reach him.

But Herod did have a serious problem. He was doubleminded. As William Barclay points out, Antipas "was an odd mixture. At one and the same time he feared John and respected him. At one and the same time he dreaded John's tongue and yet found pleasure in listening to him" (Barclay, *Mark,* p. 154). Of course, if we think about it, the rest of us aren't much different from Herod. We at the same time are attracted to and repelled by temptation and sin. Herod was a human like us. And we, like Antipas, have his potential in our own hearts.

The dichotomy in Herod's mind between a respect for goodness but a desire for evil eventually provided the crack in his character that would lead to disaster for both himself and John. It appears that the one thing Herod wasn't willing to give up under any circumstances was his adulterous relationship with Herodias. That cherished sin left him open to a complete abandonment of all that was right.

Herodias soon found her opportunity to tighten her grip on her husband. On the occasion of his birthday feast she had her daughter Salome publicly dance before his important guests. "The fact that she did so at all is an incredible thing. Solo dances in those days in such society were disgusting and licentious pantomimes. That a princess of the royal blood should so expose and demean herself is beyond belief because those dances were the art of professional prostitutes. The very fact that she did so dance is a grim commentary on the character of Salome, and of the mother who allowed and encouraged her to do so" (*ibid.,* p. 153).

It also says something about the seamier side of Herod. He was "pleased" (verse 22), so much so that he publicly promised to grant the girl whatever she desired. Asking her mother's advice, Salome requested the death of John.

To his credit, the request upset Herod (verse 26). At that point he faced the dividing line. He could either stand up and condemn such wickedness or he could succumb to it.

He caved in, thus exposing the real root of his problem—a vacillating will. "In a sense," notes J. D. Jones, "Herod was not a deliberately wicked man, but he was a weak man, and, through his weakness, he allowed himself to be swept into this awful wickedness. He is in the New Testament what Ahab is in the Old Testament. Both of them were weak and sensual men. Neither, however, if left to himself, would have steeped his hands in blood. But they both had queens of masterful will. Driven by this stronger will of their queens, both these weak men committed great and awful wickedness" (Jones, vol. 2, p. 31). Herod is a type of those who love good and evil at the same time, but whose decisions are shaped by the influence of too much "refreshment" and/or a fear of displeasing their associates.

Having made a disastrous choice, the Bible thereafter pictures Herod on a moral slide. "His fate you may read for yourselves in Luke xxiii, when it is said, 'And Herod with his soldiers set Him (i.e., Jesus) at nought, and mocked Him.' Contrast these two facts, Herod feared John—Herod set Jesus at nought and mocked Him. In the contrast you see the calamitous issue of sin. This chapter [Mark 6] is full of the most tremendous teaching about sin. The way in which it breeds—for all this tragedy sprang from Herod's unholy passion for Herodias. The way in which it haunts the conscience, as illustrated in Herod's terror-stricken outcry. The solemn fact of personal responsibility, 'John, whom *I* beheaded.' And the tragic doom of sin, 'The wages of sin is death.' It is no empty threat. It is no theological bogey. It is the inexorable law. See it working itself out. He feared John; but in a few months he had become so dead to purity and holiness that he could make a mock[ery] of Christ" (*ibid.*, p. 35).

That last thought brings us to the comparison between John the Baptist and Jesus in Mark 6:14-29. Interestingly enough, we find only two passages in the second Gospel that are not centered on Jesus. And both are about John. The first (1:2-8) presents him as Jesus' forerunner in message and ministry, while the second (6:14-29) presents the Baptist as a forerunner of His death. Jesus also will be put to death by a ruler who recognized His goodness (see 15:9, 10, 12, 14, 15) but who surrenders to public pressure (see 15:10, 14, 15).

Yet, asserts Francis Maloney, "there is a difference between John and Jesus. . . . Mark's account of John the Baptist's death closes as his body is taken by his disciples and laid in a tomb (v. 29). According to vv. 14-16, rumors of the resurrection of the Baptist are in the air, but they are only rumors. The Christian community reading this story is told that the Baptist was buried (v. 29), but believes that Jesus has been slain, buried, and has been raised from the dead (see 16:1-8). A further difference emerges. John the Baptist is buried by his loyal disciples, but Jesus, abandoned by his disciples (see 14:50), is buried by a member of the council, Joseph of Arimathea, who should have been his enemy (see 15:43-46)" (Maloney, p. 127).

But enemies there would always be. That brings us to one last look into the "real meaning" of John the Baptist. "Jesus," writes Ellen White, "did not interpose to deliver His servant. He knew that John would bear the test. . . . But for the sake of thousands who in after years must pass from prison to death, John was to drink the cup of martyrdom. As the followers of Jesus should languish in lonely cells, or perish by the sword, the rack, or the fagot, apparently forsaken by God and man, what a stay to their hearts would be the thought that John the Baptist, to whose faithfulness Christ Himself had borne witness, had passed through a similar experience!" (White, *The Desire of Ages,* p. 224).

25. Feeding the 5,000 and the Crisis of the Christ

Mark 6:30-56

[30]*And the apostles gathered around Jesus and reported to Him all that they had done and taught.* [31]*And He said to them, "Come to a deserted place by yourselves and rest a while." (For many were coming and going, and they did not even have time to eat.)* [32]*And they went away privately in the boat to a deserted place.* [33]*But many recognized them and saw them going. They ran from all the cities on foot and arrived there before them.* [34]*Jesus, getting out of the boat, saw a large crowd and had compassion on them because they were like sheep without a shepherd. And He began to teach them many things.* [35]*When it grew late the disciples approached Him, saying, "This is a lonely place and it is late.* [36]*Send them away so that they may go into the surrounding farms and villages and buy themselves something to eat."* [37]*But He answered, saying to them, "You give them something to eat." And they said to Him, "Are we to go and buy 200 denarii worth of bread and give it to them to eat?"* [38]*And He said to them, "How many loaves do you have? Go look." And when they knew, they said, "Five, and two fish."* [39]*And He instructed them to seat everyone in groups on the green grass.* [40]*They sat down in groups of hundreds and of fifties.* [41]*And taking the five loaves and the two fish, He looked up to heaven and blessed and broke the loaves and gave them to the disciples to set before the people. And the two fish He divided among them all.* [42]*They all ate and were satisfied.* [43]*And they took up 12 baskets full of broken pieces and of the fish.* [44]*Those who ate the loaves were 5,000 males.*

[45]*And immediately He compelled His disciples to get into the boat and to go before Him to the other side, to Bethsaida, while He dismissed the crowd.* [46]*Saying farewell to them, He departed to the mountain to pray.*

[47]And when evening came the boat was in the middle of the lake and He was alone on the land. [48]And He saw them in distress as they rowed, for the wind was against them. About the fourth watch of the night He came toward them walking on the lake, meaning to pass them by. [49]But they saw Him walking on the lake. Thinking that it was an apparition, they cried out. [50]Everyone saw Him and they were terrified. But He at once spoke to them, saying to them, "Have courage, it is I. Do not be afraid." [51]He went into the boat with them and the wind stopped, and they were exceedingly astonished, [52]for they did not understand about the loaves, but their hearts were burdened.

[53]And crossing over they came to the land of Gennesaret and anchored. [54]As they got out of the boat, the people immediately recognized Him [55]and ran all around the countryside and began to carry those who were ill on sleeping mats to wherever they heard He was. [56]And wherever He entered into villages or into cities or into the countryside, they laid the sick in the marketplaces and begged Him that they might touch even the fringe of His garment. And as many as touched Him were healed.

Mark 6:30 is the only place in Mark's entire Gospel that calls the Twelve apostles. The reason is that it is the only time that they are sent forth (literally *apostled*). For the rest of the Gospel they are not messengers or preachers but students or disciples.

But they had had their first exposure to being sent (see 6:7-13), and had now returned. As the rest of Mark's story will show (see 6:52), they have still a lot to learn. They need a lot more discipling before they will be adequate apostles.

Jesus realized that it was time for a new level of education. So after they returned from their mission and told "Him all that they had done and taught," He explained that they needed to go to a deserted place by themselves (6:30, 31). It was now time, R. T. France suggests, "for 'learning' again. They have been through a demanding and exhausting time of mission, and it is time to recharge" (France, *Mark,* Doubleday, p. 80). Jesus had sent them out to serve. Now it was time for communion with Him. Combined, service and communion stand at the center of a healthy Christian ministry.

But the needed time apart with His disciples was not to be. People ran from all over to the other side of the lake, so that when Jesus arrived a large crowd had already assembled. As the day wore on that crowd became the occasion of the feeding of the 5,000, or what we might better describe as the feeding of the 20,000, since Mark counts only adult males (Mark 6:44).

The Balanced Ministry

"Communion that does not end in service is unhealthy, but service without communion is sterile and barren, and in the long run impossible" (Jones, vol. 2, p. 48).

The miracle itself must have made a deep impression on the disciples, because it is the only one reported in all four gospels. Yet as A. B. Bruce points out, this particular miracle seems to have no adequate reason for even taking place. It certainly didn't result from any requirement on the part of the multitude. That is where the feeding of the 4,000 of Mark 8:1-10 differs from the feeding of the 5,000. The author describes the feeding of the 4,000 as an act of necessity. They had gone without food for three days and had nothing to eat. But the 5,000 had only been away from home a few hours and could have bought food from nearby villages (see A. B. Bruce, *"Kata Mapkon,"* p. 393).

The reason for the importance of this miracle story occurs in Mark 6:52, in which Jesus reprimands the disciples because they had not yet understood about the loaves, and in the fuller account of the miracle in John 6.

The miracle itself, of course, is impressive. Anyone who has ever tried to prepare food for a few thousand (or few dozen) people can vouch for that. But the meal itself was simple, consisting of the course barley loaves and salted sardine-size fishes that were the food of the poorest of the poor. Jesus supplied their need but not perhaps their gastronomic desires.

But it was not the type of food that mattered to the people, rather the fact that He supplied it—that He could do it. In that event, this One who had recently raised the daughter of Jairus, was like Elijah and Elisha, who also "raised the dead and miraculously fed the hungry" (Guelich, p. 344. See also 1 Kings 17:10-24; 2 Kings 4:32-37, 42-44). However, the scope of Jesus' miracle went way beyond those of the two Hebrew prophets. Something unique happened in the feeding of the 5,000.

One clue to that uniqueness appears in verse 45, in which Mark tells us that Jesus "compelled His disciples to get into the boat" and to depart for the other side of the lake. The reason that Jesus had to *compel* or *make* the disciples enter the boat and set sail by themselves is not evident in Mark, but it becomes clear when we consider John's account. John explains that when the people saw the miracle of Jesus feeding the 5,000, they begin to say, "Surely this is the Prophet who is to come into the world." Then follows an attempt on their part to "make him king by force" (John 6:14, 15, NIV).

The people identify Jesus as "the Prophet who is to come" because of His powerful sign or miracle. Josephus tells us that in nearly every case themes of a prophet and the working of signs accompanied first-century political uprisings by would-be liberators (see Brown, p. 249). Building on the Messianic promise that God would "raise up . . . a prophet" like Moses (Deut. 18:18, 15, RSV), the Jews at the feeding of the 5,000 believed they were experiencing a fulfillment of prophecy.

The connection made is that Moses, the great deliverer, gave their "fathers . . . manna in the wilderness" (John 6:31, RSV). In Jesus they have someone who appears to be a second Moses, a second deliverer—another prophet, who like Moses can supply bread from heaven. That is the reason for the forcefulness that lies behind the drive to make Jesus king.

Even the disciples got carried away with the possibility. Mark tells us that Jesus had to *compel* them to get into their boat and leave Him, while He dismissed the crowd alone (6:45, 46). The disciples must have clearly sensed the Messianic potential. *Now,* they must have assumed, *is the time for Jesus to make His masterstroke. Now is the Messianic movement.* With that thought in mind, it is easier to see why Jesus had to send the disciples away before He could dismiss the crowd.

The disciples' excitement and perhaps their knowledge of Jesus' "backwardness" in putting Himself forward as the Messiah undoubtedly caused some of them to consider it their job to push Jesus to the front in what they hoped would be the beginning of the Messianic kingdom of glory. After all, up through the resurrection of Jesus, they still perceived His kingdom to be a political kingdom that would overthrow the Roman oppressors.

We miss a major point of the story if we fail to see Jesus here being tempted to obtain the kingdom without a cross. He is facing His ultimate temptation. Here we have a repetition of His first wilderness temptation (Matt. 4:3, 4), but with greater forcefulness. He had demonstrated that He could indeed make bread out of "stones," and it had profoundly impressed the people—so much so that they wanted to set up His kingdom on the spot. Even Jesus' "support group" (the Twelve) was behind the movement. The situation was temptation of the first order: "Build the Kingdom, it suggests, on bread. Make it the first point in your programme to abolish hunger. Multiply loaves and fishes all the time," and the people will love you (Denney, *Jesus,* p. 210).

Here is the old seduction to establish His kingdom without a cross, without having to take the path of the rejected servant. We see the seriousness of the episode reflected in the fact that immediately after dismissing the crowds, "He departed to the mountain to pray" (Mark 6:46; see also John 6:15). Jesus needed to commit Himself anew to the accomplishment of God's will and to pray especially for His disciples, who still desired a Messiah out of harmony with God's will. Doing God's will in the accomplishment of His mission must remain central in Jesus' life. And doing God's will is always a matter of prayer.

The disciples, meanwhile, had their own struggle. They were not only extremely upset with Jesus, but they were fighting for their lives on the lake. While it is only four or five miles wide at that spot, it was already past 3:00 a.m. (the fourth watch is from 3:00 a.m. to 6:00 a.m.) and they were only part way across because of the fierce winds. They probably grumbled at least once about Jesus having forced them out there in the first place. And where was He? Didn't He care?

But Jesus knew of their struggles—both of them. Their extremity became His opportunity. Once again He saved them from a storm. And once again they were "exceedingly astonished" (Mark 6:51). Why? Because "they did not understand about the loaves, but their hearts were hardened" (verse 52). The lesson that they desperately needed to understand from the miracle of the loaves was threefold:

1. That Jesus was indeed the promised one, who could perform miracles even more impressive than those of Elijah, Elisha, and Moses.
2. But that His Messiahship was of a different order than that expected by the Jews and the disciples.
3. And, just as important, that the One who had provided the loaves could care for them in all circumstances, that they were under His protection just as much when He was hidden from their eyes as when He was present with them. That last lesson was extremely important, since He would soon be leaving them altogether.

Learning the lesson of the loaves would be a difficult one for the disciples, but one that will take up a great portion of the space remaining in Mark's Gospel. Meanwhile, in Mark 6:53-56 the author makes his third summary report (see also 1:35-39; 3:7-12) of Jesus' miracles, reminding his readers that Jesus' ministry was much larger than the few stories included in his book.

26. God's Law and Human Rules

Mark 7:1-13

¹And the Pharisees gathered together around Him with some of the scribes who had come from Jerusalem. ²They had seen that some of His disciples were eating their meal with unclean hands, that is, unwashed. ³(For the Pharisees and all the Jews will not eat unless they carefully wash their hands, thus holding to the tradition of the elders. ⁴And they do not eat anything from the marketplace unless they wash themselves. There are many other traditions they hold, such as the washing of cups and pitchers and kettles.) ⁵And the Pharisees and the scribes asked Him, "Why don't Your disciples walk according to the tradition of the elders, but eat meals with unclean hands?" ⁶He said to them, "Isaiah prophesied rightly about you hypocrites. It is written that 'This people honors Me with their lips, but their heart is far away from Me,' ⁷'yet they worship Me in vain, teaching as doctrines the commandments of men.' ⁸Abandoning the commandments of God, you hold onto the tradition of men."

⁹And He said to them, "You are good at setting aside the commandment of God so that you may keep your tradition. ¹⁰For Moses said, 'Honor your father and your mother' and 'Those who speak evil of their father or mother must certainly be put to death.' ¹¹But you say, 'If a man says to his father or mother, whatever you might have benefitted from me is corban' (meaning a gift to God)—¹²then you no longer permit him to do anything for his father or mother, ¹³thereby annulling the word of God by your tradition which you have received. And you do many similar things."

The Pharisees have not been prominent in Mark's Gospel since Mark 3:6, in which they were plotting Jesus' downfall. But with chapter 7 they return to center stage. And it is here that we see more clearly the differences that separated them from Jesus.

141

Their disagreements did not have to do with loyalty to God. Both parties had put God at the center of their lives. Neither did their conflicts involve allegiance to the law of God. Once again, both parties were clear on the importance of God's law. Rather, they differed over its nature.

To understand the situation it is important to grasp the conception of law in Pharisaic Judaism. Early in Jewish history the term "law" stood for two things. First, and most importantly, it represented the Ten Commandments. Secondly, it signified the five books of Moses or the Pentateuch.

But three or four centuries before Christ a class of legal experts known as the scribes arose. The scribes began to define what they saw as the meaning of God's law. In the process, a distinction developed between written Torah and oral Torah, that is, "between the authoritative Holy Scriptures (the OT) and an orally transmitted authoritative tradition, which interprets, supplements, and sometimes corrects the written Torah" (Bromiley, vol. 4, p. 884). By the time of Jesus the unwritten tradition had become known as "the tradition of the elders" (Mark 7:3). It had evolved into thousands and thousands of carefully defined rules and regulations governing every possible action in life. Some two hundred years after Jesus the rabbis wrote down the oral tradition in a form called the *Mishnah*.

The issue of the oral law formed the basis of many of the struggles between Jesus and the Pharisees. "It was their commitment to the oral tradition—and Jesus' equal commitment to recovering the intent of the written law—that made their differences so earnest" (Edwards, p. 209). We especially see that conflict in Matthew 5, in which Jesus repeatedly used His "You have heard that it was said to the men of old, . . . but I say to you" formula (see verses 21, 27, 33, 38, 43, RSV) to uncover the deeper intent of the law and to unmask the fact that the oral tradition dealt with externals rather than capturing the spiritual meaning of the law for human lives.

That same battle unfolds in Mark 7. In the first 13 verses the dispute involves two aspects of the oral tradition—cleanness and uncleanness and vows, both of which have ample tractates in the *Mishnah* (Tohorot and Nedarim, respectively) describing rituals associated with those practices in great detail.

Their first point of difference had to do with washing. The Pharisees complained to Jesus that His disciples did not follow the proper rules when they ate (verse 2). Then Mark goes into verses 3 and 4 in which he briefly describes the Jewish attitude to washing for his Gentile readers.

Now such washings had nothing to do with cleanliness or sanitation. Rather, they were ceremonial acts that cleansed from ritual defilement. After all, a pious Jew could become defiled by touching a Gentile, touching food touched by a Gentile, or even touching a pot handled by a Gentile. Thus strict Jews, upon returning from the marketplace, carefully went through a cleansing procedure to rid themselves of defilement.

The hand washing referred to in Mark 7 reflected the practice of pious Jews, who before every meal, and even between courses in the same meal, washed in a certain way. The water had to be ceremonially clean and had to be stored in a certain type of jar. In the washing itself, "the hands were held with the finger tips *pointing upward;* the water was poured over them and must run at least down to the wrist; the minimum amount of water was one quarter of a log, which is equal to one and a half egg-shells full of water. While the hands were still wet each hand had to be cleansed with the fist of the other." But at that stage "the hands were wet with water; but that water was now itself unclean because it touched unclean hands. So, second, the hands had to be held with finger tips pointing downward and the water had to be poured over them in such a way that it began at the wrists and ran off at the finger tips. After all that had been done the hands were clean" (Barclay, *Mark*, p. 167).

It was the failure of the disciples in carrying out such ritual washings that provided the occasion for the Pharisees to condemn them to Jesus (Mark 7:5). Jesus responded with a quotation from the Septuagint (Greek) version of Isaiah 29:13, which claims that some of God's ancient people had worshiped Him with their lips but not with their hearts and that they were "teaching the commandments and doctrines of men" (LXX). His conclusion was that when the Pharisees were worshiping they were in effect teaching human commandments rather than divine ones (Mark 7:8), that they were worshiping in vain (verse 7), and that they were hypocrites (verse 6).

The word *hypokritēs* (hypocrite) is an interesting one. In Greek it means a play actor. One who is a *hyopkritēs* is a person whose life is one of acting, as on a stage. Thus there is no reality behind the acting, no sincerity. As a result, they are good at externals, but neglect the heart of the issue. In calling the Pharisees hypocrites Jesus was letting them know that their religion consisted of externals and that they had missed the real intent of the written Torah.

He expounded upon that thought in Mark 7:9-13 by showing how the external rules set forth in their oral tradition actually contradicted the law of God as expressed in the Ten Commandments. Jesus used the fifth commandment as His illustration. It stipulated that people were to honor their fathers and their mothers. But, He points out to the Pharisees, their tradition had a provision for *corban*. The word itself means gift. If something is *corban* to God it is dedicated to Him, it has been placed upon the altar, it is God's property. Thus it cannot be used for any other purpose, even "for the material support of aged parents." The oral tradition also had a stipulation that the giver of a *corban* could retain the gift for personal use (see Bromiley, vol. 1, p. 772).

Thus persons having made a *corban* vow to God could both retain the dedicated money and be considered as honoring their parents, even though they couldn't help them with the money they had offered to God. After all, nothing was more important than a vow to God. But in essence, as Jesus pointed out, the vow was merely a selfish excuse for not supporting one's parents in their time of need. For that reason He asserted that their tradition nullified the intent of God's law.

Jesus throughout His ministry opposed external religion. He fought anything that put ritual and human rules above caring for human beings. For Him the essence of the law was not externals but loving God and other people with all of one's mind and heart (Matt. 22:36-40). It was reaching out to help another person in spite of the legal stipulations of the law. He illustrated that in His own life by touching a leper (Mark 1:41) and healing on the Sabbath (3:1-6).

Such teachings were not new with Jesus. They constituted the heart of Old Testament theology (see Deut. 6:5; Lev. 19:18). "I despise your feasts," God said through Amos, "and I take no delight in your solemn assemblies. Even though you offer me your burnt offerings . . . , I will not accept them. . . . But let justice roll down like waters" (Amos 5:21, 22, 24, RSV). "I desire steadfast love and not sacrifice," God said through Hosea (6:6, RSV). "He has showed you, O man, what is good," was the word of the Lord through Micah, "and what does the Lord require of you but to do justice, and to have kindness, and to walk humbly with your God" (Micah 6:8, RSV).

Even though God Himself had commanded Israel to offer burnt offerings and to keep certain solemn feasts, He plainly stated that such externals were of no value without a heart religion. The curse of so-called religious people down through the ages has been a merely outward religion.

The Pharisees had not only externalized religion but they had blocked the road to true religion. "The emphatic position of . . . 'anything,'" in the new sentence, "'You no longer allow him to do anything for his father and mother,' stresses the completeness of 'nullifying the word of God by means of your tradition'" (Gundry, p. 353). For Jesus the Pharisaic teachings were not merely tangential to true religion, they actually nullified it.

If Jesus were alive today He might say the same thing to those who in their external concern for proper diet and even the Sabbath (good things in themselves) treat other people unlovingly or neglect to reach out and help them where they are.

27. The Heart of Sin

Mark 7:14-23
¹⁴And calling the crowd to Him again, He said to them, "Listen to Me, everyone, and understand: ¹⁵There is nothing outside of the man that entering into him can defile him; but the things coming out of the man are the ones that defile the man."* ¹⁷And when He had left the crowd and entered a house, His disciples asked Him about the parable. ¹⁸He said to them, "Are you also without understanding? Do you not understand that whatever enters the man from the outside cannot defile him? ¹⁹Because it does not enter into his heart but into the stomach, and passes into the latrine." (Thus He declared all foods clean). ²⁰And He said, "It is what goes out of the man that defiles the man. ²¹For from within, out of the heart of the man, come evil thoughts, fornications, thefts, murders, ²²adulteries, greedinesses, licentiousnesses, deceit, sensuality, envy, blasphemy, pride, and foolishness. ²³All these evil things come from within and defile the man."

---

*Verse 16 is not in the earliest Greek manuscripts. It reads: "If anyone has ears to hear, let him hear."

Exploring Mark

Here is a truly revolutionary passage of Scripture. But to understand it we need to go back to verse 5, in which the "Pharisees and the scribes asked Him, 'Why don't your disciples walk according to the tradition of the elders, but eat meals with unclean hands?'"

Jesus has already replied in verses 6–13 with a two-part answer:

1. That they were hypocrites in the sense that they had outward obedience but without having a heart relationship with God.
2. That by their tradition they actually contradicted the law of God.

Thus they had missed the genuine obedience that God required.

His answer was important in that it showed the Pharisees and scribes that they didn't hold God's truth in either their lives or in theory.

Jesus' response in verses 6 to 13, however, didn't really get to the root of the Pharisaic problem. As a result, in verses 14 to 23 He follows up with part two of His response to the question of verse 5. After all, any real understanding of defilement and cleansing must recognize the source of that defilement. True spiritual defilement, Jesus claimed, did not come from the outside, but rather it was caused by something on the inside of a person. Thus genuine spiritual defilement does not result from people not washing their hands properly or even by what they eat. Such a thought was a bombshell to the Pharisaic mind. They were good at the outward aspects of religion. On one occasion Jesus noted that they were like whitewashed tombs crammed with dead people's bones (Matt. 23:27). When Jesus claimed that the essence of genuine religion was a matter of the heart, He hit at the core problem of many "churchly types," whether they be Pharisees or members of a local congregation in the twenty-first century. The church has never been short on hypocrites—those who are good on outward ritual and dietary peculiarities but are void of those inward qualities that make a person a Christian in the sense that Jesus described in Mark 7.

At this point, we need to be very clear on exactly what Jesus is talking about as He answers the Pharisees' question in verse 5. His message is that nothing external to people truly defiles them *spiritually*. In verse 19 He uses food as an illustration of what He means. Food, He said, does not make a person impure because "it does not enter" the "heart but into the stomach" and from there goes into the toilet. Here Mark makes one of the very few interpretations of Jesus' words that we find in his entire Gospel.

In reflecting upon Jesus' statement about food he added that "thus He declared all foods clean."

What, we need to ask, did Mark mean by his interpretative statement? In the context of the Pharisaic question of verse 5, it appears that William Lane is correct when he writes that Jesus' expression "did not abrogate the Mosaic laws on purification or erase the distinctions between clean and unclean and declare them invalid. It rather attacked the delusion that sinful men can attain to true purity before God through the scrupulous observance of cultic purity which is powerless to cleanse the defilement of the heart" (Lane, p. 254). Again, "Jesus has no intention of denying that the purity laws occupy a significant place in the Mosaic code (Lev. 11:1-47; Deut. 14:1-20) or of detracting from the dignity of men who suffered death rather than violate the Law of God governing unclean foods (1 Macc. 1:62f.). Rather, he presses home the recognition that the ultimate seat of purity or defilement before God is the heart" (*ibid.*, p. 255). C.F.D. Moule makes much the same point when he writes that "he *declared all foods clean* (verse 19), in the sense that no foodstuff can, in itself, defile. Rather, what defiles is a foul imagination, for (verse 21) it is *out of a man's heart* that there *come evil thoughts*" (Moule, p. 56).

These interpretations are worlds apart from that of R. A. Cole, who claims that we can paraphrase verse 19b as "by saying this, He was abolishing all distinction between ceremonially clean and unclean foods" (Cole, p. 186). Such an explanation moves away from the context of verse 5, which provides the question that Jesus is answering. Jesus was not denying the distinction, but that *anything* outside of the human heart is the source of spiritual impurity.

His answer, however, did not focus on the negative. It moved on to the positive truth that is really at the center of what He wanted to say. In verse 21 He declared that genuine spiritual defilement comes "from within, from out of the heart." The heart or mind is the source of all "evil thoughts." Jesus then went on in verses 21 and 22 to list 12 fruits of evil thinking. One interesting thing to note about that list is that the first six are plural and denote evil acts, whereas the last are in the singular and denote evil attitudes. Perhaps part of the idea is that one evil attitude can spawn many evil actions. All 12 terms, however, are lodged in evil thoughts, which find their source in a corrupt heart.

Mark 7:1-23, James Edwards points out, is "the longest conflict speech in the Gospel of Mark. The length of the section is a clue to its importance. Mark labors to clarify that the essential purpose of the Torah, and hence the foundation of morality, is a matter of inward purity, motive, and intent rather than of external compliance to ritual and custom. The controversy thus cannot be interpreted as a case for Christian antinomianism but rather for the recovery of the true intent of the Torah [law]. 'Uncleanness' can no longer be considered a property of objects but rather a description of inner attitudes, a condition of the heart. The goodness of a deed depends not solely on its doing, but primarily on its intent" (Edwards, p. 214).

The teaching of Jesus in Mark 7 on the locus of human sin surfaces throughout the Bible. Take the case of Eve back in Genesis 3. Did she sin when she took and ate the forbidden fruit or before she took and ate?

Think about it for a moment. God had told her not to eat it (Gen. 2:17). His command was plain. It is also clear from Genesis 3 that she did what God had forbidden. But note, before she committed the sinful action, something happened in her mind and heart. First she rejected God and His word to her. Second, she placed herself and her own authority at the center of her life. Only then did she reach out and pick the fruit (3:1-6).

Thus the beginning of her rebellion was internal. In her heart she turned against God. The eventual result of her internal "heart problem" was a sinful act. But before then she had already sinned against God in her heart and mind.

> "Education, culture, the exercise of the will, human effort, all have their proper sphere, but here they are powerless. They may produce an outward correctness of behavior, but they cannot change the heart; they cannot purify the springs of life. There must be a power working from within, a new life from above, before men can be changed from sin to holiness. That power is Christ. His grace alone can quicken the lifeless faculties of the soul, and attract it to God, to holiness" (White, *Steps to Christ*, p. 18).

That theology of sin stands over against the popular Pharisaism of Christ's day (and ours). It also forms the heart of the New Testament message on salvation. Nowhere do Jesus and the apostles teach that the way to heaven is for people to clean up their actions so that they can become better and better. Even if they did manage to become a bit "better" by that route, it would merely lead to spiritual pride over their accomplishments for God. That was the problem of the Pharisee in Luke 18:9-14 who thought he was better than other people.

The Bible answer to the sin problem is not improvement but crucifixion, resurrection, and a new heart and mind (Rom. 6:1-4; 2 Cor. 5:17; John 3:7; Eph. 3:16, 17). Out of that new heart and mind will come a desire to walk with God in terms of outward practices.

The tragedy of too many is that they do the external without having undergone an inner transformation. To all such, ritual, diet, and "proper behavior" become the center of religion. The result of such an approach is exacting church members who can be meaner than the devil. That, of course, is nothing new. It was the same Pharisaic spirit that put Jesus on the cross. The only solution to the sin problem is an internal one.

Carlyle B. Haynes caught the essence of Jesus' message in Mark 7:14-23, when he wrote that Christianity "is not any modification of the old life; it is not any qualification of it, any development of it, not any progression of it, any culture or refinement or education of it. It is not built on the old life at all. It does not grow from it. It is entirely another life—a new life altogether" (Haynes, p. 10). That new life finds its source in a new heart. "Marvel not," said Jesus, "that I said unto thee, Ye must be born again" (John 3:7, KJV). The new birth with its new heart is the essential starting point of spiritual purity.

28. Reaching Out to the Gentiles

Mark 7:24–8:10

²⁴*From there He arose and departed to the district of Tyre. And He entered into a house, wanting no one to know of it. Yet He was unable to escape notice. ²⁵But a woman whose daughter had an unclean spirit heard about Him, immediately coming and falling at His feet. ²⁶Now the woman was a Greek, a Syrophenician by race, and she begged Him to cast the demon out of her daughter. ²⁷And He said to her: "Allow the children to be satisfied first, for it is not good to take the children's bread and throw*

it to the dogs." *[28]She answered and said to Him, "Lord, even the dogs under the table eat from the crumbs of the children." [29]And He said to her, "Because of this saying, go, the demon has gone out of your daughter." [30]And departing to her house, she found the child lying on the bed, the demon having left.*

[31]Again, having departed from the region of Tyre, He came through Sidon to the Sea of Galilee, within the region of Decapolis. [32]And they brought to Him a man who was deaf and mute and begged Him to put His hand upon him. [33]And taking him privately apart from the crowd, He put His fingers into his ears, and spitting, He touched his tongue. [34]Looking up to heaven, He sighed and said to him, "Ephphatha!" (which means be opened). [35]Immediately his ears were opened and the binding of his tongue was loosened and he was speaking correctly. [36]And He ordered them that they should tell no one, but the more He ordered them, the more they proclaimed it. [37]They were exceedingly amazed, saying, "He has done all things well, He has even made the deaf to hear and the mute to speak."

[1]In those days when there was again a large crowd not having anything to eat, He called the disciples, saying to them, [2]"I have compassion for the crowd, because they have already remained with Me three days and have nothing to eat. [3]If I send them away hungry to their homes, some of them, having come from far away, will faint on the way." [4]And His disciples answered Him, "Where in this remote place will anyone be able to get enough bread to feed these people?" [5]He asked them, "How many loaves do you have?" and they said, "Seven." [6]And He gave orders to the crowd to sit on the ground. And taking the seven loaves, He gave thanks, broke them, and gave them to His disciples that they might serve them, and they served the crowd. [7]They had also a few small fish. Blessing them, He ordered that they be served also. [8]And they ate and were satisfied, and there was an abundance of baskets of pieces left over. [9]There were approximately 4,000, and He sent them away. [10]And at once He boarded the boat with His disciples, coming into the region of Dalmanutha.

The common factor that each of its three sections focuses on Jesus' ministry to Gentiles binds Mark 7:24–8:10 together. At least two excellent reasons emerge for placing these stories here in Mark's narrative. First, Jesus and the disciples not only need the rest and time apart that they had been seeking since before the feeding of the 5,000 (Mark 6:30-32), but things had become more difficult for Jesus in the Jewish territories. In addition to the fact that the scribes and Pharisees had branded Him a common sinner because of His rejection of their oral tradition (7:1-23), Herod had also begun to see Him as a menace (6:14-29). Perhaps they could find the peace they needed and the time that Jesus sought to privately instruct His disciples outside of Jewish territory. A second reason is that Jesus wanted to begin to demonstrate to His disciples that His mission was larger than just to the Jews.

But Jesus could not avoid the crowds of people. His fame had already transcended national boundaries. Even in pagan Tyre "He was unable to escape notice" (7:24). Both Mark and Matthew single out for treatment one rather aggressive woman, who had a daughter with an unclean spirit. Mark describes her as a Syrophenecian, a "differentiation" that "clearly marks a pagan" (Mann, p. 320).

Her story is a perplexing one because of Jesus' seeming lack of concern for her, but even moreso because of what appears to be His harshness in speaking to her. Regarding the first of those points, Jesus in His humanity may have truly desired to avoid a healing miracle. After all, to perform such a miracle would be to invite the same sort of attention He had sought to get away from in Galilee. Thus to heal the daughter would be to frustrate the purpose of the special trip with His disciples. But, as we will see, Jesus can never overlook human need. That is good news—not only for the Syrophenecian woman but for each of us.

Regarding Jesus' apparent harshness, we need to consider three points. One is that He had told her to "allow the children to be satisfied first, for it is not good to take the children's bread and throw it to the dogs" (verse 27). Now she could have taken offense at that statement and walked off in a huff. After all, no one likes others to call them a dog and classify them as second-class citizens. But she must have seen something that Jesus' critics don't. She bounced back with the repartee that "even the dogs under the table eat from the crumbs of the children" (verse 28). The upshot is that Jesus rewards her for her "faith" (Matt. 15:28) and heals her daughter.

What is it, we need to ask, that this pagan woman saw in Jesus' seemingly harsh treatment of her that gave her hope? One thing is the word "first"—the children were to be satisfied "first." In that word she saw a world of encouragement, because the very existence of a first in the order of ministry implied a "second." The quick-witted Syrophenecian woman did not miss that subtlety. She was undoubtedly ahead of the disciples on that score. At this stage in their development they recognized no second.

But they will eventually understand. To the Jew and then to the Gentile would be the order of the apostolic mission (see Rom. 1:16; Acts 1:8).

A second thing that the Syrophenecian undoubtedly noticed in Jesus' reply to her request was the word He selected for dog. Greek has two words for dog. The first refers to scavenging street dogs, a symbol of contempt and dishonor in the ancient world. In Jewish eyes, Gentiles were dogs indeed. But Jesus didn't use that word. He chose the one meaning house pet or lap dog that we might better translate as "doggie."

Thus Jesus' very choice of words took the story out of the realm of negative appellation. The woman was quick to perceive that fact, replying that "even the dogs under the table eat from the crumbs of the children" (verse 28). A. B. Bruce suggests that those bits were "not merely the crumbs which by chance fall from the table, but morsels surreptitiously dropt by the children . . . to their pets" (A. B. Bruce, *"Kata Mapkon,"* p. 391).

A third thing that the woman would have noted in Jesus' reply was His facial expression. Facial expressions and body language always accompany words. Floyd Filson is undoubtedly correct when he states that the effect of Jesus' words on the woman "would depend much on the speaker's tone and facial expression. The woman senses that his word is not final, and she is quick to show him that he can help her without giving up his concentrated mission to fellow-Jews" (Filson, p. 180). As Ellen White puts it, "Beneath the apparent refusal of Jesus, she saw a compassion that He could not hide" (White, *The Desire of Ages,* p. 401).

All in all, Mark pictures the Syrophenecian woman as a person of remarkable faith—a faith that got rewarded in spite of her ethnicity. "Symbolically," William Barclay concludes, "she stands for the Gentile world which so eagerly seized on the bread of heaven which the Jews had rejected and thrown away" (Barclay, *Mark,* p. 183).

Mark 7:31-37 presents the second segment in the second Gospel's section on Jesus reaching out to the Gentiles. We should note four things about this section. First, that if Jesus is heading to Decapolis from Tyre through Sidon, the verse has Him traveling in the wrong direction (Mark 7:31). After all, Tyre is 40 miles northwest of Capernaum, Sidon is 26 miles north of Tyre or about 60 miles northwest of Capernaum, while Decapolis is to the southeast of Capernaum (see map on page 14). Some critics, such as Julius Wellhausen, have claimed that either Mark didn't know his Palestinian geography or Sidon is a mistranslation (see Cranfield, p. 250). But read in the context of Mark, the circuitous route, which may have taken an extended period of time, lends itself to a quite natural understanding. "The object of the long circuit," suggests Alfred Plummer, "was to gain the retirement necessary for the training of the Twelve," a goal that Jesus had already "twice failed in securing" (Plummer, p. 190; see Mark 6:31-34; 7:24). It is possible that some of that instruction may have helped Peter in coming to the conclusion that he will soon make in Caesarea Philippi regarding Jesus' identity (see Mark 8:29).

A second thing to observe is that the healing of the deaf and dumb man, though the only miracle reported by Mark in Decapolis, is one of many in Matthew's description of this segment of Jesus' ministry. According to Matthew, "great crowds came to him, bringing with them the lame, the maimed, the blind, the dumb, and many others, and they put them at his feet, and he healed them, so that the throng wondered when they saw the dumb speaking, the maimed whole, the lame walking, and the blind seeing; and they glorified the God of Israel" (Matt. 15:30, 31, RSV). That they were definitely in Gentile territory Matthew highlights in the phrase "they glorified the God of Israel," a phrase that would not have been necessary if the crowd were Jews.

A third item of importance is the reception Jesus now experienced in Decapolis. This time we find great crowds following Him. But the last time He had been there (chapter 5) the citizens, after the healing of the wild man and the economic disaster of the pigs, begged Jesus to leave their region (Mark 5:17). The healed man wanted to accompany Jesus, but He told him to return to his home and tell his neighbors "how much the Lord has done for you." That passage closes with the fact that "all men marveled" at his witness (verses 19, 20, RSV). Part of what we are seeing in the crowds that flocked to Jesus upon His return to Decapolis is undoubtedly the fruit of the healed man's witness.

A fourth thing to recognize in Jesus' healing of the deaf and mute man in Mark 7:31-37 is the consideration that He showed for him as an individual. Rather than risking possible embarrassment for this sensitive man, Jesus took him aside privately to perform the healing (verse 33). He knows each of us and treats us with tender care as individuals.

The final story in Mark's Gentile section is the feeding of the 4,000.

The general outline is the same as for the feeding of the 5,000 but with one major difference. After that latter miracle Jesus had forced the Twelve to depart while He dismissed the crowd (6:45). Nothing similar happens with the 4,000. Apparently the 4,000, being a largely Gentile audience, did not seek to turn that "bread from heaven" miracle into a Messianic event by attempting to crown Jesus king (compare with Matt. 14:22; John 6:14, 15).

Edwards concludes his comments on Mark 7:24-8:10 by saying that "the journey of Jesus to Tyre, Sidon, and the Decapolis proves that although the Gentiles are ostracized by the Jews, they are not ostracized by God. Jewish invective against the Gentiles does not reflect a divine invective. There is a lesson here for the people of God in every age, that its enemies are neither forsaken by God nor beyond the compassion of Jesus" (Edwards, p. 232).

29. Different Kinds of Blindness

Mark 8:11-30

[11]*The Pharisees came and began to argue with Him, seeking a sign from heaven from Him, to test Him.* [12]*And sighing deeply in His spirit, He said, "Why does this generation seek a sign? Truly, I say to you, no sign will be given to this generation."* [13]*Leaving them, He then embarked and departed to the other side.*

[14]*Now they had forgotten to take bread, and, except for one loaf, they did not have anything with them in the boat.* [15]*And He instructed them, saying, "Watch out! Beware of the leaven of the Pharisees and the leaven of Herod."* [16]*Now they were arguing among themselves because they did not have any bread.* [17]*And knowing this, Jesus said to them, "Why are you arguing about the fact that you do not have bread? Do you not perceive or understand yet? Do you have a hardened heart?* [18]*Having eyes, do you not see, and having ears, do you not hear? Do you not remember* [19]*when I broke bread for the 5,000, how many baskets full of pieces you picked up?" They said to Him, "Twelve."* [20]*"When I broke the seven for the 4,000, how many baskets full of pieces did you pick up?" They said to Him, "Seven."* [21]*And He said to them, "Don't you yet understand?"*

[22]*They came to Bethsaida. And they brought a blind man to Him, begging Him to touch him.* [23]*Grasping the hand of the blind man, He took him outside the village, and spitting in his eyes and putting His hands on*

*him, He asked him, "Do you see anything?" ²⁴And looking up, he said,
"I see, I see people as trees walking." ²⁵Then He again placed His hands
on his eyes. And when he opened his eyes, he was restored and saw everything clearly. ²⁶And He sent him to his house, saying, you may not go into
the village.*

*²⁷And Jesus and the disciples went to the villages of Caesarea Philippi.
On the way He questioned His disciples, asking them, "Who do people
say I am?" ²⁸And they told Him, saying, "John the Baptist, and others
Elijah, but others one of the prophets." ²⁹He asked them, "But you, who
do you say I am?" Peter answered and said to Him, "You are the
Christ." ³⁰And He warned them that they should tell no one about Him.*

One theme—blindness—holds the four paragraphs of Mark 8:11-30
together. Verses 11 to 13 treat the blindness of the Pharisees. Next,
verses 14 to 21 deal with the blindness of the disciples.

Up to that point we find no talk of healing. That changes with verses 22
to 26, in which a physically blind man receives his sight, but in two stages.
After his healing, verses 27 through 30 indicate that the spiritual blindness of
the disciples has also been healed. But, like the case of the blind man, their
initial healing is only partial, a fact evident in verses 31-33, in which Jesus
rebukes Peter for his blindness. The next stage in the disciples' healing from
blindness begins in verses 34 and 35 and extends for the rest of Mark's Gospel
as Jesus prepares them for what will take place in Jerusalem.

The Logic of Mark 8:11-35

1. The Pharisees are blind (verses 11-13).
2. The disciples are blind (verses 14-21).
3. A "real" blind man is healed, but in stages (verses 22-26).
4. The blindness of the disciples is healed (verses 27- 30).
5. But, like the two-stage healing of the blind man, the disciples are
   only partially healed (verses 31-33).
6. The task of Jesus thereafter is to bring the healing of their
   blindness to completion (verse 34 to the end of the Gospel).

Mark 8:11-13 finds Jesus again contending with the Pharisees. This
time they ask for some sign or miracle that will demonstrate that He is the
one who was to come. Perhaps, like Elijah, they wanted Him to call fire

down from heaven (2 Kings 1:12). But Jesus will have none of that. He gets into a boat and leaves them behind.

And why didn't He perform a sign for them? For one thing, that is exactly what Satan had desired Him to do in the wilderness temptation (Matt. 4:3-6). Now the Pharisees were playing the part of the devil in requesting a sign on demand. But even more to the point is that He had been constantly performing signs or miracles for other people throughout His ministry. That is, His ministry consisted of one long chain of miraculous signs, but they were too blind to see them for what they were.

Verses 14 to 21 pick up the theme of blindness, but this time in the disciples. The occasion for the story is the fact that somebody had blundered in not bringing any food for their journey except one small loaf. That worried the disciples greatly, and Jesus knew it. So while they had their mind on the topic of bread, He told them to beware of the leaven of the Pharisees and of Herod, referring to their false ideas about true power—ideas that could lead the disciples' minds astray on the true nature of His Messiahship. After all, the people had been looking for a powerful earthly king rather than a suffering servant. Their teaching, as we saw at the feeding of the 5,000, was a real temptation for the disciples. Such thoughts, like leaven or yeast, could easily continue to permeate their minds, much as yeast spreads through dough.

But the disciples in their blindness totally missed Jesus' point. All they could think about was literal bread or food (verse 16). Their failure demonstrates their dullness in understanding and calls forth the stern rebuke of Mark 8:17, 18. "This rebuke," writes Larry Hurtado, "is the harshest comment on the dullness of the disciples thus far in Mark (cf. 4:13, 40; 6:52) and describes them in language borrowed from the O[ld] T[estament] where rebellious Israel is condemned for disobedience to God and an unwillingness to hear his prophetic word" (Hurtado, p. 126). Mark 8:18 is an allusion to Jeremiah 5:21, in which God condemns the ancient Jews in the same manner that Jesus does the Pharisees. It warned the disciples not to follow their ancestors' path, or, in the words of verse 15, accept their leaven into their minds.

Jesus goes on in verses 19 and 20 to refer them back to His feeding of the 5,000 and the 4,000, thereby demonstrating that He had had no problem with supplying food in time of need. In effect, the twice-repeated reminder declares, "Haven't you learned anything yet?" The answer in this paragraph seems to be negative. Whether they know it or not, the disciples appear to be as blind as the Pharisees.

Mark 8:22-26 shifts the focus from blindness to its healing. While only Mark reports this miracle, it is unique among all of those performed by Jesus in that it is the only one that took place in stages. And it is no accident that it appears where it does in Mark's Gospel, placed between sections describing the blindness of the disciples (verses 14-21) and its partial healing (verses 27-35).

While the healing of the blind man in two stages first applies to the disciples, it also highlights a more general truth. None of us see fully when we become Christians. While we have a new perspective on life, as new converts we are still partly looking through the old lenses. Christianity is a growing experience. And part of that involves learning to see God more clearly. And as we do so we will have clearer perceptions of our selves and our shortcomings and needs. Clear vision comes about through Bible study and practicing Christian living in the everyday world. The Bible not only provides us with perspective, but also with feedback on the nature of our experience. Other biblically informed Christians help us in the process.

One of the genuine tragedies of many Christians is that they are satisfied with a partial healing. Somehow their healing got arrested and they have never allowed Jesus to finish His work. Many in the church have only a dim view of what He can do for them. They do not recognize either their problems or the world's. Needing the second touch of Jesus, they still see "people as trees walking" (verse 24).

The good news is that He is able and desirous to bring to completion what He has begun if we are willing to let Him work in our lives.

Mark 8:27-30 carries the theme of healing from blindness into the lives of the disciples. With these verses we have come to what is in many respects the most critical episode in the life of Jesus. The passage stands at the center of Mark's Gospel, and rightly so. It comes at the apex of the first half of Mark's narrative of Jesus.

As William Barclay points out, this episode occurs at "the crisis of Jesus' life. Whatever His disciples might be thinking, He knew for certain that ahead there lay an inescapable cross. Things could not go on much longer. The opposition was gathering itself to strike. Now the problem and the question confronting Jesus was this—had He had any effect at all? Had He achieved anything? Or, to put it in another way, had anyone discovered who He really was?" (Barclay, *Mark,* pp. 196, 197).

The only way to find out was to ask those closest to Him, those who would soon, unbeknownst to them, take over His movement as true apostles. The question at this point was whether they had learned the basic thing they needed to know as disciples, since without the understanding that Jesus had sought to give them as disciples they could not be apostles.

So Jesus asks what others said of Him. The disciples quickly replied that some saw Him as John the Baptist or Elijah or one of the prophets (verse 28). But Jesus really didn't care about the answer to that question. He only used it to get them thinking and talking about an issue that was crucial to Him now that He had reached the critical point of His ministry.

So He raises the fundamental question that underlies everything: "Who do you say that I am?" (verse 29). Everything rode on their answer. With relief Jesus heard Peter respond, "You are the Christ." At that point Jesus knew that He had not failed. The eyes of the disciples had at last opened.

But as verses 31 through 35 demonstrate, their vision was still imperfect. They understood that Jesus was the Christ, the Messiah, but they didn't know what that meant.

As a result, Jesus told the disciples that "they should tell no one about Him" (verse 30). That seems like a strange command, but it was a necessary one. As Ralph Martin points out, Peter still "has no understanding of what Jesus' true office is" (Martin, *Mark,* p. 129). He still had the conquering-king perspective. And that is quite normal, since, as James Brooks indicates, "there is no evidence that any Jew in pre-Christian times thought of a suffering Messiah." Thus, although Peter's confession was correct, it "was also inadequate" (Brooks, p. 135). Peter and the other disciples, like the partially healed blind man of verses 22 to 26, still need the second touch of Jesus.

Part III

Act Two

Understanding and Embracing the Costs and Expectations of God's Rule on the Road to Jerusalem

Mark 8:31–10:52

30. The Tempter Reappears

Mark 8:31-33

> *[31] And He began to teach them that it is necessary for the Son of Man to suffer many things and to be rejected by the elders and the chief priests and the scribes and to be killed and to rise again after three days. [32] He spoke plainly about this. And Peter took Him aside and began to rebuke Him. [33] But turning around and seeing His disciples and Peter, He said, "Get behind Me, Satan, because you are not thinking the things of God but human things."*

With Mark 8:31 we come to one of the great turning points in Mark's Gospel. From this point on Jesus *begins* to teach them that it was *"necessary"* for Him to

1. "suffer many things,"
2. "be rejected by the elders and the chief priests and the scribes,"
3. "be killed," and
4. "rise again after three days" (verse 31).

It wasn't as if He hadn't alluded to some of these events before. He had, after all, told them that a time would come when the bridegroom would be taken away from them (Mark 2:20), but such statements were not "straight talk." They were veiled words whose meaning the disciples could recognize only after His death and resurrection, but not at the time. Thus the significance of the words "He began" was that now for the first time Jesus taught them openly about what would happen to Him.

And why, we need to ask, did Jesus choose this precise time to set forth such an important teaching? A direct connection exists between

Peter's statement in verse 29 that Jesus was the Christ and Jesus' plain speech regarding His forthcoming rejection and suffering. That confession meant that Peter and the other disciples had begun to gain their sight. But Jesus knew that, like the restored blind man in verses 22-26, they did not yet see clearly. It was one thing for them to confess that Jesus was the Messiah, but quite another for them to understand the nature of that Messiahship. The disciples pictured it as glorious and triumphant, but Jesus knew that His end would be death and rejection. As He saw the plotting of the religious and political powers, He realized that it was vital to instruct His followers on the true nature of His mission.

Why the urgent necessity? First, as J. D. Jones points out, "if Christ had allowed His death to come upon Him without a word of warning to His disciples, it would completely have shattered their faith. Even as it was, it went far towards doing it. But He told them all about it before it came to pass, so that when it did come to pass they might believe" (Jones, vol. 2, p. 169).

Second, it was safe at this point to tell them the disaster that lay ahead of Him. But if He had done so at first, given the universal belief of the Jews in a kingly Messiah, the disciples would have rejected Him outright. They would have refused to believe because, as far as they were concerned, Jesus didn't even know what Messiahship was all about. But things had changed now. They *had already* come to the conclusion that He was the Messiah. Peter had made that plain. Because of that acceptance, and only because of it, it was now safe for Him to redefine the nature of His Messiahship to them. They had at last come to the place where they could bear the straightforward announcement of the cross.

It is important for us to note that Jesus claimed that it was *necessary* for Him "to be killed." From His perspective, the cross was not an option but mandatory. He had come to earth not only to live a sinless life, but "to give his life as a ransom for many" (Mark 10:45, RSV). "This is my blood of the covenant," He told His disciples at the Last Supper, "which is poured out for many" (14:24, RSV). Christ's death was not an optional part of the plan of salvation. It was central. Without His substitutionary death there would be no plan of salvation. Because of that necessity He began to teach them plainly. But as events in the next few verses and in the rest of the Gospel show, it would be a difficult task.

And why? Because everything in the disciples' tradition went against it. In their understanding the Messiah would "arise from the posterity of David" to "deliver in mercy the remnant" of God's people and at the same time destroy their enemies (4 Ezra 12:32-34). He would come "to smash the arrogance of sinners like a potter's jar; to shatter all their substance with an iron rod; to destroy the unlawful nations with the word of his mouth" (Ps. of Sol. 17:23, 24).

The Jews of Christ's time knew nothing of a suffering Messiah. As a result, the sequence of Mark 8:29-31 caught the disciples totally off guard. In response to Peter's declaration that Jesus was the Messiah or Christ He strangely taught them that He must suffer and die. No line of reasoning could have been more foreign to the thinking of the disciples. From their perspective such ideas just didn't belong together. A suffering Messiah whose end would be rejection and death was an impossibility. Israel's history consisted of three great bondages: the Egyptian, the Babylonian, and now the Roman. The first two had had political solutions. First-century Jews would hardly regard as genuine a Messiah who did not at least deliver the nation politically. They were not ready for a Messiah who had come to save them from their sins (Matt. 1:21) rather than from their Roman oppressors.

With such thoughts in mind, it is not difficult to see why Peter "took [Jesus] aside and began to rebuke Him" (Mark 8:32). Jesus was obviously confused, didn't see things correctly, and needed a bit of help in understanding His mission as Messiah. Peter was absolutely sincere in his attempt to straighten Jesus out.

But it was the disciple who had the blurred vision. He may have correctly identified Jesus as the Messiah, but he had not the foggiest idea of what that meant. Thus the beginning of Jesus' instruction to him and the other disciples in verse 31. And thus the brutal rebuke in verse 33. Never in all of the gospels do we find a more scathing or sterner rebuke than that handed out to Peter when he was only trying to help Jesus see things correctly.

Why the forcefulness of the rebuke? Because Peter had usurped the role that Satan had earlier taken in the wilderness temptation. Both of them had suggested that Jesus could fulfill His mission without His death on the cross. And to both Jesus exclaimed, "Get behind Me Satan!" (see also Matt. 4:8-10).

We miss the point if we imagine that Jesus thought Peter was Satan. Rather, He saw Satan speaking through His chief disciple. Peter was playing the part of the tempter. And the temptation was the central one in Jesus' life. In fact, He undoubtedly found the thought of His forthcoming death to be even more distasteful than did Peter. Jesus had seen crucifixions in His travels, and, like any normal human being, He had no desire to exit the world by the excruciating death of the cross. He would have found it much easier to become the political Messiah that the Jews and the disciples expected. Beyond that, Jesus had no desire to bear the judgment of the world by becoming sin for all humanity in the sacrifice on Calvary (John 12:31-33; 2 Cor. 5:21). The thought of separation from God while bearing the sins of the world on the cross was abhorrent to Him in the extreme.

The lure to do His own will by avoiding the cross was the *great temptation* of Jesus' life. He had encountered it after the feeding of the 5,000 when they tried to make Him king (see the discussion on Mark 6:30-44 in section number 25), and He would face it again in Gethsemane, where He would repeatedly pray, "If this cannot pass unless I drink it, thy will be done" (Matt. 26:42, RSV). The forcefulness of Jesus' rebuke to Peter implies the importance of the cross in His ministry.

Not only had the temptation come, but it had emerged from the mouth of a friend. It is a sad fact of life that Satan can use Jesus' followers—even His ministers—to do his own work. As Christians we not only have the potential of betraying Jesus, but also one another. We also can guide fellow Christians in the wrong direction and discourage them from doing God's will by advising them to avoid all dangers to themselves and inconveniences to our selves. Lest we also play the role of Satan, we need to be more aware than Peter.

Think About It!

If you would have been Peter, how would you have responded to Jesus' assertions? What would you have been thinking as He turned toward Jerusalem? Would you have even desired to go with Him?

Peter's experience can teach us yet other lessons. One is that we as Christians are a mixed bag. In one moment I can have a divine insight, then in the next I can be a tool of the devil. At the best we are fallible creatures, partly controlled by knowledge and partly by ignorance. All of us have one foot in the kingdom. We have been saved in the sense that we have accepted Jesus, but the plain fact is that He has a lot more saving to do in us.

Another lesson is that we need to be careful not to cast people off because of their stupidity and errors. Jesus in the days and weeks to come on the road to Jerusalem would demonstrate almost infinite patience in working with His erring disciples. Sherman Johnson has pointed out that "only a miraculous stupidity could keep them from understanding" (Johnson, p. 150), but they managed to do exactly that until after the resurrection. Jesus, however, did not abandon them. It is significant that Mark tells us in 8:31 that Jesus *"began* to teach them." He didn't give up on the disciples. He hasn't given up on me. And we shouldn't give up on one another.

31. The Real Meaning of Discipleship

Mark 8:34–9:1

[34]And He called together the crowd along with His disciples, saying to them, "If anyone desires to follow after Me, let him deny himself and take up his cross and follow Me. [35]For whoever desires to save his life will lose it, but whoever loses his life for My sake and the gospel's will save it. [36]For what does it profit a person to gain the entire world and to forfeit his soul? [37]For what will a person give in exchange for his soul? [38]For whoever in this adulterous and sinful generation is ashamed of Me and My words, the Son of Man will also be ashamed of when He comes in the glory of His Father with the holy angels." [1]And He said to them, "Truly I say to you that there are some standing here who will not taste death until they see the kingdom of God coming in power."

When Jesus "began to teach them that it is necessary for the Son of Man to suffer . . . and to be killed" (Mark 8:31) He was truly only commencing His instruction, because a new understanding of Messiahship dictates a new insight to the meaning of discipleship. And if the new interpretation of Messiahship was distasteful to Peter and His followers, the new concept of discipleship would be equally abhorrent. "If anyone desires to follow after Me," they heard Jesus say, "let him deny himself and take up his cross and follow Me" (verse 34).

That verse contains two of the most difficult words that a person will ever have to face—"deny" and "cross." When we think of self-denial we imagine abstaining from certain luxuries for a certain period of time, while at the same time, perhaps, congratulating ourselves on how well we are doing in being self-controlled and/or generous.

But that is far from what Jesus meant by "deny." It is a sharp and demanding word. Kenneth Wuest suggests that in verse 34 it means "to forget one's self, lose sight of one's self and one's interests" (Wuest, vol. 1, p. 170). And Halford Luccock writes that "the denial of *self* is something deeper" than mere self-denial. "It is making ourselves not an end, but a means, in the kingdom of God. It is subordinating the clamoring ego, with its shrill claim for priority, its preoccupation with 'I,' 'me,' and 'mine,' its concern for self-assertion, its insistence on comfort and prestige; denying self, not for the sake of denial as a sort of moral athletics, but for Christ's sake, for the sake of putting the self into his cause" (Luccock, p. 770).

Thus there is a huge difference between self-denial and denying one's self. The first is a minor surface operation, while the second is a matter of the heart—or, more specifically, a change of heart.

The second difficult word in verse 34 is "cross." The bad news to Peter and the rest of the disciples (including us) is that Jesus' cross is not the only one. He goes on to say that each of His followers will have his or her own cross.

To fully understand the statement that each person must take up the cross, we need to put ourselves in the place of those first disciples. The idea of a cross or of being crucified doesn't do much for our twenty-first century imaginations. We have never seen a crucifixion. To us, "crucifixion" is a word that has lost most of its emotional connotations. But that was not true for the disciples. When they saw a knot of Roman soldiers escorting a person through town carrying or dragging part of a cross, they knew it was a one-way trip. To Jesus and the disciples, the cross symbolized nothing but death. For the disciples, to carry the cross meant one horror-producing thought: "They were to go to Jerusalem like a procession of condemned criminals with halters round their necks" (Dodd, pp. 94, 95).

It is with that realization that the word "cross" and the word "deny" intersect. The cross, like the concept of denial of the self, has been trivialized by the Christian community. For some people bearing the cross is wearing it as an ornament around their neck. For others it means putting up with some discomfort or inconvenience in their life, such as a nagging spouse or a physical impediment. Jesus does not have in mind that caricature of cross bearing. He is speaking of the cross as an instrument of death—not of physical death for most of His hearers, but for the crucifixion of the self, the denial of the center of our life and our primary allegiance to our self. Ellen White points out that "the warfare against self is the greatest battle that was ever fought" (White, *Steps to Christ,* p. 43). And James Denney emphasizes that "though sin may have a natural birth it does not die a natural death; in every case it has to be morally sentenced and put to death" (Denney, *Doctrine of Reconciliation,* p. 198). That sentencing is an act of the will under the impulse of the Holy Spirit. Jesus and Paul repeatedly refer to it as a crucifixion.

> "When Christ calls a man, he bids him come and die" (Bonhoeffer, p. 99).

Paul is especially clear on that topic in Romans 6, in which he describes becoming a Christian as a crucifixion of the "old self" and a resurrection to a new way of life with a new center—Jesus and His will (see verses 1-11). It is that death that is implicit in Jesus' command to deny one's self. Baptism by immersion is the symbol of spiritual death and resurrection to a new life centered on God (see John 3:5-7; Rom. 6:1-4).

Four "fors" follow the command to deny self and take up the cross. First, "for whoever desires to save his life will lose it, but whoever loses his life for My sake and the gospel's will save it" (verse 35). That passage had special meaning for Mark's first audience in Rome. At times during the various Roman persecutions of Christians they could literally save their life if they would deny Christ and proclaim that Caesar was Lord. It was a tempting thing to do, especially in the face of the consequences. Many did so. But while they may have saved their physical life they lost their connection with the source of eternal life.

The second "for" appears in verse 36: "For what does it profit a person to gain the entire world and to forfeit his soul?" It is clearly related to the third "for": "For what will a person give in exchange for his soul?" (verse 37). Here we have two great unanswered questions. Scripture leaves them open-ended because they apply to more than just those first-century disciples. They are questions for you and me. We all find ourselves confronted by the alternatives set forth by Jesus—the world or the soul. And it is all too easy to sacrifice the soul to the world. Some of us, William Barclay suggests, are willing to exchange honor for profit. It is all too easy to cheat just a bit if we think no one will discover it. Others are willing to give up "principle for popularity." But the real question is not what people think of us but how God regards us. And yet others may "sacrifice eternity for the present." It is all too easy to live for the present, especially if our willful self is still at the center of our lives. But people would save themselves endless pain if they always evaluated their actions and their things in the light of eternity (see Barclay, *Mark,* pp. 211, 212).

That is what Dives failed to do in the parable of the rich man and Lazarus. He had more possessions than he could ever use, but, Jesus tells us, "the rich man also died" (Luke 16:22, RSV). And when he did he lost everything. The old proverb "You can't take it with you" is no joke. You really can't. We must make all of our choices in the context of everlasting values and eternal truths. Whether we like it or not, one of the central truths of this life is that everything and everyone eventually passes away.

The fourth "for": "For whoever in this adulterous and sinful generation is ashamed of Me and My words, the Son of Man will also be ashamed of when He comes in the glory of His Father with the holy angels" (Mark 8:38). Here we come to the reality that Dives neglected to consider, Christ's final acceptance of our choices in the judgment at the end of time. "Son of Man," Jesus' favorite title for Himself in the book of Mark, comes from Daniel 7, in which the "Son of Man" and the "Ancient of Days" pass judgment in favor of the saints and against those who have opposed God and His values (verses 13, 22, 26). After that pre-Advent judgment "the kingdom and the dominion and the greatness of the kingdoms under the whole heaven shall be given to the people of the saints of the Most High; their kingdom shall be an everlasting kingdom" (verse 27, RSV).

Part of the good news of the judgment is that God and Jesus force no one to believe anything, accept anything, or do anything. They respect human individuality and the right of every person to choose for himself or herself. God respects our decisions in the judgment. He compels no one to live by His principles and values for eternity. If we cling to those things that pass away, God honors our choice. The same goes for those who accept the eternal things. But, according to Jesus, a day of reckoning will come.

After that foreshadowing of the final judgment, Jesus makes the perplexing statement that some standing with Him would not see death before "they see the kingdom of God coming in power" (Mark 9:1).

The explanations of that passage have been many, and the immediate context suggests two of them. One is that it refers to the Transfiguration that follows in Mark 9:2-13. Another is that it has in mind the Second Advent prediction of Mark 8:38. That latter explanation, however, forces one to see Mark 9:1 as a failed prediction. Thus of the two contextual explanations, the Transfiguration as a foreshadowing of the kingdom of glory is the most satisfactory.

But while the Transfiguration explanation is helpful, it may not uncover the full meaning of the prediction. Herman Ridderbos offers the insightful suggestion that prophecy "often compresses the distinct phases of the future into a unity" (Ridderbos, pp. 314, 315). We have already seen, for example, that Jesus preached the nearness of the kingdom of heaven (Matt. 4:17; cf. Mark 1:15). But He did not make clear the kingdom's progressive nature by explaining that the kingdom of grace aspect would precede the kingdom of glory aspect by at least 2,000 years. In like manner, the pre-resurrection Gospel narrative does not differentiate the segments of Jesus' exaltation experience.

Only after Jesus' resurrection did the disciples begin to realize that His exaltation would take place in stages. They would live to see the beginning stages of His coming in glory in His resurrection and ascension, but would not remain alive to witness the later stages, such as the Second Advent. Thus it appears that a combination of Ridderbos's compression insight with the idea of the Transfiguration as a foretaste of the kingdom of glory offers the best solution to the meaning of Mark 9:1.

But until the fullness of the kingdom arrives, we as Jesus' disciples need to stay on our crosses and keep our values in line with those of the coming King.

32. A Glimpse of Heaven

Mark 9:2-13

²After six days Jesus took Peter and James and John and led them to a high mountain by themselves. And He was transfigured before them. ³His garments became gleaming white, such as no bleacher of cloth on earth could whiten them. ⁴Elijah along with Moses appeared to them, and they were talking with Jesus. ⁵And Peter said to Jesus, "Rabbi, it is good for us to be here. Let us make three tents, one for You, and one for Moses, and one for Elijah." ⁶For he had not known what to say, because they were terrified. ⁷A cloud came and overshadowed them, and a voice came out from the cloud, saying, "This is My beloved Son, listen to Him." ⁸Suddenly, looking around they no longer saw anyone with them but Jesus only.

⁹As they were coming down from the mountain, He ordered them that no one should tell what they had seen until the Son of Man had arisen from the dead. ¹⁰And they kept the topic to themselves, discussing what it meant to rise from the dead. ¹¹And they were questioning Him, saying, "Why do the scribes say that it is necessary for Elijah to come first?" ¹²He said to them, "Elijah must come first to restore all things. Yet how has it been written concerning the Son of Man that He must suffer many things and be rejected? ¹³But I say to you that Elijah has indeed come and they did to him whatever they desired, just as it has been written concerning him."

The transfiguration is intimately connected with what has gone before, that is, Peter's confession that Jesus was the Christ (Mark 8:29) and Jesus' devastating prediction of His death and resurrection and His statement about His disciples' crosses (verses 31-34). The glorious event itself, Mark tells us, took place about a week (Mark 9:2 says 6 days, while Luke 9:28 says 8) after the events at Caesarea Philippi. The site was probably Mount Hermon, which rises to an elevation of 9,200 feet and is approximately 12 miles from Caesarea Philippi.

The event is different from any other miracle story in the Gospels. In all the others Jesus is the giver of grace. But in this one He is the recipient of glory.

Mark doesn't tell us why Jesus went up on the mountain, but Luke does. Luke 9:28 claims that He took Peter, John, and James "up on the mountain to pray" (RSV). He certainly had plenty to pray about. By now

He had fully committed Himself to go to Jerusalem and the cross that awaited Him there. How much it horrified Him we find out in His struggle in Gethsemane. He also had a burden to pray for His noncomprehending disciples, men whom He would soon leave behind to head up His church on earth. And what weak individuals they were at this stage. Luke tells us that they did on the Mount of Transfiguration what they would later do in Gethsemane—they slept while Jesus prayed (9:32). And these were His three closest disciples. If they were operating spiritually at such a low level, what must have been the condition of the other nine? No wonder Jesus felt the need to pray.

It was while they were sleeping that the Transfiguration began to take place. By the time the disciples had awakened, Jesus' appearance had altered and His clothing had already taken on its glorious brightness (Luke 9:29; Mark 9:3). Not only the brightness but also the presence of Elijah and Moses must have startled them. "They are here, not as competitors with Jesus—only he is said to be arrayed in glistening white garments. . . . The appearance of Elijah," writes Robert Gundry, "gives an eschatological signal to the three disciples," because the Jews firmly believed on the basis of Malachi 4:5, 6 that "Elijah is to come back before the Day of the Lord" (Gundry, p. 458). Mark 9:11, 12 indicates that the disciples shared a similar belief.

And why is it that Moses and Elijah were present? A.W.F. Blunt suggests that it was because they "represent [the] Law and Prophets" of the Hebrew Bible that pointed forward to Jesus (Blunt, p. 206). Alternately, Ellen White suggests that Moses "represented those who shall come forth from the grave at the resurrection of the just," while Elijah, who had been translated to heaven without seeing death, "represented those who will be living upon the earth at Christ's second coming," and who will be translated to heaven without seeing death. There "upon the mount the future kingdom of glory was represented in miniature" (White, *The Desire of Ages,* pp. 421, 422; cf. 1 Thess. 4:13-18; 1 Cor. 15:51-53).

The purpose of the Transfiguration was to encourage both Jesus and the disciples, who were in a "tailspin of bewilderment" (Edwards, p. 262) due to Jesus' recent redefining of Messiahship and discipleship (Mark 8:31-38). First and foremost, it strengthened Jesus Himself. Please note that God did not take the bitter cup away from Him. Rather, He sustained Him so that He would have courage and assurance as He moved toward Jerusalem.

Christ's encouragement took place on three levels. First was the glorious brightness that had been His environment in the heavenly kingdom. Second was the presence of Elijah and Moses, the special envoys of heaven to Him, individuals who had also experienced stress and rejection on earth as God's servants. Luke tells us that they spoke to Jesus "of his departure" (9:31, RSV), which He was to accomplish at Jerusalem.

Interestingly, they did not speak of Jesus' death, but rather of His departure. The Greek word translated as departure is *exodon,* from which we get the English word exodus. Thus they are looking beyond the death and tomb and even the resurrection to His ascension back to heaven. The emphasis is not on what Jesus was to suffer but on what He was to achieve. Exodus suggests emancipation and deliverance. The conversation of Elijah and Moses with Jesus concerned victory rather than defeat. Jesus in His humanity needed that good word.

Then there was the voice from heaven—the same voice that Jesus had heard at His baptism when He was just starting out on His mission. Now, He hears it again at the very point His ministry turns its direction toward Jerusalem. "This is My beloved Son, listen to Him" (Mark 9:7). God had put His stamp of approval on Jesus' decision and His course of action. It was as if the Father were saying, "Go ahead, You made the right choice. I will be with You." That is just the encouragement that Jesus needed as He approached His hour of trial.

But the Transfiguration wasn't only for Jesus. It was also for His shattered disciples who had been bewildered since Caesarea Philippi. R. T. France points out a progression in God's announcements of His pleasure in Jesus between Mark 1:11 and 9:7. "The earlier declaration was apparently to Jesus alone (hence the second-person address), whereas here it is a third-person pronouncement to the three disciples; the secret is being shared, even if still to only a handful of chosen disciples" (France, *Mark,* NIGTC, p. 347). They had heard Jesus' statement that He was going to Jerusalem to die. Now they had God's witness that Jesus was doing the right thing and that the Father was behind Him. Thus the command to them to "listen to Him" (Mark 9:7). They might not as yet understand what was happening, but God had provided them with an anchor to stabilize them in the stressful time soon to overwhelm them.

Peter, in usual fashion, didn't know how to respond to the situation. So he suggested that they make three tents for Jesus, Moses, and Elijah (verse 5), hoping perhaps to prolong the incident or even make it permanent. But all who have had mountaintop spiritual experiences know the impossibility of staying on a spiritual high. In actuality, such experiences are not meant to be permanent. Rather, we from time to time get a glimpse of God so that we might be better prepared to descend the mountain into the world of service.

The Transfiguration ended as quickly as it had begun. The disciples were left with God's command to listen to Jesus ringing in their ears. And He did indeed have something to tell them. He ordered them to remain silent about what they had seen until He had arisen from the dead. The last thing Jesus needed was for the Jews to know that Elijah had appeared in person. More than anything, that fact would have set off a Messianic revolution. They were not to reveal it to anyone, Jesus ominously told them, until after His resurrection (verse 9). By that time it would be obvious to all that His kingdom was not the sort the people expected. Only then would it be safe to repeat the details of the Transfiguration.

Meanwhile, it left the three disciples more confused than ever. The grip of their preconceptions left them with no understanding of what it meant for Jesus to rise from the dead (verse 10).

Not knowing how to respond, they changed the topic, asking Jesus why the scribes claimed that Elijah would return before the establishment of the Messianic kingdom (verse 11). Here was a topic much more to their liking. After all, they had just seen the Old Testament prophet.

But Jesus' response to their question hardly left them anything to rejoice over. To the contrary, it reiterated the topic that they didn't want even to contemplate. For Elijah too, Jesus claimed, endured suffering. "Elijah," He reported, "has indeed come and they did to him whatever they desired" (verse 13). "This statement," James Edwards reports, "surely sent a shock wave to Jesus' hearers, for they were as unprepared for the suffering of Elijah as for the suffering of the Son of Man. Apart from only vague references (1 Kgs. 19:2, 10), there was no hint that Elijah would suffer before the Day of the Lord. The reference to the suffering of Elijah is, of course, a reference to the death of John the Baptist, as Matt. 17:13 makes explicit. . . . If Herod had dealt severely with the forerunner of the

Messiah (6:14-29), should there be any surprise about the fate of the Messiah?" (Edwards, p. 275).

The disciples on the mountain top had glimpsed a bit of heaven. But as so often happens following such experiences, they would soon get a peek at hell. Whether we like it or not, life in this world isn't everything it should be. But we can thank God that He provides us with periodic views of heaven to help us navigate the more difficult times.

33. A Glimpse of Hell

Mark 9:14-29

[14]*When they came to the disciples, they saw a great crowd around them and the scribes arguing with them.* [15]*Immediately when all the crowd saw Him they were amazed and ran up to Him and were greeting Him.* [16]*He asked them, "What are you discussing with them?"* [17]*One of the crowd answered Him, "Teacher, I brought my son to You, for he has a mute spirit.* [18]*And whenever it seizes him it throws him down and he foams at the mouth and grinds his teeth and becomes stiff. I told Your disciples so that they might cast it out, but they were not able."* [19]*And He answered them, saying, "O faithless generation, how long will I be with you? How long shall I endure you? Bring him to Me."* [20]*And they brought the boy to Him. When he saw Him, the spirit immediately convulsed him, and falling on the ground he rolled around, foaming at the mouth.* [21]*And Jesus questioned his father, "How long has this been happening to him?" He said "From childhood,* [22]*and often it throws him into fire and into water that it might destroy him. But if you can do anything, have pity on us and help us."* [23]*And Jesus said to him, "If you are able, all things are possible for one who believes."* [24]*Immediately crying out, the child's father said, "I believe, help my unbelief."* [25]*And, Jesus, seeing the crowd rapidly assembling, commanded the unclean spirit, saying to it, "Mute and deaf spirit, I command you, come out of him and enter him no more."* [26]*Crying out and convulsing him, it came out and he was like a dead person, so that many said, "He is dead."* [27]*But Jesus, taking hold of his hand, lifted him up, and he stood.* [28]*And entering into a house, His disciples privately questioned Him, "Why were we not able to cast it out?"* [29]*And He said to them, "This kind cannot come out except by prayer."*

What a contrast! On the mount of Transfiguration Jesus and the "Three" had witnessed a bit of heaven. Now they glimpse a bit of hell in the life below. To say the least, they descend to find a difficult situation.

In fact, it was exactly the kind of circumstances that Peter had hoped to avoid when he said, "it is good for us to be here, let us make three tents" (Mark 9:5). If Peter could have had his way he would have stayed up there forever.

But Jesus had not forgotten His mission. The purpose of the Transfiguration had been to strengthen Him and encourage Him for that goal. So He descended.

He arrived just in time to face a serious problem. The nine disciples had publicly failed in healing a boy with what may have been a severe case of epilepsy. The scribes had taken advantage of their lack of success, casting doubt not only on the ability of the disciples but, by extension, on Jesus who had commissioned them (verse 14). The crowd was amazed to see Him—probably because He had arrived just at the apex of the argument between the assertive scribes and the humiliated disciples (verse 15).

A major theme in the story and in Mark's portrayal of the disciples thus far is their lack of faith and their need for instruction. Those points are clear. But why had the disciples failed so dismally on this particular occasion? Not because of a lack of potential power. Jesus had already given "them authority over the unclean spirits" (6:7, RSV). Upon returning from their first mission experience without Jesus they had reported that they had "cast out many demons, and anointed with oil many that were sick and healed them" (6:13, RSV). But yet they couldn't heal this time. Something had definitely changed, something was wrong.

What was now different? A first suggestion is that Jesus' announcement a week earlier that He would be rejected and die had destabilized and even shattered their faith (8:31). As a result, they were suffering from a spiritual stupor that had robbed them of their vitality. They couldn't give what they didn't have.

Beyond that was the fact that their prayer life was weak (see verse 29). We know that Peter, James, and John had slept while Jesus prayed on the mountain (Luke 9:32). And if the three closest to Jesus were in such a condition, what were the rest of them like? The devil would like nothing better than for the followers of Jesus to neglect that prayer which strengthens the soul.

> ## Our Greatest Need
>
> "With Him we may do all things. Without Him we can do nothing at all. With Him we may overcome the greatest temptations. Without Him the least may overcome us" (Ryle, p. 182).

Of course, the disciples' discouragement and their lack of prayer were not unrelated. Most people stop praying when they become discouraged. Yet that is the very time we need to pray more than ever. We must let God transform the downward spiral of discouragement into the upward one of faith-inspiring prayer. And no matter how discouraging our circumstances, we need to remember that prayer has power, and that we have a choice as to which spiral we will ride.

The events at the foot of the mountain took a different direction when Jesus arrived. He asked about the nature of the difficulty, and the boy's father described both his son's problem and the failure of the disciples. At that point Jesus raised one of the great themes in Mark when He exclaimed, "O faithless generation, how long will I be with you? How long shall I endure you?" (verse 19). One question that jumps out of that verse is to whom did Jesus refer in calling them a faithless generation? A.E.J. Rawlinson is correct when he claims that it includes "the scribes, the multitude, the disciples, and the contemporaries of Jesus as a whole" (Rawlinson, p. 124). Jesus could now put His disciples and the scribes in the same camp. That situation raised in His mind the central problem of this part of His ministry—"how long will I be with you?" He knew the answer. And He also recognized the stupendous needs of all of His disciples. How to reach them and teach them had become His greatest challenge.

Jesus sees an avenue for further teaching of the Twelve in the plight of the father. When they brought the boy to Jesus the child immediately went into a violent fit, rolling on the ground and foaming at the mouth (verse 20). We would have expected Jesus to heal the boy at once. After all, here was an agonizing human need. But He did something that must have troubled the father. Yet He had a purpose behind it.

Instead of instantly healing the boy, Jesus entered into a discussion with his father at the very time that the boy was convulsing on the ground in front of them (verse 21). Strange time for a discussion. But it was a crucial move for both the father and the disciples (and even for us).

Perhaps the main miracle that day was not the healing of the boy, but the restoration of the father's faith. As James Edwards points out, "Jesus can expel demonic forces at a word, but the evoking of faith is a much harder matter" (Edwards, p. 279).

The man had apparently had some faith when he began his journey. After all, he had brought his son so that Jesus (not the disciples) could heal him (verse 17). But the bungling performance of the disciples had robbed him of most of that faith. Now both the disciples and the man were in the midst of a crisis of faith—one that the scribes were busily exploiting. At that juncture most of us would have probably shaken the dust off our feet and left the whole bunch of them standing in the street. But Jesus never gives up. Instead of scorning the lack of faith in the man and in the disciples, He begins to rebuild it.

The father's statement *"if* you can do anything" (verse 22) indicates the condition of his faith. But Jesus doesn't operate on "ifs." Rather, He drew the father out a bit by saying that "all things are possible for one who believes" (verse 23). That encouraging statement was enough for the father. "I believe, help my unbelief," he cries out. As his struggling faith sought to rise to the surface, Jesus honored it and healed the boy (verses 25-27).

Jesus always meets us where we are. He doesn't demand perfect faith before He acts on our behalf. Rather, He honors us in our weakness by responding to our partial and even broken-down faith. There is a wideness in God's mercy that extends down to you and me as He gives us not what we deserve but what we need. That is grace.

That thought takes us back to the Twelve. Talking to Jesus privately, they asked what had gone wrong. They wanted to know why they hadn't been able to perform the miracle, as they had on previous occasions. Jesus' answer is to the point: they weren't men of prayer—or faith for that matter. The implication is that they didn't stay close to God the Father. They were not only like the partially healed blind man, who could only see half the truth (8:24, 25), they were also like the father in this story, who only half believed in Jesus (see Hooker, p. 224). Like his, the disciples' faith needed to grow and develop. It is to that faith development that Jesus will turn again in Mark 9:30-50.

Meanwhile, it is important to admit that we also are half seeing and half believing. Those who don't believe that claim need the lesson of humility that Jesus will give in the rest of chapter 9. But the remainder of us can be thankful that "what Jesus looked for long ago," He still seeks in us: *"faith— even 'little faith' which can grow"* (Martin, *Where the Action Is,* p. 83).

34. A Lesson on Greatness

Mark 9:30-50

[30]From there they passed through Galilee. He did not want anyone to know about it [31]because He was teaching His disciples, saying to them, "The Son of Man will be betrayed into the hands of men, and they will kill Him, and when He has been killed, after three days He will rise." [32]But they did not understand the statement and feared to question Him.

[33]And they came to Capernaum. When He was in the house He asked them, "What were you discussing on the way?" [34]They were silent, for on the way they had been debating with one another which of them was the greater. [35]Sitting down, He called the Twelve and said to them, "If anyone wishes to be first, he shall be last of all and the servant of all." [36]And He took and set a child in the midst of them. Taking it into His arms, He said to them, [37]"Whoever receives such children in My name, receives Me. And whoever receives Me, receives not Me but the One who sent Me."

[38]John said to Him, "Teacher, we saw someone casting out demons in Your name, and we forbade him, because he was not following us." [39]But Jesus said, "Do not forbid him, because there is no one who shall do a miracle in My name who will be able soon afterward to speak evil of Me. [40]For those not against us are for us. [41]For whoever gives you a cup of water to drink because you bear the name of Christ, truly I say to you, he will by no means lose his reward.

[42]"And whoever causes one of these believing little ones to stumble, it would be better for him if a heavy millstone were hung around his neck and he be thrown into the lake. [43]If your hand causes you to stumble, cut it off; it is better for you to enter life crippled than to go into hell (into the inextinguishable fire) having two hands.* [45]And if your foot causes you to stumble, cut if off; it is better for you to enter into life lame than to be cast into hell having two feet.* [47]And if your eye causes you to stumble, pluck it out; it is better for you to enter the kingdom of God one-eyed than, having two eyes, to be cast into hell, [48]where their worm does not die and the fire is not extinguished. [49]For everyone will be salted with fire. [50]Salt is

good. But if salt becomes unsalty, how will you use it to season? Have salt in yourselves and be at peace with one another."

★Verses 44 and 46 are not in the most reliable Greek manuscripts. The text in each case is identical to verse 48.

Jesus has reached another major turning point in His ministry. Having left the country to the north, where He had been relatively safe, He has begun His last extended journey, advancing through Galilee toward Jerusalem where He knew the cross awaited Him.

The last thing He wanted now were crowds, because He desperately needed to teach His disciples. The topics of His lectures were three in particular:

1. that the Son of Man would be betrayed,
2. that He would be killed,
3. that He would rise after three days (Mark 9:31).

He had plainly taught points 2 and 3 to all the disciples at Caesarea Philippi (8:31, 32) and had alluded to them when coming down the mountain with John, James, and Peter (9:9, 10).

But point 1 is new. For the first time Jesus begins to teach His disciples that He would not only die but that He would be "betrayed" (9:31). He knew that they had a traitor in their midst. Even now, suggests William Barclay, "he could see the way in which the mind of Judas was working. Maybe He could see it better than Judas could himself." Perhaps His raising the issue was an appeal to the man who would betray Him (Barclay, *Mark,* p. 227).

If they could have really "heard" what Jesus was saying, it might have encouraged them. But how could they possibly grasp resurrection when they couldn't even understand the necessity of His death. And that latter point was something they simply wished would go away. But they weren't as ignorant as they might appear. G. A. Chadwick points out that "they comprehended enough to shrink from hearing more. They did not dare to lift the veil which covered a mystery so dreadful; they feared to ask Him [9:32]. It is a natural impulse, not to know the worst" (Chadwick, p. 250).

We may fault the disciples for their blindness and their perverse "stupidity" when Jesus repeatedly warned them. But we are not so much different. Denial is a popular human sport in all ages. We all participate in the amazing ability of the mind for rejecting that which it does not wish to see.

Nothing shows how distant the Twelve were from understanding the true nature of Jesus' mission than the incident reported in Mark 9:33, 34. "What an amazing and startling contrast we have here!" writes J. D. Jones. "The Lord is in front, absorbed in thoughts of His cross and passion, thinking of the death He was to taste for every man; His disciples, following a little behind, quarrel and wrangle about precedence and position" (Jones, vol. 2, p. 237).

Perhaps the stimulus for the argument concerning who was the greatest was Jesus' selection of Peter, James, and John to accompany Him up the mount of Transfiguration (Mark 9:2). Then again, perhaps it was the Lord's blessing of Peter for identifying Him as the Christ at Caesarea Philippi a few days before (see Matt. 16:17, 18). But on a deeper level, the question resides at the center of the sinful human heart. The desire for egocentric greatness fuels both the world's stunning accomplishments and its great sins. The craving to stand out, to be superior, to have people look at and admire us is part of the great rebellion of humanity against God. It was also the root of Lucifer's sin in heaven. He had said in his heart, "I will raise my throne above the stars of God. . . . I will make myself like the Most High" (Isa. 14:13, 14, NIV). Competitiveness and egocentricity have not lost their edge in the past 2,000 years. Like the disciples, we also struggle with the natural pull of the human heart.

Yet for all of their love of this favorite argumentative topic, the disciples realized that their attitude and desire was wrong. How do we know? Because when Jesus asked them what they had been arguing about "they were silent" (verse 34).

It is an interesting fact that what had seemed quite proper among themselves as they jockeyed for position suddenly appeared shabby and disreputable when Jesus put the spotlight on it. How different things look in the radiance of the cross, in the light that shines from the life and attitude of Jesus. "It would do us good to bring our ambitions and desires and plans constantly into the presence of the lowly Jesus, and test them there" (Jones, vol. 2, p. 238).

In Mark 9:35-37 Jesus presents His much needed lesson on servant leadership—that the greatest would be the servant of all. But the disciples weren't sure they liked the way the discussion was going. So John, who was at the forefront of bickering about greatness (see 10:35-45), jumped in and changed the subject to something he thought would be more comfortable (9:38).

But he didn't find much relief in his attempted diversion. Rather, he got more instruction. This time on tolerance rather than humility (verses 39-41). Perhaps, however, the two topics are really quite closely related. After all, why is it that we don't want others who are not of our "group" teaching and healing in Christ's name? Could it be kind of a collective pride that says my church is "greater" than yours? Jesus' mild rebuke to John should help us be cautious in regard to ecclesiastical arrogance and intolerance. While some churches may have a larger proportion of truth than others, none of them are totally free from error, and none have a monopoly on truth. "The story is impressive," Craig Evans writes, "because Jesus' name is so powerful that someone outside of his circle [of disciples] can invoke it to good effect" (Evans, p. 66). It is an experience that we need to keep in mind as we "do church." The temptation to "greatness" is not only an individual problem, it also seduces institutions and denominations.

At first glance it appears that verses 41 to 48 don't seem to have any connection to the incident about the "stranger" healing in Jesus' name. He had concluded His previous lesson by noting that "those not against us are for us" (verse 40). Then He went on to say that those who help His disciples by even giving them a cup of cold water would surely not lose their reward (verse 41). That appears to be a blessing on the "stranger." Thus the one whom the disciples had denounced Jesus now blessed.

It is in that context that Jesus warned His disciples about causing "one of these believing little ones" to stumble (verse 42). "Little ones" here does not mean children but "the humblest members of the community" (Taylor, p. 410). It refers to followers of Jesus who may not be as "great" as the Twelve—to "immature, weak, and perhaps new believers" (Brooks, p. 152).

Jesus' warning couldn't have been firmer. Those who offended such "little" ones because of their arrogance or other attitudes and actions did not partake of the humble servant spirit of God's kingdom. As such, they could not expect the reward of Jesus' followers. To the contrary, He promised them hell (the reward of the wicked), "where their worm does not die and the fire is not extinguished" (verse 48, which is an allusion to Isa. 66:24).

The Greek word that Jesus used for hell is *Gehenna*. *Gehenna* refers to the valley of Hinnom outside of Jerusalem, where people had once offered human sacrifices to the false god Moloch. The reformation of King Josiah declared the valley of Hinnom an unclean place (2 Kings 23:10). The inhabitants of Jerusalem later used it, Morna Hooker notes, as a city rubbish dump, "where fires burned continually, and so came to be a symbol for the place of future destruction for the wicked. It should be noted that nothing is said here about eternal punishment: on the contrary, the image seems to be one of annihilation, in contrast to life; it is the *fire,* and not the torment, which is *unquenchable"* (Hooker, p. 232).

Jesus' warning to the disciples is clear. They needed to employ their God-given blessings to build up the little ones rather than to injure them through arrogance or intolerance. The contrasting spirits of service and arrogance would have opposite rewards—heaven or hell. That is the essential lesson of Mark 9:42-48. It was a needed lesson, but one that has proven difficult to learn by disciples in all ages.

Commentaries have long debated the meaning of the three cryptic proverbs of verses 49 and 50. But the final words, "be at peace with one another," are clear enough. That saying, argues Evans, "harks back to the very beginning of this chain of materials, namely, to the discussion between the disciples in vv. 33-34 regarding who was the greatest among them. . . . If they take to heart Jesus' teaching in vv. 35-50, they will indeed be at peace with one another and will cause neither themselves nor others to stumble" (Evans, p. 74).

35. A Lesson on Cardiology

Mark 10:1-16
> [1]*Arising, He went into the region of Judea and beyond the Jordan. And again the crowds came to Him, and again He taught them as was His custom.* [2]*The Pharisees approached Him, asking Him if it is lawful for a man to divorce His wife, thus testing Him.* [3]*And He answered them saying, "What did Moses command you?"* [4]*And they said, "Moses permitted a man to write a certificate of divorce and to divorce her."* [5]*But Jesus said to them, "He wrote you this commandment because of your hardheartedness.*

⁶But from the beginning of creation He made them male and female. ⁷'For this reason a man shall leave his father and mother, ⁸and the two shall be one flesh.' So they are no longer two, but one flesh. ⁹What therefore God has joined together, let no one separate."

¹⁰And when He was in the house again, the disciples questioned Him about this. ¹¹And He said to them, "Whoever divorces his wife and marries another commits adultery with her, ¹²and if she divorces her husband and marries another, she commits adultery."

¹³And they brought children to Him, that He might touch them. But the disciples rebuked them. ¹⁴But seeing them, Jesus was angry and said to them, "Let the children come to Me, do not prevent them, for of such as these is the kingdom of God. ¹⁵Truly, I say to you, whoever does not receive the kingdom of God like a child will never enter into it." ¹⁶And taking them into His arms He blessed them, placing His hands on them.

Jesus now inescapably heads toward His destiny. Mark 10:1 infers that after leaving Capernaum (9:33) He passed through Galilee and then went over to the east side of the Jordan River to travel through Peraea in order both to avoid complications in Samaria and to find time to further instruct His disciples. In typical Jewish fashion, He will recross the Jordan at Jericho (10:46) as He heads up to Jerusalem (11:1; see map on p. 14).

Jesus' teaching on discipleship will intensify in chapter 10, the last bit of time He has before arriving in Jerusalem. Verses 1-16, building on Mark 9:33-50, deal with some of the most crucial characteristics of discipleship, verses 17-31 discuss a potential disciple who failed to have those characteristics, and verses 35 to 45 treat the misconceptions of the disciples in the context of the servanthood of Jesus. Inserted into the midst of the chapter in verses 32 to 34 is Jesus' third prediction of His death and resurrection. The chapter closes with the healing of blind Bartimaeus (verses 46-52), a healing that the disciples still desperately needed in their spiritual lives.

At first glance it is not clear as to why Mark placed the section on marriage (verses 2-12) where it is in chapter 10, or what connection it has with the rest of the chapter. One answer to that arrangement, of course, is that the Pharisees raised the issue. But that reply doesn't help us understand why Mark selected that particular incident rather than some other one to put in this particular spot.

Upon closer examination, however, the relationship becomes clear.

The main link between verses 2–12 (marriage) and 13–16 (children) is not family matters but rather matters of the heart. The marriage verses center on "hardheartedness" (verse 5), while the children verses discuss simplicity of heart. The heart-centeredness of those two passages is why I have selected "A Lesson on Cardiology" as the title for this section of Mark. Cardiology comes from two Greek words *kardia* and *logos,* which literally means heart knowledge or knowledge of the heart. It is that knowledge that the disciples need—especially knowledge of their own hearts as Mark 9:33–50 and 10:35–45 indicate.

The reappearance of the Pharisees sets the stage for the first half of the "heart lesson." They had a question that they hoped they could use to trip Jesus up: Is it, they asked, "lawful for a man to divorce his wife?" (10:2). That was a hot issue at the time, having split the Jewish community. Deuteronomy 24:1 stipulated that a man could write a certificate of divorce and send his wife away if "he has found some indecency in her" (RSV). The Pharisees had divided over the question of what "some indecency" meant. The school of Shammai interpreted it strictly, holding that "some indecency" was adultery and adultery alone. The school of Hillel, on the other hand, explained the phrase as widely as possible. Thus if a woman burnt her husband's food or spoke disrespectfully to him she could legally be put away.

The Pharisaic "test" (verse 2) looked like a good one. It appeared that Jesus was on the horns of a dilemma no matter how He answered. If He said yes to the divorce question, they could undermine His moral authority by holding Him up as being morally lax. But if He said no they could denounce Him as rejecting the law of Moses. Beyond that, a negative reply might put Him in conflict with Herod, who had divorced his wife and remarried. The Pharisees may have surmised that if they could stir up sweet little Herodias against Jesus, then she and her pliant husband might take care of their "Jesus problem" in the same way they had gotten rid of John the Baptist over the same issue.

Not a bad strategy. But it didn't work. Jesus shifted the ground of the argument by moving beyond Jewish tradition and even Mosaic law to God's original ideal. In the process, He "transferred the whole discussion from the realm of 'is it lawful?' into the higher realm of the purpose of God, and the moral and spiritual realities of the marriage relationship" (Luccock, p. 795).

A Lesson on Cardiology

James Edwards expands upon that point when he writes that "Jesus does not conceive of marriage on the grounds of its dissolution but on the grounds of its architectural design and purpose by God. Human failure does not alter that purpose (Rom. 3:4). The intent of Jesus' teaching is not to shackle those who fail in marriage with debilitating guilt. The question is not whether God forgives those who fail in marriage. The answer to that question is assured in 3:28, '"All the sins and blasphemies of men will be forgiven."' There is, after all, no instance in Scripture of an individual seeking forgiveness and being denied it by God. The question in our day of impermanent commitments and casual divorce is whether we as Christians will hear the unique call of Christ to discipleship in marriage. In marriage, as in other areas to which the call of Christ applies, will we seek relief in what is permitted, or commit ourselves to what is intended by God and commanded by Christ?" (Edwards, p. 305).

In the process of uplifting God's lofty ideal on the sanctity and permanence of marriage, Jesus also discussed why God through Moses even gave the divorce regulation of Deuteronomy 24:1 in the first place. It wasn't to permit divorce, but to control it, to make it more difficult, to provide steps so that people couldn't act in the heat of the moment. The hardheartedness of the Israelites in irresponsible marriage unions and divorces had triggered Moses' statement on the topic (Mark 10:5). But reflecting that ancient hardheartedness is that of the Pharisees, who were at that very moment plotting against Jesus, and the hardheartedness of the disciples, who were arguing about who was the greatest despite His prediction of His imminent death (9:30-37), who were denying the rights of others to proclaim Jesus, and who were hurting the "little ones" in the faith (9:38-50).

It is that hardheartedness that links Jesus' teaching on marriage in Mark 10:2-12 to His instruction regarding the spirit of a child in verses 13 to 16. He was quite clear that "whoever does not receive the kingdom of God like a child will never enter into it" (verse 15).

And what is it about children, we need to ask, that makes their attitude the only one acceptable in the kingdom? What did the disciples need to learn from them as they traveled with Jesus toward Jerusalem? In the setting of Mark 9 and 10, Donald Juel argues, the childlike quality that they required "has mostly to do with status. The disciples are portrayed as exceedingly concerned about position; they argue about who is the greater."

> ## A Prayer
>
> "Lord, make us more like children in our relationship with you, and more ready to welcome and value those whom society does not regard as important" (France, *Mark,* Doubleday, p. 131.

But in the ancient world a child had "no status" (Juel, p. 141). They were small, powerless, and without sophistication, and ancient societies (unlike most modern ones) undervalued if not actually despised them. Exposing unwanted infants to the elements of nature to get rid of them, for example, was widespread. "To receive the kingdom of God as a child is to receive it as one who has no credits, no clout, no claims. A little child has absolutely nothing to bring, and whatever a child receives, he or she receives by grace on the basis of sheer neediness rather than by any merit inherent in him- or herself" (Edwards, p. 307).

Disciples then and now need the lesson of little children more than almost any other. When we finally realize that we bring nothing to the salvation table but problems, that salvation is all by God's grace, then we will become more humble in our opinion of ourself and more gracious toward others.

The disciples, as they walked toward Jerusalem, still failed to understand both of those lessons. Their abrasiveness in forbidding the children to come to Jesus (verse 13) demonstrated beyond a shadow of a doubt that they had not successfully processed Jesus' teaching in Mark 9:42-48 about not offending one of God's "little ones."

According to Mark's picture of Jesus, Sharyn Dowd writes, people enter God's realm "not in a proud triumphal procession, but in complete vulnerability, with no claim to any rights or status. It was not what the disciples had in mind, and the next incident" in chapter 10 "proves even more devastating to their preconceptions" (Dowd, p. 104). The case of the rich young ruler (verses 17-31) will pound home the lessons that Jesus has emphasized throughout Mark 9 and 10.

Meanwhile, before leaving Mark 10:1-16, we should note that Jesus conferred upon children and women a dignity and rights that they didn't have in the ancient world. The fact that He was kind to the socially powerless tells us a great deal about Him. In the process, He modeled that which He attempted to teach His disciples.

36. A Lesson on Salvation

Mark 10:17-31

[17]As He set out on His journey, a man ran to Him and knelt, asking Him, "Good Teacher, what shall I do to inherit eternal life?" [18]Jesus said to him, "Why do you call Me good? No one is good except God alone. [19]You know the commandments: 'Do not kill, Do not commit adultery, Do not steal, Do not bear false witness, Do not defraud, Honor your father and mother.'" [20]And he said to Him, "Teacher, I have kept all these from my youth." [21]Jesus, looking at him, loved him, and said to him, "One thing you lack. Go sell all you possess and give to the poor, and you will have treasure in heaven; and come, follow me." [22]But he was saddened by that statement and went away grieving, for he had many possessions.

[23]And Jesus, looking around, said to His disciples, "How difficult it is for those having riches to enter into the kingdom of God." [24]The disciples were amazed at His words. But Jesus, answering again, said to them, "Children, how difficult it is to enter into the kingdom of God. [25]It is easier for a camel to go through the eye of the needle than for a rich man to enter into the kingdom of God." [26]They were exceedingly astonished, saying to themselves, "And who can be saved?" [27]Looking at them, Jesus said, "With people it is impossible, but not with God; for all things are possible with God." [28]Peter said to Him, "Look, we have left everything and followed You." [29]Jesus said, "Truly I tell you, there is no one who leaves house or brothers or sisters or mother or father or children or farms for My sake or for the sake of the gospel, [30]who will not receive a hundredfold now in this time, houses and brothers and sisters and mothers and children and farms, along with persecutions, and eternal life in the age to come. [31]But many of the first will be last, and the last, first.

The most remarkable thing about this man is that he approached Jesus at all. Matthew tells us that he was young and rich (Matt. 19:20, 22, 23), while Luke says that he was a ruler (Luke 18:18). It is that very class that Jesus had the most difficult time with. The poor and the prostitutes and the tax collectors flocked to Him, but not the Jewish aristocracy in either the religious or the political realms.

The man not only came but he "ran." And not only that, he knelt before Jesus (Mark 10:17). Here was a person who defied his social class, an individual willing to face the scorn of his peers. Now other rich men of the ruling class found themselves drawn to Jesus. One thinks of Nicodemus and

Joseph of Arimathea. But they were discreet. Nicodemus, for example, came to Jesus secretly "by night" (John 3:2, KJV). And Joseph quietly went to Pilate to request permission to bury Him (Matt. 27:57, 58). One can hardly imagine them running up to Jesus and kneeling before Him in the dust. This young man had something special about him, a zeal that is refreshing.

The aristocrat also had a concern, one that blinded him to everything else. He was in earnest about salvation. Addressing Jesus as "Good Teacher," he inquired what he had to *"do"* to inherit eternal life (Mark 10:17). Obviously he saw behavior as the key to religion.

Before giving an answer, Jesus questioned him on why he had described Him as good. After all, Jesus noted, "no one is good except God alone" (verse 18). Apparently Jesus was seeking to get the young man to be explicit as to where he stood on His identity. Was He merely a teacher or was He God, as the use of the term "good" implied? The rich young ruler had undoubtedly heard Jesus before. But he was still in the valley of decision on His identity. Jesus' question was a gentle nudge to force him to come to grips with the issue.

The man expected a behavioral answer to salvation and Jesus gave him one, telling him that if he "would enter life" he should "keep the commandments" (Matt. 19:17). Then Jesus lists several of the Ten Commandments (verses 18, 19; Mark 10:19).

The list itself helps us begin to unpack the young man's problem. We should note at least four things about the list. First, the commandments cited all come from the second table of the law and deal with the way people treat others. That selection provides a hint that his problem probably centered on his relationship to other people rather than on his dedication to God.

Things to Note About Jesus' Listing of the Commandments

1. They all came from the second table of the law.
2. They are listed in order, except for number five.
3. Number 10 is missing.
4. There is a new one: "Do not defraud."

Each of those points helps us unpack the rich young ruler's problem.

Second, Jesus lists the commandments in order: the sixth, seventh, eighth, and ninth (Mark 10:19). But then, to our surprise, he lists the fifth after the ninth. Why? Undoubtedly to call attention to it. The rich young ruler may have been among those Jesus condemned in Mark 7:11-13 for using the human tradition of *corban* to avoid caring for his parents' material needs in their old age.

Third, we find a command that is not one of the Ten Commandments: "Do not defraud" (10:19). The term is "used of keeping back wages from one hired" (Rogers, p. 89). He may have gained at least some of his wealth at the expense of the poor.

Fourth, Jesus does not mention the tenth commandment (dealing with covetousness) at all. It will soon be evident that covetousness stands at the very center of the man's spiritual problem.

In Matthew's account Jesus adds a quotation from Leviticus 19:18 ("love your neighbor as yourself") to the commands to be kept (Matt. 19:19, RSV). Once again, Jesus uses a text that was important in Judaism and at the core of the young man's problem.

With confidence the aristocrat replies that he has obeyed all of those commandments from his youth (Mark 10:20). Apparently not embarrassed by that claim, he truly did seem to be a shining example of a certain type of moral person. But he will soon discover that mere morality is not enough to gain entry into the kingdom of heaven. Jesus would probe a bit further, demonstrating that the individual's obedience was outward and legal rather than inward and spiritual.

Before moving to that examination, we should note that Mark tells us that Jesus "loved him" (verse 21). Obviously He saw something special in him. Perhaps it was a heartfelt appreciation of his evident sincerity, fearlessness, and enthusiasm. Here was a man, Jesus may have thought, who could truly do something for the kingdom.

It was at that point that Jesus extended to the young man an invitation to become a disciple. "Come," He said, and "follow me" (verse 21). But there was a condition: "Go sell all you possess and give to the poor." With that unexpected command Jesus cut to the heart of the rich man's problem. Mark tells us that "he was saddened by that statement and went away grieving, for he had many possessions" (verse 22). It would be just as true to say that his possessions had him. The center of his life, they were the one thing that he would not give up, even for the kingdom.

As Jesus with a heavy heart watched the man depart, He provided another instructional shock to the disciples. He told them that it was difficult for those with wealth to enter the kingdom of God. "It is easier for a camel to go through the eye of the needle than for a rich man to enter the kingdom of God" (verse 25). The disciples weren't ready for that bit of pedagogy. It caught them completely off guard. All their lives their culture had taught them just the opposite, that property was a sign of God's favor, an indication of the truly good person. And hadn't they themselves been looking forward to material rewards—princedoms and thrones. Yet here Jesus declared that the very things they had been anticipating could be a curse. Jesus recognized their confusion. "Children," He tenderly addressed them (verse 24).

Who, then, they wanted to know, could enter heaven if it was just as impossible for a rich person to be saved as it was for the largest of Near Eastern animals (the camel) to squeeze through the smallest of openings (the eye of a sewing needle)? Jesus replied that what was impossible for people was not so with God, "for all things are possible" for Him (verse 27). Even though they didn't fully understand it at the time, Jesus was teaching that "salvation is completely beyond the sphere of human possibilities" (Lane, p. 370). He was bordering on a theology of grace without being explicit.

One thing that we should keep in mind is that Jesus was not categorically condemning wealth in Mark 10. He did not make the same request of Nicodemus or Zacchaeus or other people of means that He dealt with. But wealth was the danger for this man. It was his idol, the thing that kept him from God. As Halford Luccock points out, "Jesus was not laying down poverty as either a requirement or an ideal for everyone. He was a Good Physician, and did not prescribe the same pill for every patient. He looked on this patient and loved him with an individual love, a love which saw him as a person with a specialized need. Then he prescribed the action that would free him from the thing that was holding him back. In this case it was wealth" (Luccock, p. 804). For you or me it may be something different. But all must meet the same requirement—total surrender of all that we are and all that we have to God's will so that He is truly Lord of our life.

That thought brings us back to Peter. He is still hung up on what he is going to "get" since, unlike the rich young ruler, he and his fellow disciples had given up all to follow Jesus (Mark 10:28; cf. Matt. 19:27, where Peter asks "what do we get").

Jesus' answer is fourfold (Mark 10:29-31). First, those who have had to relinquish their earthly families receive the larger fellowship of God's family here on earth. Second, they have the promise of eternal life. Third, and certainly more problematic for disciples then and now, they will have persecutions while on earth. And fourth, Jesus' reply has a cryptic warning to Peter and the other disciples (made much more explicit in Matthew 19:30 through 20:16) not to become overly confident in their position in the kingdom just because they were the first of Christ's followers. If they continue to fixate on pride of position and fail to learn the lessons of humility, tolerance, and total surrender that Jesus has desperately been trying to teach them, they could end up last, even though they thought they were first. And to be "last," if one follows the logic of Matthew's extended illustration on this topic, means to be left on the outside of the kingdom.

From Mark 10:16-31 we learn what we need to do to gain eternal life. We must surrender our total self to God and let Him do for us through grace that which it is impossible for us to do for ourselves. Only those who do so will be first in the kingdom of God.

37. A Lesson on Blindness

Mark 10:32-45
32They were on the road, going up to Jerusalem, and Jesus was going before them; and they were amazed, and those following were afraid. Taking the Twelve, He again began to tell them the things about to happen. 33"Look, we are going up to Jerusalem, and the Son of Man will be betrayed to the chief priests and to the scribes, and they will condemn Him to death and will deliver Him to the Gentiles. 34And they will mock Him and spit on Him and will whip Him and kill Him, and after three days He will rise again."

35And James and John, the two sons of Zebedee, approached Him, saying to Him, "Teacher, we desire that You will do for us whatever we ask." 36And He said to them, "What do you wish Me to do for you?"

[37]And they said to Him, "Give us the honor of sitting, one on Your right and one on Your left, in Your glory." [38]Jesus said to them, "You do not know what you are asking. Are you able to drink the cup which I drink, or to be baptized with the baptism with which I am baptized?" [39]And they said to Him, "We are able." And Jesus said to them, "The cup which I drink, you shall drink, and you shall be baptized with the baptism with which I am baptized. [40]But to sit on My right or on My left is not Mine to give, but it is for those for whom it has been prepared." [41]Hearing this, the ten began to be angry with James and John. [42]And Jesus called them to Him, and said to them, "You know that those who are regarded as rulers of the Gentiles lord it over them and their great ones exercise authority over them. [43]But it is not to be so among you. But whoever desires to become great among you shall be your servant, [44]and whoever among you desires to be first shall be slave of all. [45]For even the Son of Man came not to be served but to serve and to give His life a ransom for many."

Something is going on and everybody seems to know it, even if they don't understand what. The disciples were amazed and the whole crowd was afraid (verse 32). Amazed and afraid of what? R. Alan Cole suggests that it was "something in the face and manner of Jesus" (Cole, p. 240). One clue internal to Mark's passage is that Jesus was "going before them" rather than being in their midst as usually seems to have been the case. Perhaps, knowing that His hour had come (John 13:1; 16:32; 17:1), He was traveling with a grim but unwavering determination that they hadn't seen before as He progressed toward His cross. While it is impossible to fully describe what He was doing at that time, Mark makes it quite clear that a great deal of tension filled the air among His followers.

Sensing the need to help His disciples better understand the situation, Jesus separated the Twelve from the larger group and for a third time predicted His death and resurrection. But this was no mere rehash of what He had told them the first two times. Each time He mentioned His forthcoming crisis He added further details. In Mark 8:31 He made a mere announcement, while in 9:31 Jesus supplied the idea of betrayal. But in Mark 10:33, 34 He included the grisly details that He would be mocked, spit upon, and whipped. He went on to provide one other piece of bitter information. Not only would Israel reject its Messiah but its leaders would "deliver Him to the Gentiles" (verse 33). That is the ultimate rejection.

It was the understanding of His death and resurrection that Jesus wanted His disciples to see more than any other truth. In some ways it was a dismal picture. But not totally as Jesus saw it. He might have to journey through "the valley of the shadow of death" (Ps. 23:4, KJV), but He never lost sight of His ultimate triumph.

The Increasing Detail of Jesus' Predictions of His Passion			
	8:31	9:31	10:33,34
(1) Delivered to the chief priests and scribes	-	(X)	X
(2) Sentenced to death	(X)	-	X
(3) Delivered to the Gentiles	-	-	X
(4) Mocked, spit upon, scourged	-	-	X
(5) Executed	X	X	X
(6) Resurrected	X	X	X
(adapted from Lane, p. 375)			

There is something special in Jesus' confidence in His ultimate triumph. The good news is that He extends that assurance to each of His followers down to the end of time. They may face problems and even a martyr's death, but even though life has its crises and discouragements, ultimate victory is certain. The Christian faith has an optimism that we do well to remember, especially when the going gets tough.

The message of Mark 10:32-34 is that Jesus above all things wanted to give His disciples sight—He wanted them to see the events surrounding His death and His ultimate triumph. But verses 35 to 45 indicate that they were blinder than the proverbial bat. It is more than significant that Mark regularly interspersed among Jesus' predictions of His forthcoming death scenes in which the Twelve jockeyed for position (see 9:33-35; 10:35-45). The tension between the passion predictions and the disciples bickering about who was the greatest stands at the very center of not only Mark's narrative, but of all of life. Only two possible kingdoms can ever exist: the one based on self-sacrifice and selfless service and the one built on selfishness and self-aggrandizement. All potential disciples experience the struggle between those two kingdoms as they decide on whether to follow Christ or not.

It is also no accident that Jesus' predictions of His death in Mark 8:31 and 10:33 and the related stories of striving for supremacy appear between two stories of healing the blind (8:22-26; 10:46-52). Blind disciples desperately need healing in order to be able to see the true meaning of Christianity and the principles of Christ's kingdom that make it different from the kingdom of this world.

We should note that just as Jesus' predictions of His death become progressively more detailed, so do the struggle for supremacy scenes among the disciples. The one in Mark 10:35-37 is by far the most blatant attempt at a power takeover by any of the disciples. James and John didn't beat around the bush. They wanted nothing less than the two most powerful positions in Jesus' forthcoming kingdom. Their request is Mark's ultimate example of human self-centeredness in contrast to Jesus' humility and self-sacrifice.

Part of the reason for their request at this particular time was that they greatly feared that Peter, their nearest competitor as they saw it then, might grab first place before they did. Not only was Peter the third member of Jesus' inner circle (9:2), but Jesus had praised him for his statement at Caesarea Philippi (Matt. 16:17, 18).

Their petition tells us a great deal about the Zebedee brothers. On the negative side, it was presumptuous and selfish. But it, surprisingly, also had positive aspects. For one thing, it reflected a deep faith that Jesus was who He claimed to be and that He would triumph in spite of His confusing statements about death. In addition, it displayed an element of courage and dedication in the sense that they had no intention of abandoning Jesus in what He claimed would be difficult times. While the negative aspects of their request must have perplexed Jesus, the positive gave Him a bit of room to see some possible hope in them.

Most of all, however, the brothers' request indicated to Jesus that they had not yet understood the nature of His kingdom or the principles that undergirded it. It was on that point that Jesus would focus His instruction.

Matthew 20:20, 21 tells us that the mother of James and John asked the favor of Jesus for her sons. But whatever role she may have played, Mark's treatment indicates that the two disciples were ambitious on their own behalf. And since Jesus knew that the request ultimately came from them, He answered them directly, asking them if they could drink His cup and be baptized with His baptism (Mark 10:38). They glibly answered that they could. But if they could have visualized that within a week Jesus would be uplifted not on a throne but on a cross, with one to His right and left, they might not have replied with so much confidence. Eventually, however, both would drink the cup as Jesus predicted in verse 39, with James perishing from the sword at the command of Herod (Acts 12:1, 2) and John being thrown into a vat of boiling oil, if tradition is correct, and eventually being exiled for the gospel on the island of Patmos.

What must have been the ultimate discouragement to Jesus in an already disheartening time was that His other 10 disciples became furious with the Zebedees over their request (Mark 10:41). Their anger did not result from any sense of its wrongness, but rather because they each harbored the same unholy ambition to be the first, the greatest, to have the honored seat of power in the kingdom.

Sin breeds sin. The wrongheaded ambition of James and John had stimulated intense jealousy in the rest of the disciples. The little band had reached a crisis point right at the edge, so to speak, of Jerusalem. They were torn apart by tensions that might permanently separate them and frustrate Jesus' purpose in calling them in the first place.

We don't know if Jesus felt tempted to give up on them, call them blockheads, and walk away. But certainly, as we find in other places in Mark (see, e.g., 8:12), He must have sighed deeply as He once again began to instruct the Twelve on the basic principles of His kingdom. He went on to give His most profound teaching on the concept of the leader who is a servant rather than a domineering ruler (10:42-44). And with it He made clear the foundation of a Christian ethic based upon love and service to others, an ethic opposed to the power over others concept undergirding all human societies.

But beyond the service in love ethic, Jesus' answer to the Twelve moved into new territory when He claimed that His service to His followers even went so far as His giving "His life a ransom for many" (verse 45). Here is one of the clearest teachings of the substitutionary sacrifice in the four Gospels. As Walter Wessel notes, "The entire phrase 'to give his life a ransom for many' emphasizes the substitutionary element in Jesus' death. He takes the place of the many. What should have happened to them happened to him instead" (Wessel, p. 721). Ellen White said it a little differently when she penned that "Christ was treated as we deserve, that we might be treated as He deserves. He was condemned for our sins, in which He had no share, that we might be justified by His righteousness, in which we had no share. He suffered the death which was ours, that we might receive the life which was His" (White, *The Desire of Ages,* p. 25).

38. A Lesson on the Importance of Vision

Mark 10:46-52

⁴⁶They came to Jericho. And as He was leaving Jericho with His disciples and a large crowd, Bartimaeus the son of Timaeus, a blind beggar, was sitting by the road. ⁴⁷Hearing that it was Jesus of Nazareth, he began to cry out and say, "Jesus, Son of David, have mercy on me." ⁴⁸And many rebuked him, telling him to be silent. But all the more he cried out, "Son of David, have mercy on me." ⁴⁹And Jesus stopped, saying, "Call him." And they called the blind man, saying to him, "Have courage, stand up, for He is calling you." ⁵⁰So he threw off his garment, jumped up and came to Jesus. ⁵¹And answering him, Jesus said, "What do you wish me to do?" And the blind man said to Him, "Rabboni, that I may see again." ⁵²And Jesus said to him, "Go, your faith has healed you." And immediately he saw again and followed Him on the road.

Jesus now neared the end of His journey that had started north of Galilee. He had recrossed the Jordan, passed through Jericho, and was setting out on the last 18 miles of His long journey to Jerusalem (see map on p. 14). A crowd of disciples and others often surrounded and listened to distinguished Jewish teachers as they walked. So it was with Jesus as He passed through Jericho. In addition, it was almost Passover, and custom had it that crowds would often line the streets of towns on the road to Jerusalem to greet the pilgrims traveling to the holy city. Then again, Jesus was no ordinary teacher. He was well known as both a healer and teacher and also as a man who fearlessly challenged the religious status quo. If any teacher on a pilgrimage could attract a crowd it was Jesus.

It was such a situation that caught the attention of a blind beggar named Bartimaeus. Now before going any further, we need to note that all three synoptic gospels tell this story, but each does so differently. Matthew, for example, mentions two blind men (Matt. 20:30) while Mark only tells of one. And Luke says the miracle took place as Jesus entered Jericho (Luke 18:35), while Mark and Matthew agree that the miracle took place as He left the city (Mark 10:46; Matt. 20:29). There is a side lesson here that we need to learn. Inspired writers were not so concerned with the marginal details of a story as they were with its main point(s). Those interpreters who make a career out of pushing every detail in the Bible to its "logical" conclusion need to remember the purpose of Scripture and its writers (see 2 Tim. 3:15-17).

Meanwhile, in Mark 10:46-52 one detail especially stands out. Mark is the only one of the three synoptic authors to mention Bartimaeus by name. That is probably because Bartimaeus, having become a follower of Jesus (verse 52), must have been (like Rufus in Mark 15:21; cf. Rom. 16:13) well known to Mark's first readers in Rome. But we need to note something else about Bartimaeus. He is the only healed individual named in the synoptics—and not merely once, but twice. Please note that the name Bartimaeus comes from two Aramaic words: *bar,* which means son of, and *Timaeus.* He was the son of Timaeus. But after giving his name as Bartimaeus (son of Timaeus), Mark goes on to describe him as the "son of Timaeus" (Mark 10:46). James Edwards claims that "son of Timaeus" may have been a translation given for the benefit of Mark's Gentile readers (Edwards, p. 329). But R. T. France appears to be more on target when he asserts that the readers really wouldn't be all that interested in the meaning of a man's name (France, *Mark,* NIGTC, p. 423). Rather, it appears that the real purpose of Mark is for one reason or another to emphasize this particular man and his name.

And Bartimaeus was an extraordinary person with a remarkable story. As Edwards points out, Bartimaeus is a "blind beggar who ironically sees Jesus more clearly than those with two good eyes." What he lacks "in eyesight he makes up for in insight" (Edwards, pp. 328, 329). It is the story of this special person that Mark selects to climax his section on Jesus' teaching on faith and discipleship. Chapter 10 is full of references to discipleship but none of the disciples demonstrate the faith and clear vision of the blind Bartimaeus.

All in all, Mark paints this marginal person in a most attractive light. For one thing, he pictures Bartimaeus as a person who recognized opportunity when he saw it. Unlike some who have followed Jesus down through the ages in a sort of fuzzy sentimentality, Bartimaeus knew precisely what he wanted.

A second thing to note about him is that Bartimaeus was a person of aggressive faith. "It is evident," writes William Lane, "that Bartimaeus has heard about Jesus of Nazareth and that his relentless crying of 'Son of David, have mercy on me' reflects a conviction, formed on the basis of what he had heard, that Jesus could restore his sight" (Lane, p. 387).

It is significant that this blind beggar saw in Jesus what most Jews did not. He had concluded, as had Peter in Mark 8:29, that Jesus was the Messiah. His use of the term "Son of David" was no accident. Ever since God's promise in 2 Samuel 7:12, 13 that God would raise up a king in David's line and would "establish the throne of his kingdom for ever" (RSV), the Jews had equated the Messiah with the Son of David. It is only through the mouth of Bartimaeus that Mark's Gospel calls Jesus the Son of David.

Other people might refer to Him as Jesus of Nazareth, but He is the Son of David to Bartimaeus (Mark 10:47). "Physically blind though he was," J. D. Jones writes, yet "he saw further into spiritual things than the multitude. He had heard about Jesus, about His wonderful words, and still more wonderful deeds. He had meditated upon it all in his heart. And while other people were quarreling and debating who Christ was, this blind man had made up his mind that this Jesus Who was giving sight to the blind, and cleansing to the leper, and life to the dead, was none other than the promised Christ. . . . The faith of his soul expresses itself in his cry, 'Jesus, Thou Son of David, have mercy on me!' " (Jones, vol. 3, p. 49).

The uproar Bartimaeus created was an embarrassment to everyone, and they did their best to shut him up. But he knew what he needed and he recognized who Jesus was and what He could do. Bartimaeus was not one to let the opportunity of a lifetime pass by while he kept his mouth shut. The more they tried to quiet him, the more he shouted (verse 48). He is like the person much in prayer who desires God's blessing with all the heart.

And Jesus did bless Bartimaeus. He has ears to hear the cry of need, the cry of faith. But Jesus didn't heal him immediately. First, Jesus asked Bartimaeus the seemingly obvious question of what he wanted Him to do for him (verse 50). It's not that Jesus didn't know. Rather, He desires us to come to Him personally and form a trusting and loving relationship with Him in our time of need. And that is just what Bartimaeus did, addressing Jesus as Rabboni rather than Rabbi. "Rabboni," suggests Ralph Martin, is a term of endearment that might be translated as "dear Master" rather than merely "Master." The same word was used by Mary Magdalene to address Jesus in John 20:16, it was a personalization of Bartimaeus' faith (Martin, *Where the Action Is,* p. 94). Jesus doesn't desire disciples in the abstract. He wants us to form a close relationship with Him.

Not only did Jesus restore Bartimaeus' sight, He also blessed him: "Go, your faith has healed you" (Mark 10:52). As we noted earlier, the Greek word for "healed" *(sōzō)* also means "saved." The blind beggar received both a physical and a spiritual healing. "Immediately, he saw again and followed Him on the road."

It is little wonder why Mark's Gospel not only mentions Bartimaeus' name but emphasizes it, while that of the rich young ruler has been entirely forgotten. France points out that "the last potential recruit [for discipleship that] we met was an admirable, respectable, and wealthy man (10:17-22), but to the disciples' consternation he has not been welcomed into Jesus' entourage. Now we meet a man at quite the other end of the scale of social acceptability, a blind beggar. And it is he, rather than the rich man, who will end up following Jesus . . . , with his sight restored, whereas the rich man has gone away 'blind'" (France, *Mark,* NIGTC, p. 422).

But the young ruler wasn't the only blind one. "The significance of this story," writes Ray Stedman, "lies in what Bartimaeus did. That is the reason Mark placed it here. Here was a blind man who was conscious of his blindness, whereas the disciples were not conscious of theirs" (Stedman, *Ruler Who Serves,* p. 109).

As we noted earlier, Mark has bracketed the entire section running from Mark 8:31 to 10:45 with two healings of blindness (8:22-26; 10:46-52). That is no accident. The disciples were blind to Jesus' repeated emphases on His forthcoming death (8:31; 9:9, 31; 10:32-34) and their wrongness in struggling for supremacy (9:33, 34; 10:35-45). But they didn't see it. He wanted to heal them as He did the physically blind. But in that He failed. As a result, they would pass through an unnecessary crisis at His arrest and crucifixion. The healing would not take place until after His resurrection.

One of the tragedies of the church down through the ages is that it has had all too many blind disciples, disciples oblivious to their own faults, to Jesus' power to heal and restore both spiritually and physically, and to their need to cry out to the "Son of David" in the persistent voice of faith.

Part IV

Act Three

Facing Persecution and Death in God's Service

Mark 11:1–15:47

39. The Entrance of the Servant King

Mark 11:1-11

¹And when they were approaching Jerusalem, that is, to Bethphage and Bethany, near the Mount of Olives, He sent two of His disciples, ²saying to them, "Go into the village opposite you, and immediately as you enter it you will find a colt tied, upon which no person has yet sat. Untie it and bring it. ³And if anyone says to you, 'Why are you doing this?' say, 'The Lord has need of it, and He will send it back here immediately.'" ⁴And they went and found a colt tied in the street near a door, and they untied it. ⁵And some of those standing there said to them, "What are you doing, untying the colt?" ⁶And they told them what Jesus had said, and they let them go. ⁷They brought the colt to Jesus and laid their garments upon it, and He sat on it. ⁸And many spread their garments on the road. But others spread leafy branches that they had cut from the fields. ⁹And those leading the way and those following were crying out, "Hosanna! Blessed is the One coming in the name of the Lord. ¹⁰Blessed is the coming kingdom of our father David. Hosanna in the highest."

¹¹And He entered into Jerusalem, into the Temple, and after looking around at everything, the hour being late, He went to Bethany with the twelve.

With chapter 11 we have come to a major turning point in Mark's Gospel. The first eight chapters he devoted to helping people experience the blessings of God's rule through presenting Christ as an authoritative healer and teacher. Through His gracious acts and teachings readers gained a sense of who Jesus was and the nature of the blessings of His kingdom. That long section came to an end with Peter's exclamation that Jesus was the Christ, the Messiah (Mark 8:29).

But what did it mean to be the Christ? That question became the Gospel's focal point from Mark 8:31 to 10:52. Rather than being the conquering warrior Messiah of Jewish thought, Jesus repeatedly taught that He would be put to death and then resurrected.

Whereas Mark placed the first eight chapters in Galilee, Jesus' special instruction for His disciples regarding the nature of His messiahship in chapters 9 and 10 is situated on the long and circuitous road to Jerusalem. But now they are arriving at their destination. Mark 11:1 brings them to the last stage of their journey as they leave Jericho and arrive at Bethphage and Bethany (villages outside of Jerusalem) and finally at the great city itself. The climax of Jesus' ministry will take place in Jerusalem.

Mark 11-16 make up one-third of Mark's Gospel, but they represent only one week in Jesus' life. The disproportionate amount of space devoted to the events of that week by Mark and the other gospel writers suggests its importance in understanding the meaning of Jesus' mission and purpose. What takes place in Jerusalem in those few days is central to the Christian message.

The last six chapters of Mark divide into three sections. Chapters 11-13 deal with the escalating conflict between Jesus and the Jewish leaders. Their spurning of Him and His rejection of their views and ways of approaching things sets the stage for chapters 14 and 15, in which Jesus passes through Gethsemane on His way to His cross. The final section (chapter 16) focuses on the resurrection of Jesus and brings the good news to a climax.

The story of the crucified and resurrected Messiah is the focal point of the Gospel. Without chapters 11-16 the rest of Mark would never have been written. Jesus would have been merely a miracle worker and remarkable (if somewhat deluded) teacher. But with the story of the cross and the resurrection Mark is able to present the good news that Jesus died for our sins (10:45) and was resurrected as one who had won the victory over death (Rev. 1:17, 18), a victory that His followers knew that He would share with each of those who believed in Him (1 Cor. 15). It was that message that would help Mark's first readers stand up against the atrocities of the Neros of the empire and would fortify Christians in distress down through history. With chapter 11 we enter that part of Mark's book that truly makes it a gospel—good news.

In Mark 11:2-6 we find the interesting story of the colt. Some people have seen that event as an example of Jesus' foreknowledge. But William Lane is probably closer to the truth when he suggests that "Jesus himself took the initiative in preparing for his entry into the city" (Lane, p. 393). He had apparently made prior arrangements with the owner of the colt, who was probably one of the unnumbered disciples, telling him that a time would come in the near future when He would need a colt that no one had yet ridden.

We must remember that the important point in the story is not how Jesus acquired the colt, but rather that He had decided beforehand that He would ride into the city in the first place. Here was a man who has just walked from north of Galilee. Certainly He had no physical need to ride the last two miles. Furthermore, Jesus had always walked. This is the only time we find the adult Jesus riding in any of the Gospels. As R.C.H. Lenski points out, *"he always went on foot until this time when, by his own orders,* the beast *was found for him"* (Lenski, *Matthew,* p. 806; italics supplied).

The key to understanding Jesus' unusual act is that it is deliberate. Here we find the Man who repeatedly sought to keep His Messianic identity a secret ready to make a public statement. He knew precisely what He was doing. In the process, He let the prophecy of Zechariah 9:9 guide His actions:

"Rejoice greatly, O daughter of Zion!

Shout, Daughter of Jerusalem!

See, your king comes to you,

righteous and having salvation,

gentle and riding on a donkey,

on a colt, the foal of a donkey" (NIV).

Even though, unlike Matthew, Mark doesn't quote that text in his account of Jesus' entry into Jerusalem, the force of the act is the same. The reason that Jesus *deliberately* made arrangements for the colt is that He knew that the time had come to make a public Messianic claim. The ride asserted His kingship.

The crowd didn't miss its implications. Their spreading of their garments and palm branches (John 12:13; Mark 11:8) on the road as He passed echoed the coronation of Jehu (2 Kings 9:13) and the entry of Simon Maccabaeus into Jerusalem after he had smashed Israel's armies in battle. Of the latter incident we read that "it was on the twenty-third day of the second month in the year 171 that the Jews entered the city amid a chorus of praise and the waving of palm branches, with lutes, cymbals, and zithers, with hymns and songs, to celebrate Israel's final riddance of a formidable enemy" (1 Macc. 13:51, REB).

And, as we noted earlier, the Jews had hoped that their forthcoming Messiah would be just such a conquering king who would rid the nation of the formidable Romans. But by deliberately utilizing the symbolism of Zechariah 9:9 in His entry, Jesus was not only claiming kingship but was asserting that He would be a certain type of king. The prophecy specified that the Messiah King would be "gentle," rather than the warlike leader expected by later generations. Entrance on a horse would have signified a warlike leader, but a donkey's colt symbolized the peaceful arrival by the Messiah as the "Prince of Peace" (Isa. 9:6, NIV). The book of Revelation symbolizes Jesus as arriving on a horse at His second coming. Then He will come as the conquering Messiah the Jews expected at His first advent (Rev. 19:11-21).

But the people who caste down their garments and palm leaves before Him seem to have been oblivious to the full implications of Zechariah's prophecy as they sang their hosannas to the one coming in the name of the Lord (a Messianic phrase), the one who would set up the kingdom of their father David (Mark 11:9, 10). Hosanna, we should note, is not a praise term, but one that means "save now."

Jesus would save alright. But that salvation would be from sin rather than from the hated Romans (see Matt. 1:21).

The events of Mark 11:1-11 indicate two important things about Jesus. First, that He was a person of courage. He knew the risk that He took in entering into Jerusalem the way that He did. The Romans did not take even threats of insurrection lightly.

Second, verse 11 demonstrates that Jesus was operating with great deliberation rather than with passion or by being carried along with the flow of events. Unlike Matthew, whose presentation gives the impression that Jesus cleansed the Temple on the same day that He entered Jerusalem (see Matt. 21:1-13), Mark helps us see that He merely visited the Temple that particular day. On that visit He sized up the situation and made a decision regarding what needed to be done. He returned the next day to put His plan into action (Mark 11:19, 20, 27).

Jesus was in command of the situation, even as He advanced toward

His death. His cleansing of the Temple would be, like the riding of the donkey's colt, a deliberate action. William Barclay notes that "Jesus was not recklessly plunging into unknown dangers" (Barclay, *Mark,* p. 279). To the contrary, He planned His actions step by step.

40. Challenging the Establishment

Mark 11:12–25

> [12]*On the next day, when they had left Bethany, He was hungry.* [13]*And seeing a fig tree in leaf from a distance, He went to see whether He might find something on it. And when He came to it He found nothing except leaves, for it was not the season for figs.* [14]*And He said to it, "May no one ever eat fruit from you again." And His disciples were listening.*
>
> [15]*And they came to Jerusalem. Entering the Temple, He began to drive out those selling and those buying in the Temple, and He overturned the tables of the money changers and the seats of those selling doves.* [16]*And He did not allow anyone to carry things through the Temple.* [17]*He taught, saying to them, "Has it not been written, 'My House shall be called a house of prayer for all the nations'? But you have made it a refuge of robbers."* [18]*And the chief priests and the scribes heard this and sought how they might destroy Him; for they were afraid of Him, for the whole crowd was amazed at His teaching.* [19]*When it got late they went outside the city.*
>
> [20]*And passing by in the morning, they saw the fig tree withered from its roots.* [21]*And Peter, remembering, said to Him, "Rabbi, look, the fig tree that you cursed has withered."* [22]*And Jesus answered, saying to them, "Have faith in God.* [23]*Truly I say to you that whoever says to this mountain, 'Be lifted up and thrown into the sea,' and does not doubt in his heart, but believes that what he says will happen, it will be so for him.* [24]*For this reason I say to you, all things for which you pray and ask, believe that you have received them, and it will be so for you.* [25]*And when you stand praying, forgive if you have anything against anyone, in order that your Father, the One in heaven, may forgive you your transgressions."**

---

*Verse 26 does not appear in the most ancient manuscripts of the Greek New Testament. It is probably an insertion from Matthew 6:15. It reads: "But if you do not forgive, neither will your Father who is in heaven forgive your trespasses" (NASB).

Not the easiest passage in Mark's Gospel to understand.

But it is easy enough to see why Jesus was hungry. After all, He came to earth as a human being that He might truly understand us and be able to sympathize with us in our weaknesses (Heb. 2:17, 18).

But what is the point of this business about the fig tree? To put it bluntly, if Jesus knew "it was not the season for figs," why did He curse the tree? Bertrand Russell, one of the famous outspoken atheists of the twentieth century, felt incensed by Jesus' action. Russell cited such "vindictive fury" as an evidence to support his conclusions in his book *Why I Am Not a Christian.*

Now commentators have offered many explanations relating the lack of fruit to the tree's leaves and to Jesus' hunger. Probably the best is that after the fig harvest between mid-August and mid-October the trees sprout buds that remain undeveloped throughout the winter months. But in early spring these buds or *paggim* begin to swell shortly before the tree begins to produce leaves. Thus once a tree is in leaf one can expect to find *paggim,* which can be eaten even though it is not yet time for the mature, ripe fruit of summer (see Edwards, pp. 339, 340).

It was such a tree that Jesus approached in Mark 11:13. But, to His surprise, it had no *paggim* even though the branches had already leafed out. In short, it had the outward signs of fruit, but had not produced anything useful.

A Lesson From a Sandwich

1. Part 1 of the sandwich: The story of the cursing of the fruitless fig tree (Mark 11:12-14).
2. Part 2: The cleansing of the Temple (verses 15-19).
3. Part 3: The fig tree again—now destroyed (verses 20, 21).
4. The lesson: That the unfruitful Temple system was due for judgment, just as was the fruitless fig tree.

The key to understanding the meaning of the fig tree episode is to realize that Mark has split the story in two. Verses 12-14 begin the story, while verses 20-24 complete it. Sandwiched in between the two halves is the cleansing of the Temple in verses 15-19.

Victor of Antioch (fifth century) clearly saw that connection in the oldest existing commentary on Mark. According to Victor, "the withering of the fig tree was an acted parable in which Jesus 'used the fig tree to set forth the judgement that was about to fall on Jerusalem'" (see Cranfield, p. 356).

In its context the withered fig tree points to the Temple and its failure in preparing the Jewish people for the redemptive activity of the coming Messiah. Despite all that God had attempted to do through the Temple for His people, it had not borne fruit. And just as a tree that does not perform its proper function in bearing fruit gets cut down, so the Temple will meet its end. "The withering of the tree," Craig Evans asserts, "corresponds to Jesus' hint of the temple's impending doom in 11:17 and to his explicit statement to the three disciples in 13:2" regarding the destruction of the Temple (Evans, p. 160).

By extension, the parable of the fruitless fig tree has much to say to all religionists and all religious institutions characterized by promise without fulfillment, by profession without practice. Whether it be the Jewish nation, the Jewish leaders, or ordinary Christians, Jesus is adamant throughout the Gospels that outward profession is not enough. "You will know them by their fruits" (Matt. 7:20, RSV). "Every tree that does not bear good fruit is cut down and thrown into the fire" (verse 19, RSV). It is not everyone who says "'Lord, Lord,'" but those who do God's will who will be in heaven (verse 21). In Jesus' day and in ours it is all too easy to have an outward religion without appropriate fruit, to be "whitewashed tombs" full of "dead men's bones"; to "outwardly appear righteous to men" but to be "full of hypocrisy and inequity" within (Matt. 23:27, 28, RSV). The lesson of the fig tree applies to all such examples. ⋏

It has become fashionable for Christians to focus on the gentleness and kindness of Jesus and the Father to the exclusion of the "wrath of the Lamb" (Rev. 6:16, RSV). But, as J. D. Jones points out, "the indulgent father, the father who is never severe, the father who never steels his heart to punish, is not a good father. He is a weak father and a foolish father, and from the child's standpoint, a bad father. In the same way exactly a God who winked at and never punished sin would not be a good God" (Jones, vol. 3, p. 75).

The plain fact is that the God of love calls His children to wake up before it is too late. If the Lord is truly loving He cannot perpetually allow the effects of sin to destroy people's lives. There must come a time when

He says enough is enough and puts an end to the sin problem. Thus even what the Bible refers to as God's wrath is a function of His love. Eventually He will terminate sin and create a new heaven and a new earth in which the disastrous effects of sin are no more (see Rev. 21:1-4).

And just as Jesus judged the barren fig tree and the Temple, so He will someday judge the world. In fact, no one in the entire Bible had more to say about judgment than Jesus.

His cleansing of the Temple in Mark 11:15-19 is a judgment on the religious leadership. For financial gain the leading priests had created a commercial atmosphere in the Court of the Gentiles—the only part of the Temple complex open to non-Jews. Not only did the high fees extracted from pilgrims when they sought to change their local currencies into the only coinage acceptable to pay the Temple tax involve corruption, but the authorities had so manipulated things that pilgrims were literally compelled to buy their sacrificial animals at artificially inflated prices. And the whole dishonest business took place inside the walls of the Temple. Beyond that, other merchants used the Court of the Gentiles as a short cut to transport their wares from one place to another, disturbing its sacredness.

Jesus' response was to overturn the tables of the money changers, knock over the seats of the pigeon vendors, and forbid the short-cut commercial traffic through the Court of the Gentiles (Mark 11:15, 16). So much for the myth of the perpetually gentle and quiet Jesus. The time had come for Him to act—and act He did. But even His judgment in the Temple was an act of mercy. It was a wake-up call to the religious leaders before it was too late.

But the cleansing of the Temple was even more than that. The evening before He had surveyed the situation in the Temple, only to withdraw to Bethany. But He knew that He would return the next day. And on the way back to the Temple He cursed the fig tree. Then came the cleansing of the Temple. With it Jesus took the battle into the heart of the enemy camp. If His entry into Jerusalem had Messianic overtones, so did the cleansing. It was a premeditated challenge and an assertion of His Messianic authority at the very heart of Judaism.

At that point His challenge had become impossible for either the leaders or the common people to ignore. Matthew has the children in the Temple crying out "Hosanna to the Son of David" (Matt. 21:15, RSV), while Mark has the chief priests and scribes seeking "how they might destroy Him" and the crowd being "amazed at His teaching" (Mark 11:18). Jesus' actions had brought Him to what we might think of as a point of no return. The cross now loomed closer than ever.

That thought brings us back to the withered fig tree in Mark 11:20. Peter points out its fate in verse 21. At that time, it would have seemed that Jesus should have given His disciples a lesson on the importance of being faithful and bearing fruit. Rather, He wanders off into what at first seems to be the unrelated realm of faith and prayer, utilizing a Jewish proverbial saying about faith being able to move mountains.

R. T. France suggests that one mountain that Jesus had had to face was the Temple mount, still visible in the distance as He spoke, "whose 'removal' Jesus" would "shortly predict (13:2)" (France, *Mark,* NIGTC, p. 449). That supposition may or may not be accurate. But certainly Jesus was telling them of the need for and the efficacy of faith and prayer in the light of both His present challenge to the religious leaders and the disciple's soon coming commission to take the gospel message to all the world (Matt. 28:19, 20). To fulfill that mandate they would need both faith and prayer. And they had Jesus' promise that if they had genuine faith while working to accomplish God's work, God would honor their faith and answer their prayers (Mark 11:24). The book of Acts records that fulfilled promise. After Pentecost the apostles truly did move "mountains," just as their Master did in standing up to the authorities in Jerusalem.

We in the twenty-first century still have "mountains" to move before Jesus can come. The good news is that when we pray in genuine faith, God still hears, answers, and helps us move any mountain that impedes the accomplishment of His work on earth.

᷉

41. The Counter-Challenge

Mark 11:27-33
    [27]*They came again into Jerusalem. And when He was walking in the Temple the chief priests and the scribes and the elders came to Him. [28]They said to Him, "By what authority are You doing these things, or who gave You this authority to do these things?" [29]Jesus said to them, "I will ask*

you one question, answer Me and I will tell you by what authority I do these things. [30]The baptism of John, was it from heaven or from men? Answer Me." [31]And they debated among themselves, saying, "If we say, 'From heaven,' He will say, 'Why then did you not believe him?' [32]But if we say, 'From men'?"—they were afraid of the crowd, for everyone considered John to be a real prophet. [33]And they answered Jesus, saying, "We do not know." And Jesus said to them, "Neither will I tell you by what authority I do these things."

According to Mark's account it is the third day in a row that Jesus has visited the Temple. On Sunday He went to it to observe (11:11), on Monday He challenged the abuses He saw there (11:15-18), and now on Tuesday He is back again, walking and presumably teaching (11:27). Once again we need to note the deliberateness of Jesus' actions and His courage. If He had felt concerned at all with His safety, the Temple would have been the last place He would have gone. But mission rather than safety motivated Him. He knew what He was doing and why.

Beginning with Mark 11:27-33 we find a series of seven conflict stories between Jesus and the religious leaders. Extending to the end of chapter 12, these accounts resemble those of Mark 2:1-3:6. In both series Jesus acts with authority. The leaders challenged that authority in both. And in both Jesus asked questions that they could not answer (see, e.g., 3:4 and 11:29, 30). But certain things have changed. Whereas the earlier series took place in provincial Galilee, now the scene of action has shifted to the very center of Judaism—the Jerusalem Temple itself. And whereas in the earlier series the Pharisees and Herodians discussed how they might eliminate Him (3:6), now He was facing the reality of that destruction itself.

Mark 11:27 has a delegation of chief priests, scribes, and elders—the three groups that made up the Sanhedrin, the highest governing body of the Jewish nation—confronting Jesus. They ask Him two questions:

1. "By what authority are You doing these things?"

2. "Who gave You this authority to do these things?" (verse 28).

Please note what they did not question. For one thing, they didn't challenge the facts that He had authority or that He had been doing authoritative things. Of course, the closest antecedent to "these things" is the cleansing of the Temple on the previous day. They could hardly deny that He had acted authoritatively. But that cleansing was only the latest in a long series of such deeds by Jesus. Among other things, He had earlier forgiven sins (Mark 2:10) and claimed supremacy over the law and the Sabbath (2:23-3:6). He had also exhibited control over nature (4:35-41), over demonic powers (5:1-20), over disease (5:21-34), and even over death (5:35-43). No one could deny that Jesus exercised authority. The fact of His authority is an underlying theme throughout Mark. Even Jesus' most deadly enemies had to admit that He has authority.

A second thing that the delegation from the Sanhedrin did not question was the rightness of Jesus in cleansing the Temple. They knew that they had allowed things in the Temple courts that were simply wrong.

On the other hand, they couldn't ignore what Jesus had done. After all, He had on Monday acted as if He were the Lord of the Temple and had a right to do what He did. In that He was usurping their prerogatives.

Thus they had reasons to legitimately question Him. No one could deny them the right to challenge Him on the source of His authority for His Temple-cleansing actions. After all, Jesus had no official standing. He didn't belong to the Sanhedrin, He wasn't a priest, or even a scribe, and He held no office among either the Jews or the Romans.

By asking "by what authority" the Sanhedrin was not questioning what Jesus did, but rather His legimacy to do it. And beyond that they sought to get Him to make a statement regarding the source of His authority.

Their challenge, however, had a hook in it. As William Barclay points out, "They hoped to put Jesus into a dilemma. If He said He was acting under His own authority they might well arrest Him as a megalomaniac before He did any further damage." Yet "if He said that He was acting on the authority of God they might well arrest Him on an obvious charge of blasphemy" (Barclay, *Mark,* p. 291).

Jesus was quite aware of the trap in which they hoped to force Him. "His reply was to put them into a dilemma which was still worse" *(ibid.).* He did that through a counter-question, a technique often used by the rabbis of His day. Jesus, as the Gospels indicate, was a master at answering a tricky question by responding with one of His own that was impossible to answer. The religious leaders eventually came to the place where "no one dared to ask him any question" (Mark 12:34, RSV) since Jesus could best them at their own game.

His counter question in Mark 11:29, 30 was a stroke of genius. The query regarding the source of John the Baptist's authority, while seemingly irrelevant to the delegation's question, actually was central to it. After all, the Baptist was also an unauthorized teacher who owed nothing to Jerusalem.

Here the delegation of Jewish leaders found itself in a tight spot. They could hardly acknowledge that God had sent John, because the Baptist had repeatedly witnessed to Jesus' Messiahship, claiming on one occasion that He was "the Lamb of God, who takes away the sin of the world" (John 1:29, RSV). Thus to admit that John had a divine calling was to make the same admission about Jesus. To capitulate to the perspective that John's commission came from heaven would have left Jesus fully open to ask the question regarding why they didn't accept John's witness about Him. Such an answer would hardly do.

Yet the alternative wasn't much better. It was risky to deny John's divine commissioning since the people believed the Baptist to be a real prophet. Thus both horns of their dilemma were equally sharp and problematic.

That reality led them into an argument as to how to answer Jesus. Some students have interpreted the "Answer Me" at the end of Mark 11:30 as a gentle push by Him to get them to break off their debate and give an answer.

Be that as it may, they finally stammered out the rather helpless and feeble confession that "We do not know" (verse 33). With that awkward comment they in effect gave away the company store.

Think about the significance of their reply. "They confessed themselves," J. D. Jones points out, "incapable of telling whether John was a charlatan or not; they confessed themselves incapable of distinguishing between a genuine and a sham religious movement. They confessed that in these high spiritual matters they could not judge. And by that miserable confession they put themselves clean out of court." They had come to Jesus proposing to make a decision about His claims and His authority. "But who were they, to be able to decide upon the claims of Jesus, when they confessed themselves incapable of deciding upon the work of John? These things are spiritually discerned, and they had pronounced themselves spiritual incapables, blind leaders of the blind. 'Neither tell I you,' was our Lord's rejoinder, 'by what authority I do these things' (ver. 33)" (Jones, vol. 3, pp. 116, 117).

James Edwards points out that the leaders' answer of "We do not know" was not entirely true. It is more to the point that they were *"unwilling* to know." Their judgment of truth had been "clouded by fear of popular opinion" and vested interest. Edwards concludes by suggesting that "those who cannot be honest with themselves cannot be honest about Jesus" (Edwards, p. 353).

Barclay takes us a step further when he observes that "the whole story is a vivid example of what happens to men who will not face the truth. To avoid facing the truth they have to twist and wriggle and in the end get themselves into a position in which they are so helplessly involved that they have nothing to say. The man who faces the truth may have the humiliation of saying that he was wrong, or the peril of standing by the truth, but at least the future for him is strong and bright. [But] the man who will not face the truth has nothing but the prospect of deeper and deeper involvement in a situation which renders him helpless and ineffective" (Barclay, *Mark,* p. 291, 292).

X

42. New Tenants for an Old Farm

Mark 12:1-12
    [1]*And He began to speak to them in parables: "A man planted a vineyard and he put a hedge around it and dug a wine vat and built a tower, and he leased it out to tenant farmers and went on a journey.* [2]*And he sent a slave to the farmers in the harvest time in order that he might receive the fruits of the vineyard from the farmers.* [3]*And they took him and beat him and sent him away empty.* [4]*And he again sent another slave to them. That one they wounded on the head and insulted.* [5]*And he sent another. That one they killed. And so with many others. Some were beat and others killed.* [6]*He still had one other, a beloved son. Finally he sent him to them, saying, 'They will respect my son.'* [7]*But those farmers said to themselves, 'This one is the heir. Come, let us kill him and the inheritance will be ours.'* [8]*And they took and killed him and cast him outside the vineyard.* [9]*What will the lord of the vineyard do? He will come and destroy the farmers and give the vineyard to others.* [10]*Have you not read this Scripture: 'A stone which the builders rejected, that one has become the capstone of the corner.* [11]*This came from the Lord and it is wonderful in our eyes'?"*
    [12]*And they sought to seize Him, yet they feared the crowd, for they knew that He told the parable against them. They left Him and went away.*

Exploring Mark

In Mark 11:28 the representatives from the Sanhedrin challenged Jesus on the source of His authority. He avoided giving them a direct answer, but rather questioned them regarding the authority of John the Baptist. If one reads between the lines it seems clear that Jesus was essentially telling the religious leaders that His and John's authority had the same source—God. But the matter never came to a head because the leaders refused to answer His question.

With Mark 12:1-12, however, Jesus transforms His implicit answer in 11:27-33 into an explicit one. By the time He finishes telling the allegory of the wicked tenant farmers, there is no doubt as to the source of authority. In that passage He claims both to be God's son and to have been sent by Him (12:6). Thus in answer to the questions put to Jesus in Mark 11:28, His claim was that He operated on the authority of none other than God the Father.

But Jesus didn't say that in so many words. Rather, He told a story, the only major parable in Mark's Gospel outside of chapter 4. The story itself was straightforward enough. A rich landowner planted a vineyard and put a hedge (probably of thorn bushes) around it to keep out sheep and goats and to discourage trespassers. Then he excavated a winepress right on the property and undoubtedly lined it with plaster. The harvesters would press the grapes, when ripe, with bare feet and the juice would flow into a vat where it could later be collected into large jars. The owner even went so far as to build a tower that not only provided shelter for the farmers but also served as a lookout post for a guard during the harvest time (see Malina, p. 200). All and all it was a first class operation.

Jesus' story presented something that no informed Jew could miss. He had painted a picture straight out of Isaiah 5:1-7. And His listeners would not have overlooked the fact that in Isaiah "the vineyard of the Lord of hosts is the house of Israel" (verse 7, RSV).

Jesus at that point had the ears of every Jewish person within the sound of His voice. He then went on to give a concise but accurate parallel of the nation's past history. The owner repeatedly sent servants (the Old Testament frequently referred to the prophets as God's servants or slaves. See, e.g., 2 Sam. 3:18; Amos 3:7; Jer. 7:25; Zech. 1:6), who were ignored and/or mistreated (Mark 12:2-5). And so it was in Israel's *past history*. But the real point of the parable took place in verse 6, in which Jesus shifted the focus from past events to *present history*. The owner at that point sent his son, whom they killed.

Isaiah on God's Vineyard

"Let me sing for my beloved
 a love song concerning his vineyard:
My beloved had a vineyard
 on a very fertile hill.
He digged it and cleared it of stones,
 and planted it with choice vines;
he built a watchtower in the midst of it,
 and hewed out a wine vat in it;
and he looked for it to yield grapes,
 but it yielded wild grapes. . . .
What more was there to do for my vineyard,
 that I have not done in it? . . .
. . . The vineyard of the Lord of hosts
 is the house of Israel."

Isaiah 5:1, 2, 4, 7, RSV

It was a powerful story in the loaded context of Jesus' ongoing and escalating conflict with the religious leaders in Jerusalem. After their embarrassment in not being willing to answer Jesus' public question regarding John's authority, they probably desired a bit of space to lick their wounds and think things through. But Jesus, according to Mark, didn't give them that breathing room. To the contrary, He took the offensive and publicly pressed them to the wall.

The parable itself tells us a great deal about Jesus. For one thing, it indicates that He was quite certain about His identity. He was not merely a prophet, but rather the Son of God (verse 6).

A second thing that it informs us is that He knew that the religious leadership would put Him to death. Of course, that is nothing new to the readers of Mark's Gospel. So far in Mark He had specifically predicted His death three times (8:31; 9:31; 10:33, 34) and alluded to it several more times. But in Mark 12:7, 8 Jesus did not announce His death to His chosen disciples but rather to the religious leaders. In fact, He went further.

He declared that He knew that they would be instrumental in putting Him to death. Such straight talk should have been a wake-up call to them.

Third, the story revealed that Jesus was sure of His ultimate triumph as He moved into *future history*. That too is not new. He had repeatedly mentioned His forthcoming resurrection to His heedless disciples (Mark 8:31; 9:31; 10:34). But we find no reference to resurrection here. Rather Jesus presented in Mark 12:10, 11 a quotation from Psalm 118:22, 23 featuring the rejected stone that eventually became the most important building block of all, the one that held the others in place.

In its original context the psalm had the nation of Israel as the rejected stone. The great nations of the world had regarded little Israel as a nothing, as unimportant. But the psalmist pictured despised Israel as eventually becoming "the head of the corner," the most important of all nations.

To the shock of the listening people, Jesus applied Psalm 118:22, 23 to Himself. As A. B. Bruce points out, "the men who have just been compared to vine-dressers now become builders, and the heir cast out of the vineyard and murdered is now a stone thrown aside as useless" (A. B. Bruce, *Parabolic Teaching,* p. 458). It would not be the Jewish nation that God would raise to heights of glory as the rejected stone that becomes the cornerstone, Jesus was claiming, but rather Himself. In short, as Bruce notes, Jesus was intimating to "His hearers that in killing Him they will not be done with Him" *(ibid.).* Thus in Mark 12 Jesus' victory over death is implicit rather than explicit. But He did not have the slightest doubt about the fact of His final victory.

Jesus on History in Mark 12

1. *Past history:* The rejection of the message of the prophets.
2. *Present history:* The rejection of Jesus.
3. *Future history:* The victory of Jesus and the creation of a new people.

But Jesus hadn't finished with His antagonists yet. He not only applied Psalm 118 to Himself, but He plainly told the Jewish leaders that, as unfaithful tenants, they would be destroyed and the vineyard given to others (Mark 12:9). Or as Matthew's version of the story put it, "the kingdom of God will be taken away from you and given to a people who will produce its fruit" (21:43, NIV). That new people or "nation" (RSV) would be the Christian church, made up of both Jews and Gentiles (see Rom. 9-11).

Jesus couldn't have said it stronger or made it plainer. The Jewish leaders, Mark tells us, "sought to seize Him . . . for they knew that He told the parable against them" (Mark 12:12). Luke puts their reaction more graphically when he has the leaders exclaim "God forbid!" (Luke 20:16, RSV).

So Jesus has finally answered the question raised in Mark 11:28 as to the source of His authority. It is straight from God His Father.

Meanwhile, the coming showdown between Jesus and the Jewish leaders is rapidly looming. It had long ago reached the point of no return. They knew it and so did He.

Yet in spite of His soon coming death, Jesus still had full confidence in final victory. His first readers, witnesses of that resurrection victory, undoubtedly felt encouraged by His faith in future history as they also faced difficult times in Rome and other places. His confidence in future history still comforts those of us 2,000 years later who await the consummation of His kingdom.

43. A Question on Government

Mark 12:13-17
> [13]*They sent some of the Pharisees and the Herodians to Him so that they might trap Him in a statement.* [14]*And coming to Him they said, "Teacher, we know that you are truthful and are not concerned about anyone's opinion. For you are not swayed by outward appearances, but rather you teach the way of God in truth. Is it permissible to pay a poll tax to Caesar or not?* [15]*Should we pay or not pay?" But He, knowing their hypocrisy, said to them, "Why are you testing Me? Bring Me a denarius so that I may look at it."* [16]*And they brought one, and He said to them, "Whose image is this and whose inscription?" And they said to Him, "Caesar's."* [17]*And Jesus said to them, "Give to Caesar the things of Caesar and the things of God to God." And they were amazed at Him.*

"They sent."

Mark doesn't tell us who the "they" are, but it is undoubtedly those members of the Sanhedrin that Jesus had bested in their attempt to trap Him on the issue of authority (Mark 11:27-33). Presumably those same leaders were also on the receiving end of the story of the wicked tenants (12:1-11).

Having recently lost two rounds in their contest with Jesus, they were becoming more desperate in their desire to find evidence to discredit Him. In this third confrontation they decided not to approach Jesus themselves, but rather to send a mixed delegation of Pharisees and Herodians.

The group's composition was itself a strange one. After all, those two factions were on opposite sides of the religio/political fence. The Pharisees belonged to the patriotic party, were strict in their religious observance, and saw the Roman rule as a distasteful yoke. In short, they were anti-Rome. The Herodians, on the other hand, were lax in their religious observances and generally supportive of Roman rule, from which they benefitted through their connection with the Herodian rulers.

Ordinarily one would not find the Pharisees and the Herodians working in concert. But a common enemy had linked them together at least temporarily. That same dynamic would later that week have the same effect on Herod and Pilate. Luke, in speaking of the events leading to Jesus' death, noted that "Herod and Pilate became friends with one another that very day; for before they had been enemies with each other" (Luke 23:12, NASB). A common foe can make strange bedfellows.

Certain leaders in the Sanhedrin not only sent the Pharisees and Herodians, but they were probably also responsible for the wording of the question to be asked. At least it posed the same kind of dilemma as the one they asked concerning the source of Jesus' authority in Mark 11:27-33. Both questions posed a two-horn dilemma in that whatever way Jesus answered the leaders could condemn Him.

Now the choice of representatives from opposing parties to raise the question was a wise move. It could appear as if they had been arguing over the answer and had gone to Jesus for a solution.

And look at the way they came. Whereas the delegation from the Sanhedrin in dialog over Jesus' authority had talked down to Him (Mark 11:27, 28), these men treated Jesus as a rabbi, an authoritative teacher (12:14). Their approach was not only respectful, it also oozed with flattery. By emphasizing His courage, integrity, and honesty, they sought to place

Jesus in a position in which it would be impossible for Him to avoid giving an answer without losing His reputation.

They had carefully thought out their preparations for the question. Mark tells us that the aim was to "catch" or "trap" Jesus (12:13). And in this case they had camouflaged the trap as best they could.

The question itself was an excellent one. It was a live issue in the Jewish community, one crying for an answer.

The issue of paying taxes to Rome had fractured the unity of the Jewish people for more than two decades. It began in 6 A.D. when the Romans deposed Archaelaus, son of Herod the Great, for misgovernment and transformed Judea into a Roman province under the direction of a procurator appointed by the emperor.

With direct government from Rome came direct taxation. The tax was unpopular, and before long Judas the Gaulonite (also known as Judas the Galilean, see Acts 5:37) led a violent revolt against the Roman government in Judea. Judas aroused his fellow Jews by claiming that "they were cowards if they would endure to pay a tax to the Romans, and would . . . submit to mortal men as their lords" (Josephus, *Wars*, 2.8.1). Rome soon put down Judas and his fellow insurgents with its usual efficiency, but his ideas did not die with him. According to the first century Jewish historian Josephus, Judas founded the "fourth sect of Jewish philosophy," a faction that claimed that "God is to be their only Ruler and Lord" (Josephus, *Antiquities*, 18.1.6). Josephus thus placed Judas as the founder of the party in Judaism that would eventually become known as the Zealots. They took the position that the Jews should pay no tax to Rome. Their vigorous and violent opposition to the Roman government would lead to the destruction of Jerusalem in 70 A.D.

Thus when the Pharisees and Herodians came to Jesus with their question on whether it was permissible to pay taxes to Caesar, it was a loaded one, with the Herodians being definitely in the affirmative and the Pharisees seeing it as problematic even though they paid their poll tax.

Jesus' opponents had carefully laid their trap, and it appeared inescapable. No matter which way Jesus answered He would be in trouble. If He took the side of the Herodians and answered "Yes, it is lawful," the Pharisees could denounce Him as a traitor and destroy His popularity with the people. After all, the political Messiah of Judaism " 'that was to deliver the children of Israel from the Caesars and all oppression'" could hardly be one who commanded "'them to pay tribute'" (V. G. Simkhovitch, in Rawlinson, p. 165).

Yet if Jesus took the Pharisaic position and declared that it was not lawful to pay the Roman poll tax, the Herodians could immediately report Him as a traitor to the Roman authorities. It was a no win situation for Jesus. The trap itself was a stroke of genius.

But so was the non-answer. Instead of giving a direct reply, Jesus asked to see a denarius, so that He could examine it. And what did He see? The coin not only had the image of Tiberius on one side, but on its edges were stamped the words "Tiberius Caesar, son of the divine Augustus." The other side of the coin had the Latin inscription "pontifex maximus," meaning high priest (see Bromiley, vol. 3, p. 409).

It is impossible to see the full implication of the taxation issue without understanding the philosophy of coinage in the ancient world. The minting of coins was an act of political dominance. A coin was valid in the realm of the ruler. To accept and use the coin of a ruler was to recognize his sovereignty.

Because many of the Roman procurators were sensitive to Jewish beliefs about images and claims to divinity, some of the small coins minted in Judea bore symbols that were more acceptable to them (see *ibid.,* p. 408; Rawlinson, p. 166). But it was no accident that the Roman poll tax had to be paid with a silver denarius that bore the image of Tiberius and the offensive wording. To pay the tax with such a coin was an act of allegiance to the Roman ruler.

Thus when Jesus asked to examine the coin needed to pay the tax He out-maneuvered His opponents by not only avoiding their carefully laid trap but also by publicly putting them in an embarrassing position. As Bruce Malina and Richard Rohrbaugh point out, Jesus "tricked" His hypocritical opponents "into revealing their possession of unclean (engraved) . . . coins" and then obligating them to answer His counterquestion—"Whose image is this and whose inscription?" (Malina, p. 201; Mark 12:16).

They had no choice but to answer "Caesar's." And by that response they had answered their own question on the legality of paying taxes to Rome. By placing the Jewish leaders in a position in which they had to admit that they themselves paid taxes to Rome Jesus had neutralized their trap.

At that point He was in a place where He could offer some constructive teaching. He went on to His famous "render to Caesar the things that are Caesar's, and to God the things that are God's" (Mark 12:17, KJV). In effect, He claimed that people who accept the advantages of government have responsibility to be good citizens who support that government. Paul would later expound upon that teaching in Romans 13:1-7.

But the remarkable part of His answer was that Jesus claimed that human government had only limited authority. That is, human government has no control and influence in the realm of God. J. D. Jones points out that "the Pharisees were right in thinking that when the State made demands which clashed with their sense of what was due to God, it might be their duty to disobey the State. But that point had not been reached by this demand for tribute." Here the state was still "well within its rights," according to Jesus (Jones, vol. 3, p. 144). Later, however, when the authorities sought to forbid the apostles from preaching the message of Jesus to the people they responded in line with Jesus' dictum that "we ought to obey God rather than men" (Acts 5:29, KJV).

Given His time in history, one of Jesus' most radical teachings was that the state had definite restrictions to its power. Meanwhile, persecuted Roman Christians could utilize His teaching on responsible citizenship to defend Christianity from the charge of being disloyal to the state.

ﭏ

44. A Question on Resurrection

Mark 12:18-27

> [18]*And the Sadducees, who say there is no resurrection, came to Him. And they questioned Him, saying,* [19]*"Teacher, Moses wrote to us that if anyone's brother dies and leaves behind a wife, and leaves no child, the brother may take his brother's wife and raise up children for his brother.* [20]*There were seven brothers. And the first took a wife, and died without leaving a child.* [21]*And the second took her and died, leaving behind no child. And the third likewise.* [22]*And all seven left no child. And last of all the woman died.* [23]*In the resurrection, when they are raised, which of them will she be the wife of? For all seven had her as a wife."*

> *²⁴Jesus said to them, "Is this not the reason that you are mistaken, that you do not know the Scriptures nor the power of God. ²⁵For when the dead raise they do not marry, nor are they given in marriage, but they are like the angels in the heavens. ²⁶But concerning the raising of the dead, have you not read in the book of Moses how God spoke to him at the bush, saying, 'I am the God of Abraham and the God of Isaac and the God of Jacob'? ²⁷He is not the God of the dead but of the living. You are greatly mistaken."*

Here we have the only mention of the Sadducees in Mark's Gospel. On many issues they opposed the Pharisaic position. The Sadducees were the priestly and aristocratic party. As such they were on much more agreeable terms with Rome and the other ruling groups in Palestine than were the separationistic Pharisees.

One of the most significant differences between the two leading Jewish parties was that the Sadducees rejected the oral tradition that was so close to the Pharisaic heart. In fact, the Sadducees had a narrow view of Scripture that accepted only the five books of Moses as authoritative. That position led them to a denial of such teachings as angels, demons, and the resurrection, which they did not believe that the Pentateuch taught.

Thus a great deal of tension existed between the two parties on such topics as the resurrection. Paul took advantage of that disagreement in Acts to shatter the decorum of his trial before the Sanhedrin by declaring that he held for the Pharasaic position on the resurrection. At that point "the assembly was divided" and the "dissension" on the topic between the two parties "became violent" (Acts 23:6-10, RSV).

Feelings ran high regarding the resurrection. The Pharisaic party eventually codified in the *Mishnah* that those who claim that there is no resurrection from the dead "have no portion in the world to come" (m. Sanhedrin 10:1).

Thus as in the question regarding taxation, the one the Sadducees put to Jesus on the resurrection was no merely academic matter. Morna Hooker is undoubtedly correct when she writes that the Sadducees "assumed that his views on this matter would agree with those of the Pharisees" (Hooker, p. 282). Thus they sought not only to put Jesus in a tight spot but to take a swipe at the Pharisees at the same time.

The question itself may have found its inspiration in the apocryphal book of Tobit, in which a woman is given in marriage to seven husbands.

But in that case each husband died before the marriage could be consummated (Tobit 3:7-15). The Sadducean version is a bit different. In their argument the woman sequentially consummates the marriage with all seven brothers but dies childless.

Now that story might come across to the twenty-first century mind as a little strange. But it was not in the ancient Near East, where there existed a widespread custom known as levirate marriage. Moses set forth that teaching in Deuteronomy 25:5-10. The basic idea is that if a married man dies before having a son, then his brother is to take the widow as his wife. Her first son would take the name of the dead brother. In that way his line would not die out. Theoretically the process would go on with succeeding brothers until the woman bore a male child. The custom itself not only preserved the various family names but it also kept property within the family. In addition, it provided some security for the widow in a society where the death rate was high and women had few rights of their own. Levirate marriage shows up in the Bible in several places. Probably two of the most well-known occasions are that of Tamar and the sons of Judah (Gen. 38) and the story of Ruth and Boaz (Ruth 4).

The Sadducees who approach Jesus have this background in their minds. The way they told the story, of course, sought to disprove the very idea of a resurrection. After all, it is ludicrous to think of her being married to all seven brothers in heaven. In the process they hoped to embarrass Jesus in public.

A.E.J. Rawlinson may be correct when he suggests that the question was "probably one of their stock arguments . . . against the idea of a resurrection of the dead" (Rawlinson, p. 168). And since they apparently asked it jokingly and it was based upon an imaginary case, Jesus could have justifiably declined to answer.

But that wasn't His style. He took the occasion to provide a positive teaching. His answer had two prongs:

1. That they didn't understand the Scripture.

2. That they had failed to grasp God's power (Mark 12:24).

On the first point, Jesus did not utilize those portions of the Old Testament that most clearly taught a resurrection (such as Isaiah 26:19; Ezekiel 37; Daniel 12:2; or Job 19:26) because Sadducees did not accept those parts of the Bible as authoritative. Rather, He went to Moses, thereby implying that they were ignorant of the teachings of even that part of the Bible that they accepted. Going back to Exodus 3:6, in which God meets Moses at the burning bush and declares that He is the God of Abraham, Isaac, and Jacob, Jesus notes that the Lord is the God of the living and not the dead (Mark 12:26).

In other words, the God of Israel had not forgotten His covenant with the patriarchs. They did not enter the realm of nonexistence at death. To the contrary, the resurrection proves that God is the God of the living. The great patriarchs are "live to him [God]" (Luke 20:38, RSV) and await the resurrection at the end of time (see Dan. 12:2; 1 Cor. 15:51-55; 1 Thess. 4:16, 17; Heb. 11:39, 40). As Floyd Filson notes, "Jesus assumes that God will renew all things and provide a fitting place for the eternal life of his people with him, and he therefore takes it as certain that these men will be raised and given their place in that perfect eternal Kingdom" (Filson, pp. 236, 237).

The second prong of Jesus' answer is that the Sadducees didn't understand divine power (Mark 12:24). Like so many modern people they apparently thought of the future life as a slightly altered version of earthly life as we know it. As G. A. Chadwick puts it, "the Sadducee could think no better than that their new life should be a reproduction of their existence here." He goes on to note that it was a theory that they were wise to reject (Chadwick, p. 333).

The Sadducees were correct in what they repudiated, but they were wrong in that they lacked any sanctified imagination of the possibilities of a future existence—they failed to grasp the creativity of a Creator God in a world without sin. As J. D. Jones notes, "it was God the Sadducees had left out of their calculation in all their thoughts about a future life" (Jones, vol. 3, p. 153). James Edwards graphically points out that "we can no more imagine heavenly existence than an infant *in utero* can imagine a Beethoven piano concerto or the Grand Canyon at sunset" (Edwards, p. 368).

Jesus didn't tell the Sadducees what heaven would be like. Their minds couldn't have grasped it if He had. But in answer to their specific question related to levirate marriage He told them that in heaven people would neither marry nor give in marriage, but would be like the angels (Mark 12:25).

That statement has intrigued people down through the ages, especially those who see the future life in terms of a linear extension of the present one. I remember vividly the pastor in Puerto Rico who told me that if heaven didn't have sex, he didn't want to go there.

Now there is a point to ponder. But as we do, we need to remember the significance of marriage and sex as we know it on this earth. Rawlinson argues that "the purpose of marriage on its physical side is to continue the race (and that was more particularly the case with the law of Levirate marriage to which the Sadducees appealed . . .): but this is wholly relative to life in a world subjected to the prevalence of death. Where death is abolished, marriage (physically considered) and birth will be also abolished. Those who attain to the resurrection will be in this respect *as angels in heaven*" (Rawlinson, p. 168).

Thoughts on Heaven

"There every power will be developed, every capability increased. The grandest enterprises will be carried forward, the loftiest aspirations will be reached, the highest ambitions realized. And still there will arise new heights to surmount, new wonders to admire, new truths to comprehend, fresh objects to call forth the powers of body and mind and soul" (E. G. White, *Education*, p. 307).

While we don't know a lot about the future life, we do know that even if some aspects of our present life will be changed, the loving relationship that is the core of earthly happiness will be even more prominent than it is now. As Jones asserts, if we don't have marriage we will have something "more glorious and beautiful than marriage" (Jones, vol. 3, p. 154). I can't exactly think of what that might be, but I am looking forward to finding out. Jones adds that "I content myself with simply saying this, we shall miss nothing in heaven that is really worth having. Heaven will rob us of no real joy, of no genuine delight, of no enriching love. Heaven means joy at its full: happiness in its perfection" (*ibid.*, p. 155).

45. A Question on God's Commandments

Mark 12:28-34
> [28]*And one of the scribes came and heard them debating. And seeing that He had answered them well, he asked Him, "What is the foremost commandment of all?" [29]Jesus answered, "The foremost is 'Hear, O Israel,*

the Lord our God is one Lord, [30]and you shall love the Lord your God with your whole heart and with your whole soul and with your whole mind and with your whole strength.' [31]And the second is this, 'You shall love your neighbor as yourself.' There is no other commandment greater than these." [32]And the scribe said to Him, "Right, Teacher, You have truly said that there is One and there is no other except Him. [33]And to love Him with the whole heart and with the whole understanding and with the whole strength and to love one's neighbor as oneself is greater than all burnt offerings and sacrifices." [34]And having seen that he answered wisely, Jesus said to him, "You are not far from the kingdom of God." And after that no one dared to question Him.

✗

In this passage we find what at first appears to be a contradiction in the accounts of Mark and Matthew. In Mark the scribe appears to be on friendly terms with Jesus and the passage closes with a commendation of the scribe. Matthew's account, however, not only contains no commendation, but claims that the official intended to "test him" (Matt. 22:35, RSV).

The two accounts may not be as far apart as they first appear. After all, in both gospels the scribe's question falls into the same hostile context in which we find Jesus and the Jewish leaders in a series of confrontations.

It may be, as G. A. Chadwick suggests, that the scribe "probably sympathized" in the hostility of the other Jewish leaders "and had come expecting and desiring the discomfiture of Jesus" (Chadwick, p. 337). But the scribe, who had apparently been in the group of listeners who had heard Jesus' answers to the priests, Pharisees, Herodians, and Sadducees, recognized the depth and wisdom in those responses. Thus even though the man had come to put Jesus to the test, being honest at heart his aggressiveness began to progressively moderate.

As a result, the scribal expert, having seen that Jesus had answered the other questions "well," put forth one of his own in the mindset of what were becoming mixed feelings toward Jesus.

And the question, as with those previously asked, was a major issue in the Jewish community of the day. Its legal scholars had concluded that Scripture contained some 613 commandments, 365 prohibitions and 248 positive injunctions. Among those 613 the rabbis differentiated between what they saw as the "heavy" and the "light" commandments. Jesus appears to have been alluding to that distinction when He said that "whoever then relaxes one of the *least* of these commandments and teaches men so, shall be called least in the kingdom of heaven" (Matt. 5:19, RSV). Heavy commandments, as we might expect, had severer penalties attached to them.

In that context the question about the "foremost commandment" (Mark 12:29) is not concerned with numerical order but what was most necessary to be observed. However, some Jews disagreed even with the idea that certain things were more basic than others. To them, just as with some Christians today, every command held equal weight, and the same with sins. You were either with God or against Him. Such believers across time have tended toward ritualism and a behavioral perfectionism in their daily lives.

But others of the Jews disagreed and debated endlessly as to which was the most basic of all laws. The scribe in Mark 12:28 belonged to this latter group. He may have come to Jesus with a desire to test Him, but, on a deeper level, he genuinely wanted to know what was truly essential in religion. Undoubtedly he had acquaintances who were concerned with doing everything right in terms of their worship and lifestyle, but who appeared to be as "lost" as those who had no interest in God. At any rate, Jesus saw a sincerity in the question and provided the scribe with a direct answer.

Most of the bystanders probably expected Jesus to select one of the Ten Commandments, but He bypassed the Decalogue for one of the most familiar texts in Jewish culture—Deuteronomy 6:5. That verse was part of the *Shema* or Jewish confession of faith. It opened every Jewish service and formed a part of a Jew's morning prayer. In effect, Jesus defined the heart of religion as loving God with one's total being (Mark 12:30).

That answer would have been satisfactory, but Jesus chose to mention a second great commandment (verse 31). This time He quoted from Leviticus 19:18, with its injunction to love one's neighbor. The underlying assumption of both this passage and of Jesus' entire teaching is that it is impossible to truly love God without loving other people. The apostle John put the matter succinctly when he wrote that "if anyone says, 'I love God,' yet hates his brother, he is a liar. For anyone who does not love his brother, whom he has seen, cannot love God, whom he has not seen" (1 John 4:20, NIV).

We should note several points before we leave Christ's answer to the scribe. First, the observance of both injunctions is absolutely essential for the Christian. On the other hand, as James Edwards points out, "the two commandments are not blended into a compromising hybrid. The order in which Jesus declares the commandments implies that love to God is prerequisite to loving one's neighbor" (Edwards, p. 372).

Second, the rest of the New Testament builds its ethics upon Jesus' answer that the core of religion is to love. Thus Paul can write that "the whole law is fulfilled in one word, 'You shall love your neighbor as yourself'" (Gal. 5:14, RSV). He repeats the same idea in Romans 13, in which he notes that "love is the fulfilling of the law" and "he who loves his neighbor has fulfilled the law" (verses 10, 8, RSV). But in that chapter the apostle helps us see more clearly the relation of the command to love to the Ten Commandments. More specifically, he explicitly unites those commandments from the second table of the Decalogue to the second great commandment. Thus he ties such commandments as not killing, not stealing, and so on to the command to love other people (see verses 9, 10). We should also keep in mind that James' insight that "whoever keeps the whole law but fails in one point has become guilty of all of it" (2:10, RSV) builds upon the fact that all of the commandments form a unity rooted in love.

R. A. Cole is on target when he writes that "the heart of true religion [from Jesus' perspective] is seen to lie, not in negative commands, but in a positive loving attitude to God and others. This is the Pauline 'liberty' of the New Testament (Gal. 5:1). This is what St. Augustine means by saying 'Love and do as you like,' for such love towards God and others will in itself keep us from licence. If we love others, we will do nothing to work them hurt and, if we love God, what we like and choose will be to do God's will and pleasure (Ps. 40:8)" (Cole, p. 267).

A third thing that we should remember about Jesus' answer was that it wasn't unique. Rabbis Akiba (early second century A.D.) and Hillel (first century B.C.) provide similar answers in terms of Leviticus 19:8 on the weightiness of loving one's neighbors, while the Testament of Dan 5:3 and the Testament of Issachar 5:2; 7:6 (both from the second century B.C.) summarize the law as love to God and one's neighbor. While it is true that those two testaments may have undergone some Christian editing, it appears that the remarkable thing about Jesus' conclusions on the law are not their uniqueness, but that He was in essential harmony with some of the best Jewish thinkers of His day. Morna Hooker is quite correct when she writes that Mark's story about the weightiest law "reminds us again that Jesus may have been closer to some of his Jewish contemporaries than the gospels often suggest: others shared his concern for what was essential" (Hooker, p 289).

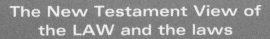

The New Testament View of the LAW and the laws

The LAW undergirding the laws = love

The two objects of love = (1) God (2) other people

Specifics on how to love = the Ten Commandments

Love to God means

1. to worship Him above all things
2. to not substitute an image for the reality
3. to honor His name
4. to honor His day

Love to other people means

5. to honor one's parents
6. to respect the lives of others
7. to respect the marriage relationship
8. to respect others' property
9. to respect the need for truth
10. not to covet anything that belongs to another

A final thing that we should learn from Jesus' response to the question about the great commandment is that the church would be a more delightful place if more of its members took Jesus' answer to heart and put it into practice. Every congregation has "pious" members who act as if they can love God while being rude to other people. Beyond that, we continually encounter those who are extremely careful about how they keep the Sabbath and/or what they eat but who are meaner than the devil himself.

The scribe of Mark 12 was one of those Jewish leaders who was in harmony with Jesus on what was central to religion. He was not of the legalistic faction that put ritual and behavior at the center. As a result, he not only praised Jesus' answer (verse 32) but alluded to such passages as 1 Samuel 15:22, Hosea 6:6, and Micah 6:6-8 in claiming that love to God and one's neighbor were "greater than all burnt offerings and sacrifices" (Mark 12:33).

The rather surprising result, given the fact that Mark is in the midst of a series of conflict episodes, is that Jesus commends the scribe for his insightful reply, saying to him, "You are not far from the kingdom of God" (verse 34). What a role reversal. The man who had come to pass judgment on Jesus ends up being judged by Him.

But what is "not far"? What happened to the scribe after meeting Jesus? Did he come close like the rich young ruler only to shy away at the last minute (Mark 10:17-22)? Or was he one of those Jewish leaders who eventually joined up with the apostles (Acts 15:5; 6:7)?

We don't know. But we do know that not to be far from the kingdom is still to be on the outside of it. As Chadwick reminds us, "we also may know, and admire, and confess the greatness and goodness of Jesus, without forsaking all to follow Him" (Chadwick, p. 340). To be "not far" is not to be partially lost but totally lost. All such individuals must close the gap and enter in. ✗

46. The Real Question

Mark 12:35-37

35And then Jesus, having answered, said while teaching in the Temple, "How is it that the scribes say that the Christ is the son of David? 36David himself said by the Holy Spirit, 'The Lord said to my Lord, sit at My right hand until I put Your enemies under Your feet.' 37David himself calls Him 'Lord'; so how is He his son?" And the large crowd listened to Him gladly.

Finally," Ralph Martin writes, "after a day of questions comes the question of the day" (Martin, *Where the Action Is,* p. 106).

The questions had come from priests, Pharisees, Herodians, Sadducees, and scribes, but Jesus had answered all of them with such ingenuity that the Jewish leaders had concluded that they had best not ask Jesus any more of them (Mark 12:34). Every question they submitted had become an opportunity for the revelation of some aspect of Jesus' understanding. He had reduced His opponents to silence. They had had enough of questions.

But Jesus hadn't. He also had a query. As Francis Moloney puts it, He "has not concluded his systematic elimination of the leaders" (Moloney, p. 243). His question would be the question of questions. It would reflect on His identity and would in fact raise publicly in the Temple of Jerusalem the issue He had brought up privately with the disciples on the road to Caesarea Philippi, when He asked them "Who do men say that I am?" (Mark 8:27, RSV).

In order to get the full picture of what happened in Mark 12:35-37 we need to turn to Matthew 22:41-45, since Mark's abbreviated version leaves out part of the scene. We discover several aspects in Matthew not evident in Mark. For one thing, we find that those to whom Jesus addresses His question are Pharisees, a party that accepted the whole of the Old Testament and looked forward to the coming Messiah with great anticipation. The second thing that we learn is that there was a prior question and an answer. Matthew quotes Jesus as saying, "What do you think of the Christ? Whose son is he?" They immediately replied that the Christ is "the son of David" (Matt. 22:42).

Now, before going any further we had better unpack some terminology if we want to grasp what the first century Jews understood from this passage. First, note that Jesus didn't use Christ as a name but rather as a position. Thus in Matthew 22:42 He asked about "the Christ." Christ *(Christos)* is the Greek word for Messiah. Both terms refer to the "anointed one." And just as kings in Bible times were anointed with oil at their coronation, so it would be for the coming Messiah.

The second term that we need to examine is "son of David." Of all the titles for the Messiah the most common was the son of David. The Jews looked forward to a God-sent deliverer of the line of David (see, e.g., 2 Sam. 7:12, 13; Isa. 9:2-7; 11:1-9; Jer. 30:9; Eze. 34:23). From their perspective, as noted earlier, the son of David Messiah would be a human being in the line of David who would be, like David, a warrior king who would free the nation from the rulership of the hated Romans.

It was no accident that the genealogies in Matthew 1 and Luke 3 trace Jesus' lineage through David. He was indeed a fulfillment of that prophecy. Blind Bartimaeus had applied the son of David title to Jesus (Mark 10:47). And the crowd had used the title for Jesus during His triumphal entry earlier in the week (11:10). There was a definite hope among some that Jesus was the long-awaited son of David who would free them from their enemies. R. T. France suggests that Jesus' failure to suppress the use of the title by Bartimaeus and the "crowd outside Jerusalem seems to indicate that he did not find it unacceptable. Indeed, the manner of his approach to the city seems to have actively encouraged it" (France, *Mark,* NIGTC, p. 483).

With those understandings in mind we can go back to Mark's account. After the Pharisees publicly identified the Christ as the son of David (Matt. 22:42), Jesus asked His question of questions: "How is it that the scribes say that Christ is the son of David" when "David himself said by the Holy Spirit, 'The Lord said to my Lord, sit at My right hand until I put Your enemies under Your feet.' David himself calls Him 'Lord;' so how is He his son?" (Mark 12:36, 37).

The argument that Jesus puts forward derives from Psalm 110:1, which He quoted in Mark 12:36. The listening Pharisees had no doubt that the passage was Messianic. Jesus had no problem with that interpretation, but His question indicated that the Pharisees, who prided themselves on their knowledge of the Scriptures, really didn't understand them. How, Jesus asked, could David call the Messiah "Lord" if he were his son?

To understand the import of the question we again need to remember that for the Jews the Messiah was to be a strictly human son in David's line. But Jesus shows them that they hadn't read the passage very carefully. David under divine inspiration, Jesus told them, called the Messiah "my Lord." And "Lord" *(kurios)* is the Greek word that the Septuagint (Greek version of the Old Testament) used to translate "Yahweh" (God) from the Hebrew Scripture. Thus David, Jesus pointed out to the Pharisees, was claiming that the coming Messiah/Christ would not only be a human being but would also be God. Thus "son of David," while being a true description of the Messiah, was an inadequate one. The Messiah would not only be David's Son but also his Lord.

Jesus accomplished at least three things in His exchange with the Pharisees. First, He publicly demonstrated their inadequacy as interpreters of Scripture. Second, He made an immense claim for Himself. As J. D. Jones points out, "Christ was David's Son according to the flesh, though, because He wore none of the trappings of royalty, the Pharisees had failed to recognise Him. But He was something infinitely greater than David's

Son. He was David's Lord. The fault with the Pharisees was not that they had thought too highly of Messiah. They had not thought highly enough. The Messiah in their thought of Him was never anything but human. Jesus here declares Him to be Divine—so Divine that the great David hails Him as Lord. And in making this stupendous and staggering claim for Messiah, Jesus was making it for Himself. He had already done it this very week by riding in lowly triumph into Jerusalem, and by claiming authority over the Temple. The Pharisees therefore knew all that was implied in this word about David's Lord" (Jones, vol. 3, p. 185).

A third implication also arises out of Jesus' discussion with the Pharisees. Larry Hurtado is correct when he argues that if the Messiah is not merely David's son, then "David's place as a model and image of Messiah is being challenged" (Hurtado, p. 204). That is, if the Messiah had only the role of son, then he could expect to follow David's example and function as a warrior-king deliverer. But if the Messiah was superior to David, then human kingship is no longer an adequate model.

And so it was with Jesus. He accepted the titles of the Messiah and the son of David, but He rejected the limitations of the Jewish definitions. Jesus never came as a warrior king, but as the Lamb of God (John 1:29). And He did not seek merely to deliver the Jews from the Romans, but to save His people everywhere from their sins (Matt. 1:21).

Mark doesn't tell us the immediate response of the Pharisees to Jesus' teaching about the Christ. But he does mention that "the large crowd listened to Him gladly" (Mark 12:37).

Jesus' use of Psalm 110:1 in Mark 12:36 reveals two more things about His understanding of His mission:

1. that He would be victorious and sit at God's right hand,
2. and that He eventually would triumph over His enemies, who would become as His footstool.

Such confidence was crucial for Mark's first readers as they faced uncertain times in Rome and other parts of the empire. In fact, it has uplifted Christians ever since the time of Christ. It is little wonder that Psalm 110 is the most quoted passage from the Old Testament in the New. Altogether the New Testament quotes or alludes to it some 33 times. Among them are Peter's great sermon on the Day of Pentecost in his argument for his ascended Lord (Acts 2:34, 35) and Hebrews' repeated use of the text as the author drives home the point that Christians can live in absolute confidence because they serve a risen Jesus who not only sits "at the right hand of the Majesty on high" (Heb. 1:3) but serves as their high priest in that exalted position. We today can also thank God that the Christ was not merely David's son but his Lord.

✗

47. A Lesson on True Value

Mark 12:38-44

[38] And in His teaching He said, "Beware of the scribes; the ones who desire to walk about in long robes and to receive respectful greetings in the marketplace [39] and to have chief seats in the synagogues and places of honor at the banquets; [40] the ones who devour widows' houses and pray long prayers for show. They will receive the greater condemnation."

[41] And having sat down opposite the treasury, He observed how the crowd put copper coins into the treasury. Many rich people put in much. [42] And one poor widow came and put in two of the smallest coins, which is one fourth of a cent. [43] He called His disciples to Him, saying to them, "Truly I say to you that this poor widow put in more than all those contributing to the treasury. [44] For they all from their abundance contribute, but this widow, out of her poverty, put in everything she had, all of her living."

Here we have two incidents that at first glance don't seem to have much in common. On closer examination, however, we find mutual themes that run through both. On the surface level a widow appears in each episode. But at a deeper level we observe such core religious ideas as values and judgment featured across the stories.

Verses 38-40, which condemn the scribes, are an abbreviated version of the woes that Jesus pronounced upon the scribes and Pharisees in Matthew 23. Perhaps the most important aspect of the paragraph is not what it says about the scribes, but what it reveals about Jesus.

The Jesus who condemns the scribes and pronounces woes on the scribes and Pharisees is not the gentle person that we like to sing about. "There is," J. D. Jones points out, "something fierce, hot, scorching about the whole of this passage. What we get here is not the gentleness of Christ, but the *anger* of Christ" (Jones, vol. 3, p. 190). Yet it is not the unreasonable, temper-based anger that other humans exhibit. Rather, it is that burning, holy indignation that the Bible labels as God's *wrath*—what Revelation 6:16 calls the "wrath of the Lamb."

The context of that phrase is important. Speaking of the end of time, it reads, "Then the kings of the earth and the great men and the generals and the rich and the strong, and every one, slave and free, hid in the caves and among the rocks of the mountains, calling to the mountains and rocks, 'Fall on us and hide us from the face of him who is seated on the throne, and from the wrath of the Lamb; for the great day of their wrath has come, and who can stand before it?" (verses 15-17, RSV). Perhaps that is the way the religious leaders felt at the end of a day of struggling with Jesus. At first they had been on the offensive. But that had changed, and by Mark 12:38-40 they have experienced a foretaste of His "other side."

"The wrath of the Lamb" sounds like a contradiction of terms. It's not. Rather, it is two aspects of one love. When we generally think of the loving Jesus we remember Him welcoming publicans and prostitutes into the kingdom or visualize Him healing Jairus' daughter or tenderly caring for broken souls.

But that is a one-side perspective on His love. That love also contains a burning indignation at those conditions and people who set the social context for prostitution and extortion, those forces that bring about blindness, illness, and death. Jesus hates anything that destroys His people.

The wrath of Jesus is the other side of His love. It is the facet that overthrows the tables of crooked dealers in the Temple and calls misleading religion by its right name. Such love will someday rid the world of sin and those who insist on clinging to it; will one day say that death and destruction shall be no more; and will eventually create a new heaven and a new earth.

Jones is right on target when he points out that "Christ's wrath is an element in the perfection of His character. We conspire to ignore it in these days under the mistaken idea that somehow or other it takes from the glory and perfection of Christ to suppose that He could be wrathful. On the contrary, it is the people who ignore the wrath who sacrifice the perfection of Christ. I will for ever refuse the epithet 'good' to the man who is incapable of a holy flame of indignation in the presence of wrong and sin. The man who is never angry is morally anaemic. He is not good; he is weak. The father who can never be wrathful with his child, who weakly smiles at his child's wrong-doing, is not a 'good' father, he is about as bad a father as a child could have. It is high time we revised our ideas of what goodness is and ceased to identify it with a weak and soft amiability. Christ's holy wrath is, then, an element in His perfection. . . . He was holy as well as tender, He was entirely good. In his passion for purity He flamed like a refiner's fire, and wicked men could not abide the day of His coming" (Jones, vol. 3, p. 192). ✗

Too many church members have forgotten the holiness of God and the wrath of the Lamb. But the scribes didn't at the end of Jesus' long day in the Temple. He told them exactly what He thought of church members who had lost their sense of values and spiritual realities.

His charges against the scribes in Mark 12:38-40 center on three areas. First, they were ostentatious in their religious practices. The long robes Jesus spoke about were the sign of a notable person. A garment in which one could neither hurry or work, it was the badge of the leisure class. As Halford Luccock observes, "Look at the economic snobbishness involved. The long robes were a sign and proof that the wearer did no manual work for a living." He continues by noting that the love of titles hasn't disappeared. People still clamor after such titles as "president," "executive," and so on. And the "best seats" syndrome hasn't died out "in restricted neighborhoods, in clubs, on preferential lists of every sort!" But "the road to greatness is still the way to service." On the other hand, Luccock queries, "What would an edition of *Who's Who* be like if it were published, not in Chicago or London, but in heaven?" (Luccock, pp. 851, 852).

Beyond ostentation, Jesus condemned the scribes for being guilty of avarice—they devoured widow's houses (Mark 12:40). In Jesus' time the experts in the law (scribes) were forbidden to ask for pay for their expertise. They had to support themselves by a trade (Paul the Pharisee was a tent maker [Acts 18:3]) or through the generosity of others. ✗

Some, however, were not above taking advantage of that situation. Larry Hurtado writes that "the reference to the scribe robbing a widow of her home (v. 40) probably has to do with a scribe sponging off devout people who felt an obligation to support a scribe as a representative of God's law. Both then and now there are examples of Jewish and Christian religious leaders who unscrupulously solicit support from simple, vulnerable people who are led to believe that they are supporting the very work of God but can ill afford to give as heavily as they are solicited to do" (Hurtado, p. 205).

A third condemnation of the scribes was that they were hypocrites. They might "pray long prayers" but it was purely "for show" (Mark 12:40). Their religion was a sham—they were play-actors on the religious scene. The church, in spite of Jesus' words, has never lacked such show-people. Of course, their script varies from person to person. For some the centerpiece is praying, for others it is giving, singing, preaching, or just being the most zealous (i.e., perfect) in the congregation.✗

The crisis of the scribes was one of perspective and values. They had a form of religion but missed its essence. As Ellen White puts it, "they occupied men's minds with trifling distinctions, and turned their attention from essential truths." They may have been strong on such things as dietary regulations, sabbathkeeping, and so on. And they may have been able to tell others where everybody else fell short. But "the weightier matters of the law, justice, mercy, and truth, were neglected" (White, *The Desire of Ages,* p. 617). Whereas the Pharisees and their scribes may have formed a distinct party in first century Judaism, it is also true that their kind also consists of a type that has plagued the church throughout its history. Jesus' evaluation of such sanctimonious people is "they will receive the greater condemnation" (Mark 12:40).

Here is one of the great paradoxes of Jesus' teaching. He reserved His sternest words and most vigorous condemnations not for the notorious sinners of the world but for religious people, especially those who formed their own so-called "holy club" that put themselves on the inside and nearly everybody else on the outside. The judgment will indeed be full of surprises. If you don't believe it, go to Jesus' portrayal of the last judgment in Matthew 25:31-46 and count the question marks.

After Jesus' remarks against the scribes in Mark 12:38-40 He started to leave the Temple for the last time. But on His way out He stopped in the Court of the Women. As He sat there He watched people put their offerings into the 13 collection boxes known as the trumpets because of their shape (verse 41).

The Bible tells us that Jesus was deliberately observing "how" people put their offerings into the receptacle. It is not only what we give that is important in God's eyes but also how. Some with a great flourish gave much in a way no one could miss. They weren't so much concerned with the gift as they were the recognition. There goes one now in a fine suit of clothes, immaculately tailored to be sure.

The Value of Unseen Gifts

"Not the great things which every eye sees and every tongue praises does God account most precious. The little duties cheerfully done, the little gifts which make no show, and which to human eyes may appear worthless, often stand highest in His sight. A heart of faith and love is dearer to God than the most costly gift" (White, *The Desire of Ages,* p. 615).

And then came the poor widow who, somewhat ashamed of her small gift, quietly deposited it and slipped away. That also caught Jesus' eye. Here He recognized true religion of the heart. And once more we encounter a judgment scene based upon internal values. For her heartfelt sincerity she received Jesus' blessing (verses 43, 44).

Please note that not a word passed between Jesus and the widow. She didn't even know He was watching. And she certainly never heard His eulogy of her. Of earthly recognition she received nothing, but of heavenly she received much.

Remarking on Jesus' kind words, Donald English writes, "This may seem to be a somewhat idyllic way to end a stormy chapter, but we should not be misled. The issue, with Jesus at the centre, is still about giving all, total trust, utter commitment" (English, p. 202).

48. A Lesson on the Signs of the Times

Mark 13:1-13

¹And as He was going out of the Temple one of His disciples said to Him, "Teacher, look what sort of stones and what sort of buildings are here." ²And Jesus said to him, "Do you see these great buildings? There is no stone upon another which will not be thrown down."

³And as He sat on the Mount of Olives opposite the Temple, Peter and

James and John and Andrew were questioning Him privately. ⁴*"Tell us, when will these things be, and what will be the sign when all these things are all to be accomplished?"* ⁵*And Jesus began to say to them, "Beware lest anyone deceive you.* ⁶*Many will come in My name, saying 'I am He,' and they will deceive many.* ⁷*But when you hear of wars and reports of wars, do not be troubled. It is necessary for these things to happen, but the end is not yet.* ⁸*For nation will rise up against nation and kingdom against kingdom, there will be earthquakes in place after place, and there will be famines. These things are the beginning of birth pangs.*

⁹*"But be alert yourselves. For they will hand you over to the Sanhedrin and you will be beaten in synagogues and you will stand before governors and kings for My sake as a testimony to them.* ¹⁰*It is necessary first for the good news to be preached to all the nations.* ¹¹*And when they arrest you and deliver you, do not be concerned beforehand what you will say. But say whatever is given to you in that hour, for you will not be speaking yourself but the Holy Spirit.* ¹²*And brother will deliver brother to death and a father his child, and children will rise up against parents and cause them to be put to death.* ¹³*And you will be hated by everyone because of My name. But the one who endures to the end, that one will be saved."*

William Lane notes two things about Mark 13. The first is that it is "the longest uninterrupted course of private instruction recorded by Mark." In fact, "it is the only extended speech attributed to Jesus by the evangelist." Second, "there is no passage more problematic than the prophetic discourse of Jesus on the destruction of the Temple" in the Gospel of Mark (Lane, p. 444).

But at least one part of Mark 13 is certain. That is the setting. Verse 1 finds Jesus leaving the Temple for the last time. As He and the disciples drift away from it they point out to Him the grandeur of the stones and the building itself. And they were correct in being impressed. The stones themselves were massive. In one place the first century Jewish historian Josephus indicates that they were 25 cubits (a cubit is 18-20 inches) long, 8 in height, and about 12 in breadth (Josephus, *Antiquities,* 15.11.2). In another place he tells us that some of the stones were up to 45 cubits in length (Josephus, *Wars,* 5.5.6). But if the stones were impressive, the Temple itself was astonishingly beautiful. Josephus writes that the outward face of the Temple "was covered all over with plates of gold of great weight, and, at the first rising of the sun, reflected back a very fiery splendour, and made those who forced themselves to look upon it to turn their eyes away, just as they would have done at the sun's own rays." At a distance, he continues, the Temple appeared "like a mountain covered with snow; for, as to those parts of it that were not gilt, they were exceeding white" *(ibid.)*.

The disciples had a right to be duly impressed. Jesus' words in Mark 13:2, therefore, caught them totally by surprise. He told His astounded followers that not one stone of the Temple would remain on another, that all would be destroyed. He hadn't been the first person to utter such a prophecy. Micah had done so in the eighth century B.C. (Micah 3:12) and Jeremiah more than a century later (Jer. 26). And it happened when Nebuchadnezzar's army took Jerusalem and destroyed Solomon's Temple in B.C. 586.

But Jeremiah's message wasn't popular. It nearly cost him his life. Jesus' prophecy wouldn't be liked either. His opponents would use it against Him both in His trial before Caiaphas (Mark 14:58) and while He hung on the cross (15:29). But popular or not, it would come to pass in 70 A.D. when Rome's legions destroyed Jerusalem and literally dismantled the Temple after it was set on fire (see Josephus, *Wars,* 6.4.7).

Four of the astounded disciples took Jesus aside and asked Him when such things would take place (Mark 13:3). Up to that point the chapter is quite clear. But after verse 3 interpreters have experienced a great deal of confusion, mainly because some of the verses seem to be primarily speaking to the destruction of the Temple and others of the second coming of Jesus. Why the Second Advent would even enter the discussion is not at all obvious from reading Mark 13, in which the disciples appear to be asking only questions related to the destruction of the Temple. But a comparison with Matthew's version of the questions will help us, because in Matthew 24:3 the disciples explicitly inquired not only about the destruction of the Temple but also about the return of Jesus and the end of the age. The following chart will help us see the difference between Mark's and Matthew's versions of the questions.

It appears from a comparison of Mark 13 and Matthew 24 that Jesus answered all of Matthew's questions in both chapters. That leaves us with the possibility that both Jesus and the disciples might have understood the *"all these things"* of Mark 13:4 as including the Second Advent and the end of the age (see France, *Mark,* Doubleday, p. 167). But that is speculation. What is not speculative is that by the end of Mark 13 Jesus has shifted His discussion from the destruction of the Temple to His second advent (see, e.g., verses 26, 27).

The Questions

1. In Mark 13:4
    A. When will the Temple be destroyed?
    B. "What will be the sign *when all these things* are all to be accomplished?"
2. In Matthew 24:3
    A. When will the Temple be destroyed?
    B. What will be the signs of Jesus' coming?
    C. What will be the sign of the close of the age?

It appears that it is almost impossible to correctly disentangle those events related to the destruction of Jerusalem from those referring to the Second Advent in many of the verses of both Mark 13 and Matthew 24. Several possible reasons may create the problem. One is that it might be that the "signs" leading up to both were to be the same. Then again, Jesus may have engineered His discourse in the way He did because He was not so much seeking to tell people *when* the prophetic events would occur as to alert His hearers that they *must live in a state of continual expectancy* as they looked forward to them. That aim appears to be especially clear in relation to the Second Advent. Both Mark 13 and Matthew 24 climax with parables that emphasize the necessity of watching and being ready.

Another possible reason for Jesus' less than precise teaching strategy is that the very lack of precision leads readers to continually rethink His teachings regarding the Second Advent as they seek to penetrate His meaning. That teaching technique is similar in some ways to His use of parables that made people ponder them as they wrestled with His meaning (see on Mark 4:10-12). Such a technique has definitely aided people to identify with the major point of His instruction—to watch and be faithful, because no one truly knows the hour of His return (Mark 13:32-37).

In response to the disciples' request for a sign (verse 4), Jesus presents several types of material. One concerns false Messiahs (verses 5, 6). That issue was so important that He repeats it in verses 21 and 22. And the years leading up to the fall of Jerusalem did see the rise of several false Messiahs (Christs). A second set of signs Jesus presented were wars, earthquakes, and famines (verses 7, 8). But Jesus told the disciples not to get overly excited about those signs, that while they must happen they did not mean it was yet the end (verse 7). Then in the next verse He added that such events were merely the "beginning" of the birth pangs.

Some interpreters have made a great deal of such signs. But the problem is that they are quite general. After all, false messiahs, earthquakes, famines, and wars have always plagued humanity. They seem to be signs in the sense that the end is coming, but they are not the final indication. It may be that such signs are similar to the rainbow that God gave to Noah as a remembrance of His covenant after the Flood. Thus every time Noah saw the rainbow he would remember the faithfulness of God, who had promised never again to destroy the earth by a flood. It was a symbol that God was faithful to His promise (Gen. 9:12-17).

So it is with many of the signs of Mark 13. Each earthquake, falling star, and so on is a remembrance of the earth's sickness and a symbol that the faithful, covenant-keeping God has not yet finished the plan of salvation. Each such disruption assures us that the end will come.

Beyond the signs of verses 5-8, verses 9-13 discuss the fact that Christians will face opposition, betrayal, and persecution because of their allegiance to Jesus. But the passage also has the comforting reality that God would be with them during that time of trial and would even, through the Holy Spirit, give them the words that they should speak (verse 11).

Such promises must have been precious to the Roman Christians to whom Mark was writing, who had just suffered persecution from Nero and might have to endure it again in the near future. They also comforted the Christians who suffered persecution from the Jewish leaders in the decades after Jesus' death, and in subsequent ages of martyrdom. In fact, they will sustain believers to the end of the age.

49. A Lesson From History

Mark 13:14-23

[14]*"And when you see the abomination of desolation set up where it should not be (let the reader understand), then let those in Judea flee to the mountains, [15]let the one on the roof not come down or enter to take anything from his house, [16]and let the one in the field not return to take his outer garment. [17]And woe to those pregnant and those nursing in those days. [18]Pray that it might not happen in winter. [19]For in those days there will be affliction such as has not been from the beginning of the creation which God created until now, and never shall be. [20]Except the Lord shorten those days, no life would be saved. But on account of the elect, whom He chose, He shortened the days. [21]And then if anyone says to you, 'Look, here is the Christ, or look there,' do not believe them. [22]For false Christs and false prophets will rise up and they will perform signs and wonders so as to deceive, if possible, the chosen ones. [23]But you are to beware. I have told you all things beforehand."*

It is in this section of Jesus' discourse on the destruction of Jerusalem, Ray Stedman notes, that "we come to His answer to the question of the disciples regarding signs. They asked, 'Tell us, when will these things happen? And what will be the sign that they are all about to be fulfilled?' The Lord puts His answer into a single brief phrase: 'When you see "the abomination that causes desolation" standing where it does not belong—let the reader understand—then let those who are in Judea flee to the mountains' (Mark 13:14)" (Stedman, *Ruler Who Serves*, p. 173).

Stedman labels the events foreshadowed in Mark 13:6-13 as "non-signs," since Jesus plainly stated that they were "the beginning of the birth-pangs" and that they must take place, "but the end is not yet" (verses 8, 7, RSV; Stedman, *Ruler Who Serves*, pp. 166-173). With verse 14 and the "abomination of desolation" (verse 14), however, we have a quite concrete event that demands a response.

The only problem is that scholars have not been able to agree on the identity of the "abomination of desolation," largely because many give a large place to Antiochus Epiphanes in the fulfillment of the prophecies of the book of Daniel. And it is in that Old Testament book that we first find the phrase (see Dan. 9:27; 11:31; 12:11). λ

The apocryphal book of 1 Maccabees ties the "abomination of desolation" to Epiphanes, who in B.C. 167 conquered Jerusalem, prohibited Jewish sacrifice, commanded that the observance of Jewish laws should cease, and destroyed copies of the book of the covenant. He also "set up a pagan altar, a desolating sacrilege, on top of the altar of burnt offerings" (Moloney, p. 259; Freedman, vol. 1, p. 270). The ultimate offense was the sacrifice of a pig within the Temple precincts (see 1 Macc. 1:54-59; 6:7). The majority of prophetic interpreters in recent times have followed 1 Maccabees in giving Antiochus Epiphanes a major role in Daniel's prophecies.

But not all have agreed with that interpretation. Josephus, the first century Jewish historian, for example, did not believe that Epiphanes' desecration had exhausted the prophecy. After noting Epiphanes' place in history in relation to the ideas in Daniel, Josephus goes on to write that "in the very same manner Daniel also wrote concerning the Roman government, and that our country should be made desolate by them" (Josephus, *Antiquities*, 10.11.7).

Luke's rendering of the parallel passage to Mark 13:14 also applies the prophecy to Rome: "But when you see Jerusalem surrounded by armies, then know that its desolation has come near. Then let those who are in Judea flee to the mountains, and let those who are inside the city depart, and let not those who are out in the country enter it; for these are days of vengeance, to fulfil all that is written. Alas for those who are with child and for those who give suck in those days! For great distress shall be upon the earth and wrath upon this people; they will fall by the edge of the sword, and be led captive among all nations; and Jerusalem will be trodden down by the Gentiles, until the times of the Gentiles are fulfilled" (Luke 21:20-24, RSV). The identifying of Mark's "abomination of desolation" with Rome by Luke also best fits the prophecy of Daniel 9:24-27.

The early Christians in Jerusalem also interpreted Mark 13:14 as applying to Rome during the Jewish war with Rome that lasted from 66-70 A.D. In fact, the course of events allowed Christians to heed Jesus warnings to flee Jerusalem when they saw it surrounded by Roman armies (Luke 21:20, 21), when the "abomination of desolation" was "set up where it should not be" (Mark 13:14).

In August of 66 A.D., Cestius (Rome's legate in Syria) attacked Jerusalem and then withdrew for some unknown reason, even though victory seemed within his grasp. Then in 67 and 68 Vespasian subdued Galilee and Judea, but delayed the siege of Jerusalem because of Emperor Nero's death. It was not until the spring and summer of A.D. 70 that Vespasian's son Titus besieged and destroyed Jerusalem. Sometime in the interval between the trouble of A.D. 66 and the destruction of A.D. 70, Eusebius (A.D. 263-339) tells us, "the members of the Jerusalem church, by means of an oracle given by revelation to acceptable persons there, were ordered to leave the City before the war began [in earnest] and settle in a town in Perea called Pella. To Pella those who believed in Christ migrated from Jerusalem" (Eusebius, *History*, 3.5.3).

Thus the Christians, following the warning of Christ in Mark 13:14 and the unnamed prophet noted by Eusebius, fled the city and avoided its destruction. And a mighty devastation it was. Jesus tells us that not one stone would remain upon another (13:2), and Josephus described the destruction as complete after "Caesar gave orders that they should now demolish the entire city and the temple" (Josephus, *Wars*, 7.1.1). Josephus depicted the almost unimaginable hardships during the final six-month siege. Not only did he claim that more than a million Jews died, but also that the Romans took nearly 100,000 more captive. The famine was so bad that a mother reportedly slew, roasted, and ate her own child (see *ibid.*, 6.3.4; also Matt. 24:21).

The final destruction of the city, including the Temple complex, brought to a fulfillment Christ's prediction of Mark 13:2. Even if Josephus' statistics were inflated, the destruction was massive. It is from that catastrophe that those Christians who heeded Jesus' words in Mark 13 escaped. He had been quite specific on the need for haste in fleeing during their window of opportunity, telling those who were resting and getting fresh air on the roof of their homes not even to go in to gather up their belongings. As William Lane points out, "at the critical moment a concern for life takes precedence over possessions" (Lane, p. 470). Haste and single-mindedness undergirded Jesus' warning (Mark 13:15, 16). He also expressed concern for those who would be slowed in fleeing by both pregnancy and the need to care for infants (verse 17). And beyond that He commanded that they should pray that their flight would not be in winter when travel conditions would be especially difficult (verse 18).

In verses 19 and 20 Jesus described the terrible time of trouble that would take place during those times. And in verses 21 and 22 He again warned of false Messiahs who would lead them astray.

When He described in verse 19 the terrible time of affliction that would accompany the fall of Jerusalem, Jesus virtually cited Daniel 12:1: "And there shall be a time of trouble, such as never has been since there was a nation till that time; but at that time your people shall be delivered, every one whose name shall be found written in the book" (RSV).

While the words of Mark 13:19, 20 and Daniel 12:1 certainly reflected the brutal realities of the destruction of Jerusalem, their context in Daniel is in the events at the end of time, when Michael arises "and many of those who sleep in the dust of the earth shall awake, some to everlasting life" (verses 1, 2). By using that quotation Jesus shifts the discussion and expands it to topics related to His second coming. That focal point dominates the rest of the chapter, becoming most explicit in Mark 13:26, 27, which picture Jesus returning in the clouds of heaven.

With that thought in mind, the sign of Jerusalem in verse 14 becomes a historical object lesson for those Christians who live in the time of the Second Advent. Both the destruction of Jerusalem and the salvation of Christians from that catastrophe have meaning for the second coming of Jesus and the end of the world. In the context of Mark 13 they function as types of the final destruction of the world and the ultimate salvation of those who believe in Jesus. Ellen White summarizes that position nicely when she writes that "the Saviour's prophecy concerning the visitation of judgments upon Jerusalem is to have another fulfillment, of which that terrible desolation was but a faint shadow. In the fate of the chosen city we may behold the doom of a world that has rejected God's mercy. . . . But in that day, as in the time of Jerusalem's destruction, God's people will be delivered" (White, *The Great Controversy,* pp. 36, 37).

50. A Lesson on the Second Advent

Mark 13:24-37

²⁴"But in those days, after the affliction, the sun will be darkened, and the moon will not give its light, ²⁵and the stars will be falling from heaven, and the powers in the heavens will be shaken. ²⁶Then you will see the Son

of Man coming in clouds with much power and glory. *[27]And then He will send the angels and He will gather His chosen from the four winds, from the ends of the earth to the ends of heaven.*

[28]"From the fig tree learn the lesson: by the time its branch has become tender and it puts forth leaves, you know that summer is near. [29]So also, when you see these things happening, know that He is near, at the gates. [30]Truly I say to you that this generation will certainly not pass away until all these things happen. [31]Heaven and earth will pass away, but My words will certainly not pass away.

[32]"But of that day or hour no one knows, neither the angels in heaven nor the Son, only the Father. [33]Be on guard, keep watch. For you do not know when the time is coming. [34]It is like a man having left his house on a journey, having given his slaves authority, to each his work, and having commanded the doorkeeper to watch. [35]You therefore are to watch—for you do not know when the master of the house will come, whether late in the day, or midnight, or at the cock crowing, or early in the day—[36]lest coming suddenly he finds you sleeping. [37]And what I say to you I say to everyone, 'Watch.'"

✗

In Mark 13:24-37 Jesus has some remarkable things to say about Himself. First, that He would return to earth in the "clouds with much power and glory." "What remarkable irony this is," James Edwards writes, "coming from a man who has predicted his humiliation and death (8:31; 9:31; 10:33-34) and who even now is preparing for his shameful treatment at the hands of Jews and Romans alike. He who will be crucified as a common criminal (Phil. 2:8) will come 'with great power and glory'" (Edwards, p. 403).

The picture of Jesus as the Son of Man (Mark 13:26) has its origin in the Old Testament book of Daniel. Chapter 7 pictures "one like a son of man" arriving "with the clouds of heaven" (verse 13, RSV). But, William Lane points out, the scene is different in Mark than it is in Daniel. "The Son of Man," Lane writes, "is not, as in Daniel, brought to God's throne. . . . Instead he comes to gather together the scattered people of God" (Lane p. 476). Thus whereas the symbolism is the same in Mark as in Daniel, the scenes are different. In Daniel the "one like a son of man" is brought to the Father during the pre-Advent judgment. It is at that time that "the court sat in judgment, and the books were opened" (Dan. 7:11), that "judgment was given for [i.e., on behalf of] the saints of the Most High" (verse 22). It is only after the judgment in Daniel 7 that the way opens for

God's children to receive the heavenly kingdom (see verse 27).

It is in the context of Daniel 7:27's giving of the heavenly kingdom to God's children that Mark places the "Son of Man coming in clouds with much power and glory" (Mark 13:26). Thus at the Second Advent Jesus will "gather His chosen from the four winds, from the ends of the earth" (verse 27). That is the second striking thing in Mark 13:24-37 that Jesus has to say about Himself. It is especially remarkable because in the Old Testament God is the one who gathers together the scattered people of His covenant (see Deut. 30:3, 4; Ps. 50:3-5; Isa. 43:6; Jer. 32:37; Eze. 34:13; 36:24). Once again we find Jesus claiming the prerogatives of God for Himself. And once again we see His self-consciousness of divinity breaking through.

But His comment about the assembling of His people from the ends of the earth at the Second Advent is not only a theological statement, it is also a firm promise. It is an assurance that has encouraged Christians down through the ages. No matter where we are, no matter how insignificant we may seem, Jesus will not forget us in that great day. He will "gather His chosen from the four winds, from the ends of the earth" (Mark 13:27).

The third great claim Jesus made in Mark 13:24-37 is that "heaven and earth will pass away, but My words will certainly not pass away" (verse 31). Once again He echoed the words of divinity. In the Old Testament it was the things of God that didn't pass away in a world of transience (see Isa. 51:6).

Within the context of those three great claims we come to Jesus' comment that "of that day or hour no one knows, neither the angels in heaven or the Son, only the Father" (Mark 13:32). Here we truly have a paradox. In the only place in Mark's Gospel where Jesus explicitly refers to Himself as "the Son" we find Him acknowledging His limitation and ignorance. In the Trinity the Father and the Son may have equality, they may both have the attributes of God, but they are different divine Persons. They have individuality. The Father knows some things that Jesus does not know, just as there are things that Jesus has experienced that the Father hasn't (e.g., being incarnated with the limitations of human flesh).

"The Olivet discourse," Edwards points out, "concludes on a note of mystery. When one reviews chap. 13 as a whole, this may seem disappointing, for the discourse began with a request for a sign (v. 4), that is, for special insight into the future. But we learn in conclusion that knowledge of the End exceeds knowability" (Edwards, p. 406).

And therein is the most important lesson on the Second Advent in Mark 13. Since no person can know the time of the coming, the emphasis is on being ready. By the way, there is probably a good reason why God has not disclosed to human beings the date of the Advent. Just think about it for a moment. If God had told humanity that it would take place at midnight on June 13, 2106, it would have led to 2,000 years of Christian inactivity. My guess is that most people would have waited until the last few days or even hours before they got their house in order. But, knowing human nature, God didn't take that approach. Rather, He through Jesus told us that we would never know the time.

Mark 13's Main Lesson

Mark 13 has some confusing passages, but the main lesson of the chapter is clear—watch, and be a faithful servant while watching, because of a certainty He will come in the clouds of heaven and gather His people from the ends of the earth.

But that isn't all that Jesus told us about that all-important event. In Mark 13:28-37 He provides us with two other pieces of counsel. First, in verse 28 He explains that we need to learn the lesson of the fig tree. "The fig tree is mentioned," Vincent Taylor notes, "because in Palestine, where most trees are evergreens [including the olive and many other leafy trees], the rising of the sap in its branches and the appearance of leaves is a sure sign that winter is past" (Taylor, p. 520). And just as people can determine from the fig tree that spring is near, so can sensitive Christians tell when the predicted event is about to take place.

But people can't learn the lesson of the fig tree unless they are awake. Thus Christ's second great lesson in Mark 13:28-37—watch! That word becomes the key to unlocking both verses 32 through 37 and the major lesson on the Second Advent in Mark 13. Examine the repeated use of watch:

1. verse 33—"Be on guard, keep watch. For you do not know when the time is coming."
2. verse 34—The doorkeeper is commanded "to watch."
3. verse 35—"You therefore are to watch—for you do not know when the master of the house will come."

4. verse 37—"And what I say to you I say to everyone, 'Watch.'"

Jesus leaves not the slightest doubt that watching is absolutely essential in the waiting time. Perhaps that is why in the chapter He talked about such things as wars, earthquakes, and astronomical events that take place in every generation. He knew that the mere mention of such events in the context of His advent would keep people thinking, studying, and watching.

But the careful reader of Mark 13:32-37 has noted that watching is not the only thing that believers need to do. To the contrary, in verse 34 He explicitly teaches that those waiting for His return must be faithful servants. Being faithful servants while we wait and watch sums up the most important lesson that Jesus gave to us regarding the Second Advent.

That disappoints some of us. We are more concerned about the time of the Advent than with being faithful. But Jesus wants us to take our minds off of that emphasis and to live every day in such a way that we will be ready when it takes place.

And how should we act if we discovered that the Second Advent would occur today? John Wesley somewhere put it correctly when he said that if he had such information he would go on doing just what he did every day in preaching God's message and loving God's people.

William Barclay points out the bottom line of the practical lesson of Mark 13. It means "that we must so live that it does not matter when He comes. It gives us the great task in life of making every day fit for Him to see, and being at any moment ready to meet Him face to face. *All life becomes a preparation to meet the King*" (Barclay, *Mark,* p. 337, italics supplied).

51. Contrasting Loyalties

Mark 14:1-11

> *[1]It was now two days before the Passover and the Feast of Unleavened Bread. And the chief priests and the scribes were seeking how to arrest Him by trickery, and kill Him. [2]For they were saying, "Not during the feast, lest there be a disturbance of the people."*
>
> *[3]And while He was in Bethany at the house of Simon the leper, reclining at table, a woman came having an alabaster vial of perfume, pure*

nard, which was expensive. Breaking the alabaster vial, she poured it on His head. ⁴But there were some angrily saying among themselves, "Why has this waste of perfume taken place? ⁵For this perfume could have been sold for more than three hundred denarii and given to the poor." And they reproached her. ⁶But Jesus said, "Leave her alone; why do you cause her trouble? She has done a beautiful work to Me? ⁷For you always have the poor with you, and whenever you want to you can do good for them, but you will not always have Me. ⁸She has done what she could; she has prepared to anoint My body for burial ahead of time. ⁹Truly I say to you, wherever the good news is preached in the entire world, what this woman did will be spoken about in memory of her."

¹⁰And Judas Iscariot, one of the twelve, went to the chief priests in order that he might betray Him to them. ¹¹And they rejoiced when they heard him and promised to give him money. And he sought how he might find an opportunity to betray Him.

Three short paragraphs. But have you noticed their positioning?

In the first we have the religious leaders and theological scholars plotting together on how they might somehow arrest Jesus and put Him to death (Mark 14:1, 2). Mark contrasts their hatred with Mary, a "religious nobody," who gives everything she has to Jesus (verses 3-9). And then there is Judas, one of the 12 chosen disciples, who agrees to betray Jesus for money (verses 10, 11).

With artistry and skill Mark has woven together a picture of contrasting loyalties. He has also told two stories still related "wherever the good news is preached in the entire world" (verse 9). Jesus, of course, made His comment about Mary's offering. But it is no less true of Judas' act. The difference is not in the notoriety of the two incidents, but rather in the fact that one was the story of ultimate love and generosity while the other was the tale of ultimate selfishness. At bottom, however, is a likeness. Both depict ultimate loyalty. The difference between the two is the focal point of that loyalty—Christ versus one's self. Each person who meets Christ even to this day faces that same choice in loyalties. And it is a decision that has no middle ground. Either our supreme loyalty is to our self or to our Lord. "No one," said Jesus on another occasion, "can serve two masters" (Matt. 6:24, RSV).

The setting for our three paragraphs is Passover, a time when hundreds of thousands of pilgrim Jews from all over the world filled Jerusalem.

Passover was a season of year when Jews remembered their miraculous exodus from Egypt. As a result, it was a time when their hopes and minds dwelled not only on deliverance from that ancient foe but also from a contemporary one—Rome. In short, Passover was an occasion when feelings of Jewish nationalism lay right on the surface.

That meant that it was a fearful time for those in responsible positions. For their part, the Romans garrisoned additional troops in Jerusalem. Meanwhile, the Jewish leaders hesitated to move against the troublesome Jesus lest a riot break out and "there be a disturbance of the people" (Mark 14:2). While the minds of the religious leaders should have been on the spiritual meaning of the celebration, they instead focused on eliminating Jesus. How to do so became their problem.

But not everybody was upset with Him. Take Simon the leper, for example. Jesus had probably healed him. If so, the feast he threw was in honor of the Healer. Not one of us wouldn't hold a party for Jesus if He had healed us from that dreaded malady.

And then there was Mary who demonstrated her devotion to Jesus in an extremely extravagant way. Now it wasn't out of the ordinary to anoint a guest's head with a few drops of oil. But Mary's was the most expensive of concentrated perfumes—spikenard, a fragrant oil used by kings and the richest classes. And she just didn't dole out a minimal dab. Rather, she poured out all that she had, perhaps partially in appreciation for the fact that Jesus had recently brought her brother Lazarus back to life (John 12:1, 3).

Mark tells us that her extravagance brought forth more than one evaluation. One was a distinct grumbling about waste and the fact that such an amount of expensive perfume could have been sold and used to help the poor (Mark 14:4, 5). Sounds good, sounds religious. After all, Jesus had a real heart for the poor.

Questions for Everyone

In what ways should we be extravagant in serving Christ? Would I have joined in the grumbling of Mark 14:5?

The second Gospel doesn't tell us how the muttering got started. But John's recounting does. He notes that it was Judas who triggered the dissatisfaction among the other disciples (John 12:4, 5). How wasteful, he claimed, and there was so much need. After all, the perfume was worth 300 denarii or about an entire year's pay for a laborer. The gospels don't portray Judas as being especially concerned with the poor, a fact that seems to have gone unnoticed by the other disciples. His point, in the light of Jesus' ministry, appeared to them as a valid one.

But John in retrospect pulls aside the curtain of Judas' motivation. The disciple, he claims, had no concern for the poor, but he did serve as the group's treasurer and periodically put his hand into their collective purse for his own purposes. In short, "he was a thief" (verse 6, RSV).

If Judas' evaluation of Mary's extravagance was one response, Jesus provides us with a second. He said that she had done a good thing (Mark 14:6). But Jesus didn't merely say that it was a good moral thing that she had done. If so we would have found the Greek word *agathos*. Instead, He employs the word *kalos,* which implies both a moral goodness and "a goodness seen on the outside as it strikes the eye, a beautiful, pleasing goodness" (Wuest, vol. 1, pp. 256, 257). Thus Jesus said, "she has done a *beautiful* work to me" (Mark 14:6). Then He went on to refer to Deuteronomy 15:11: "For the poor will never cease out of the land" (RSV). And lastly, He specifically commended Mary the sister of Lazarus (John 12:3), noting that Christians would never forget her act of devotion (Mark 14:9).

But that explicit commendation of Mary was also an implied condemnation of Judas—and he didn't miss it. The result was that Judas took a giant step forward in his journey toward betraying Jesus.

The story of Mary's extravagance tells us several things. On the one hand, it indicates that love to Jesus should not be stingy. We should not dole it out with an eyedropper. To the contrary, it is giving one's all. Such dedication Jesus evaluates as "beautiful."

The incident also teaches us another important lesson. That is, as we have seen so many times in Mark's Gospel, Jesus has a confidence in His mission and its results that not even the realization of His soon-coming crucifixion can smother. In the relating of Mary's story, He not only claimed that the anointing was for His death but He has confidence that the good news would spread to the ends of the earth (verse 9). Thus He had faith, the same kind of faith that Mark's first readers needed as they also entered into troublesome times, the same faith that we still require in similar circumstances.

But before the resurrection must come the cross. And that takes us back to Judas' betrayal in Mark 14:10, 11. The surprising part of the story is that it wasn't the Jewish leaders who came to Judas but he to them. Matthew tells us that Judas is the one that raised the issue of betrayal money: "What will you give me if I deliver him to you?" They responded with the price of a slave—30 pieces of silver (Matt. 26:15, 16).

Once again we find the issue of money looming up. It fascinated Judas, but if that had been his main motive in betraying Jesus he could have undoubtedly struck a much better bargain. After all, Jesus was worth much more to the Jewish leaders than the price of a mere slave.

So why, we need to ask, did Judas do it? What drove him on in his destructive course of action? Perhaps the best answer involves ambition. That was one thing that he shared with the other disciples. They seem to have constantly bickered about who would be the greatest in the kingdom. Judas appears to have shared that same spirit.

But then we must not forget Jesus. Always talking about dying, He now claimed that Mary had anointed Him for the grave (Mark 14:8). In Judas' mind that wasn't the way things were supposed to work out. Perhaps Jesus needed a bit of the stimulus of being in a tight spot for Him to utilize His magnificent Messianic power. The slow moving Jesus might need to be compelled to start setting up His kingdom. Judas' betrayal would force Jesus' hand.

Of all the explanations for the betrayal, that one seems to best explain all the facts. And it also helps us understand why Judas committed suicide when his plans went wrong (Matt. 27:3-7).

In the end his ambition brought him to the ultimate crisis. As noted above, all the disciples were ambitious. But, J. D. Jones reminds us, "the difference between the eleven and Judas was this, that while in the case of the eleven their love for Christ became stronger than their ambition—in Judas ambition got the better of love" (Jones, vol. 4, p. 50).

And with that thought we return to the issue of our supreme loyalty. Where, we need to ask ourselves, do we stand? Are we with the extravagant Mary, who selflessly gave her all to Jesus, or are we with the selfish Judas who saw Jesus as a tool to serve his own needs? Who has my greatest loyalty—my self or my Lord?

That is not an easy question to answer with genuine honesty, because a Judas lurks within the skin of each of us. Fortunately, there is also a Mary, with her total devotion to Jesus, residing there. As with all cases of loyalty, God gives us each individually the choice of which loyalty focus will surface in our own lives. ⚔

52. The Meaning of the Last Supper

Mark 14:12-31

[12]*On the first day of the Feast of Unleavened Bread, when they sacrificed the Passover lamb, His disciples said to Him, "Where do You want us to go and prepare so that You can eat the Passover?"* [13]*And He sent two of His disciples and said to them, "Go into the city and you will meet a man carrying a jar of water. Follow him,* [14]*and wherever he enters tell the owner of that house, 'The Teacher says, "Where is My guest room where I may eat the Passover with My disciples?"'* [15]*And he will show you a large upstairs room which has been furnished and made ready. Prepare for us there."* [16]*And the disciples went out and came into the city and found things just as He had told them, and they prepared the Passover.*

[17]*When evening arrived He came with the twelve.* [18]*As they were reclining and eating, Jesus said, "Truly I say to you that one of you eating with Me will betray Me."* [19]*They began to grieve and to say to Him one by one, "Surely it is not I?"* [20]*And He said to them, "It is one of the twelve, the one dipping with Me into the bowl.* [21]*For the Son of Man goes just as it has been written concerning Him, but woe to that man through whom the Son of Man is betrayed. It would have been better for that man if he had not been born."*

[22]*And while they were eating, He took bread, and having blessed it, broke it and gave it to them, saying, "Take, this is My body."* [23]*And taking a cup, after giving thanks, He gave it to them and everyone drank of it.* [24]*And He said to them, "This is My blood of the covenant, which is being poured out for many.* [25]*Truly I say to you that I will by no means drink of the fruit of the vine until that day when I drink it new in the kingdom of God."*

[26]*After singing a hymn they went out to the Mount of Olives.* [27]*And Jesus said to them, "Everyone of you will fall away, for it has been written, 'I will strike down the shepherd, and the sheep will be scattered.'* [28]*But after I am raised I will go before you into Galilee.* [29]*But Peter said to Him, "Even if everyone falls away, yet I will not."* [30]*And Jesus said to him, "Truly I say to you, that this very night, before a rooster crows twice, you*

will deny Me three times." ³¹But with great emphasis he said, "Even if it is necessary for me to die for You, I will never deny You." And they all spoke similarly. ⅄

Jesus has been moving toward the cross ever since Mark 8:31, in which He first told His disciples about His coming death. Events since His triumphal entry into Jerusalem in Mark 11 have begun to accelerate. Judas has already made his decision to betray Jesus (14:10, 11), and, as we saw in Mark 14:3-11, the issue of loyalty to Jesus has become central to Mark's plot. That theme will carry over into verses 12-31 as each of the disciples had to face it—at least at the intellectual level.

Mark 14:12-31 has four scenes. The first and the third deal with the Passover, while the second and the fourth treat the topic of betrayal. The time frame for the entire passage is Thursday evening, Nisan 14, which, according to Jewish reckoning, began at sundown. The Temple priests would offer the sacrificial lambs on the same date, that is on Friday afternoon (see Ex. 12:6; Martin, *Where the Action Is,* pp. 126, 127). Thus even though Jesus and the disciples will be eating a Passover meal, they will be doing so a day earlier than most people (see John 13:1; 18:28; 19:14). That earlier time was necessary since Jesus would be dead by Friday evening.

The early Passover explains why we find no mention of the lamb at the Last Supper, whereas the other parts of the meal were all in place. As a result, Jesus equated His sacrifice with bread rather than a lamb during His last supper with the disciples (Mark 14:22).

The fact that Jesus died at the Passover was no accident. It was in God's plan from the beginning. The Passover itself finds its roots at the time of the Exodus from Egypt. God instituted it to commemorate the night of the Israelites' escape from Egypt, when all the first-born of the Egyptians perished. Each family group was to slay a lamb on the fourteenth of the month and sprinkle the blood on the doorposts as a sign that the house should be passed over when sudden death invaded the homes of the Egyptians. The sprinkled blood would preserve the inhabitants of the house. And so it was that the blood of the Passover lamb spared God's people (Ex. 12).

The New Testament views the Passover as symbolic of the work of Jesus. It is no mere coincidence, for example, that the Passover lambs were slain in the Temple on Friday afternoon, the very time that Jesus also died. That timing is important, since, as Paul puts it, Jesus is "a Passover lamb sacrificed for us" (1 Cor. 5:7, Phillips). John the Baptist picked up on that same general symbolism when he pointed Jesus out as "the Lamb of God, who takes away the sin of the world" (John 1:29, RSV).

J. C. Ryle argues that "the *intentional connection between the time of the Jewish passover and the time of Christ's death"* is of great importance. "We cannot doubt for a moment that it was not by chance, but by God's providential appointment, that our Lord was crucified in the passover week, and on the very day that the passover lamb was slain. It was meant to draw the attention of the Jewish nation to Him as the true Lamb of God. It was meant to bring to their minds the true object and purpose of His death. . . .

"Did the passover remind the Jew of the marvellous deliverance of his forefathers out of the land of Egypt, when God slew the first-born? No doubt it did. But it was also meant to be a sign to him of the far greater redemption and deliverance from the bondage of sin, which was to be brought in by our Lord Jesus Christ" (Ryle, pp. 303, 304).

Jesus Himself saw His coming death in that redemptive light when He instituted what Christian's call the "Lord's Supper" to take the place of the Passover. With Jesus the genuine Lamb of God had arrived. The sacrifice of the many lambs had met fulfillment in Him who would die "once for all" (Heb. 9:26; 10:10, 12, 14). Or, as Peter would later put it, "Christ also died for sins once for all, the righteous for the unrighteous, that he might bring us to God" (1 Peter 3:18, RSV).

Peter in that verse captured the meaning of Jesus when He said, "This is My blood of the covenant, which is being poured out for many" (Mark 14:24). The "for many" appears to be an echo of Isaiah 53:11, 12: "The righteous one, my servant, [will] make *many* to be accounted righteous, and he shall bear their iniquities. . . . Because he poured out his soul to death, and was numbered with the transgressors; yet he bore the sin of *many,* and makes intercession for the transgressors" (ESV).

"Whatever else the disciples may . . . have understood," R. T. France writes, "they cannot miss the essential point that Jesus is enacting before them his own death. Even if they have not yet taken his prediction seriously, there can now be no doubt that he has meant what he has said. His body is about to be broken and his blood poured out. The bread and wine are thus symbols of death" (France, *Mark,* Doubleday, p. 182; France, *Mark,* NIGTC, p. 571).

It is in the context of His forthcoming substitutionary death that Jesus introduced the topic of the loyalty of His disciples. He did so in two stages. First, in Mark 14:17-21 He pointed out that it would be one of the Twelve who betrayed Him, indicating once again that Jesus was not a pawn of history but had control of His own destiny. The shock of that claim hit the disciples hard, with each one, including Judas, asking "Is it I?" (Matt. 26:25, RSV). It is significant that no one inquired "Is it Judas?" He must have covered his tracks quite well.

Jesus only explained that it was someone eating with Him, one of the Twelve. Jesus, of course, knew who it was. Yet He did nothing to stop him. "If," suggests France, "he had identified the traitor, no doubt Peter and the others would have made sure that Judas did not leave the room to go about his deadly business. By not identifying Judas, Jesus, not for the only time, deliberately lets slip an opportunity to prevent the course of events that will bring him to the cross. This is what he has come to Jerusalem for, and he will not now try to avoid it" (France, *Mark,* Doubleday, p. 181).

The second step in Jesus' treatment of the disciples' loyalty appears in Mark 14:26-31. Here He went beyond the fact that one disciple would betray Him to the equally devastating idea that all of them would forsake Him, citing Zechariah 13:7 as evidence. While He had no doubt as to their genuine loyalty to Him, He now dealt with the steadfastness of that loyalty. It is an unfortunate fact of life that we as humans do not fully understand ourselves until we find ourselves under pressure. So it was with the Twelve.

With such predictions as Jesus made about the disciples, it seems that He could have taken a defeatist attitude. But that was not the case. Jesus based His confidence upon His faith in the Father and not on His feelings or even His knowledge of what would soon transpire.

When all is said and done, it is the faith of Jesus that has the final word. It shines through in two places in particular. First, in verse 25 where He says, "Truly I say to you that I will by no means drink of the fruit of the vine *until that day* when I drink it new *in the kingdom* of God." No matter how bad things looked, He had no doubt of ultimate victory. Verse 25 is probably an allusion to the great messianic banquet that the Jews looked forward to in the future. Jesus echoed that anticipation in Matthew 8:11, in which He noted that "many will come from east and west and sit at table with Abraham, Isaac, and Jacob in the kingdom of heaven" (RSV). Revelation 19:9 refers to that same meal as the "marriage supper of the Lamb" (RSV).

Looking Beyond the Crisis

Jesus "ended the Supper which commemorated His dying with a confident anticipation of His triumph. The morrow, when the Cross was reared, looked like the triumph of evil. But with calm and unruffled confidence Christ looked beyond the black to-morrow and foresaw the triumph of the Kingdom of God" (Jones, vol. 4, p. 101).

Paul caught that message when he wrote, "As often as you eat this bread and drink this cup, you proclaim the Lord's death until he comes" (1 Cor. 10:26, RSV).

Jesus' second great statement of faith in the face of disaster among His disciples occurred in Mark 14:28, in which He told them, "But after I am *raised* I will go before *you* into Galilee." It comes as no surprise that Jesus never doubted His resurrection. But wonder of wonders, He told His disciples that He would meet with them at that time. That is grace. That is a promise worth remembering for each of us when we have ourselves betrayed Jesus. He did not reject them but continued to work with them in spite of themselves. No wonder Scripture calls the message of Jesus the "Good News."

53. Jesus Also Struggled With His Will

Mark 14:32-42
> ³²They came to a place named Gethsemane, and He said to His disciples, "Sit here while I pray." ³³And He took Peter and James and John with Him, and He began to be distressed and greatly troubled. ³⁴And He said to them, "My soul is grieved even to death. Remain here and stay awake." ³⁵And going a little farther He fell on the ground and prayed that

if it were possible the hour might pass away from Him. ³⁶And He said, "Abba, Father, all things are possible for You. Take this cup from Me. Yet not what I will, but what You will." ³⁷And He came and found them sleeping. He said to Simon Peter, "Are you asleep? Were you not strong enough to stay awake one hour? ³⁸Watch and pray, that you may not enter into temptation. Indeed, the spirit is eager but the flesh is weak." ³⁹Again He went away and prayed, saying the same prayer. ⁴⁰And He again came and found them sleeping, for their eyes had become heavy; and they did not know what they should answer Him. ⁴¹And He came a third time and said to them, "Sleep now and rest. It is enough. The hour has come. Behold the Son of Man is betrayed into the hands of sinners. ⁴²Get up, let us go. Behold My betrayer is drawing near."

The Gethsemane passage in a sense carries on the theme of loyalty raised in Mark 14:1-12 and continued on in verses 17-21, except this time it is the faithfulness of Jesus versus the unfaithfulness of the disciples.

Douglas Hare points out that the Gethsemane story is an important witness to the humanity of Jesus. "Here we see that Jesus was not God's robot, moving without question or emotion toward his death on the cross," that the cross "requires the willing cooperation of the human Jesus." Beyond that, "Jesus struggles with the possibility that he may resist the will of God. His obedience, like ours, is not automatic!" (Hare, p. 193).

Even though Jesus may have known the future, that does not mean that He had no choices to make regarding the bringing about of that future. Just as Caiaphas and Judas had to make their decisions about the part they would play in the final events of Jesus' life, so He also had to make a choice. He could still back out. The cross was not inevitable. He could yet walk away. Jesus had yet to make His final decision to go through with the most excruciating part of the plan of salvation. That is the significance of His struggle in Gethsemane.

After the seemingly calm manner in which Jesus had spoken repeatedly of the fate that awaited Him in Jerusalem, it is surprising to witness His agony as the prospect becomes more real. The very words that Mark used are poignant with emotion. The Greek word in Mark 14:33 that I have translated "distressed" "here denotes a being in the grip of a shuddering horror in the face of the dreadful prospect before him." And the word translated as "greatly troubled" "denotes here 'an anxiety from which there was no escaping and in which He saw no help and no comfort'" (Cranfield, p. 431). As Karl Barth points out, Jesus had withstood Satan all His life, "but it was one thing to enter and continue on this way, it was another to tread it to the end, and in this world its necessarily bitter end" (Barth, vol. 4, pt. 1, p. 266).

The time for the final decision had arrived. And Jesus was "grieved even to death" (Mark 14:34). But what was it that so greatly troubled Him? Many writers have recognized a sharp contrast between Jesus' fear of His impending death on the cross and the reaction of other famous martyrs down through history.

Not only did such ancients as Socrates, believing they had nothing to fear from death, face the ends of their lives with calmness, but Christian martyrs also encountered death serenely, and even ecstatically at times. For example, when Polycarp (c. A.D. 69-155), the second-century bishop of Smyrna, faced the proconsul who would soon take his life, he told his prosecutor to get on with the job. A letter written soon after his martyrdom in A.D. 155 or 156 tells us that as he approached his death "he was inspired with courage and joy, and his face was filled with grace, so that not only did he not collapse in fright at the things which were said to him," but he expressed a joyful reaction (*The Martyrdom of Polycarp*, 12). Such has been the experience of many martyrs down through history. Knowing they were right with God, they have had no fear of death.

And then there was Jesus! The many tranquil deaths in history force us to ask why Jesus so fearfully anticipated His. Clearly it does not involve a lack of faith, a love of earthly life, or a fear of pain, given what we know about Him.

The answer seems to lie in another direction. Ben Witherington finds "two clues. . . , one here and one at the scene of the cross," when "Jesus speaks of being God-forsaken [Mark 15:34]" (Witherington, p. 379). The one in Mark 14 has to do with the nature of the "cup" He had to drink (verse 36). The Old Testament associates the "cup" with the wrath (or judgment) of God (Isa. 51:17; Eze. 23:33, 34). Jesus' cup, John Stott points out, "symbolized neither the physical pain of being flogged and crucified, nor the mental distress of being despised and rejected . . . , but rather the spiritual agony of bearing the sins of the world, in other words, of enduring the divine judgment which those sins deserved" (Stott, p. 76). His apprehensiveness of the cross results from the fact that on it He will drink for all humanity the cup of God's judgment against sin.

Jesus' dread in Gethsemane stems from His realization of the divine hatred of sin. It is almost unbearable to Him that He must become "a curse for us" and become "sin" in God's eyes (Gal. 3:13; 2 Cor. 5:21, RSV). "He felt that by sin," Ellen White penned, "He was being separated from His Father. The gulf was so broad, so black, so deep, that His spirit shuddered before it. This agony He must not exert His divine power to escape. As man He must suffer the consequences of man's sin. As man He must endure the wrath of God against transgression" (White, *The Desire of Ages,* p. 686).

In Gethsemane the moment of decision had come. Jesus must either move forward to the cross or give up His mission. The tempter, of course, still lurked at His side, pointing out that His closest friends couldn't even stay awake to support Him (Mark 14:37, 40, 41), one of His disciples is at that very moment on the way to betray Him (verse 43), and the ungrateful people He will die for would soon crucify Him (15:21-32).

Jesus had come to His most trying hour. Fighting the temptation to do His own will and back off from the cross, He endured duress in Gethsemane that we can understand only faintly. In great agony and dread He finally made His decision: "Not what I will, but what You will" (14:37). But that initial victory was tenuous at best. Twice more He recommitted Himself to the doing of God's will (verses 39, 41) before He obtained the peace He so much needed.

The decision finally made, Jesus, exuding a calmness missing throughout His garden experience, goes back to His disciples. His decision to go forward to the cross irrevocably made, He awakened them, announcing that "the hour has come" and that His "betrayer is drawing near" (verses 41, 42).

And what about the disciples? And what about Peter who had recently sworn that he would even die with Jesus?

They had had a good (and perhaps a needed) rest, but their hearts and wills were not prepared for what was even then bursting upon them. In a short time they would all flee (verse 50), thereby deserting the captured Jesus just as they had the praying Jesus.

They weren't bad men—just unprepared men. As Jesus put it, "the spirit is eager but the flesh is weak" (verse 38). Torn between good and evil and being unprepared, they opted for the latter when the pressure was on.

Alexander MacLaren makes the interesting suggestion that "I have little doubt that if the Roman soldiers had called on Peter to have made good his boast, and to give up his life to rescue His Master, he would have been ready to do it. We know that he was ready to fight for Him, and in fact did draw a sword and offer resistance. He could die for Him, but He could not keep awake for Him" (MacLaren, *IX to XVI,* p. 201).

That is a provocative suggestion that holds some truth. Many of us in the heat of battle could (perhaps) do a great thing for God, but we have a difficult time in day to day living for Him in the common things of life. Yet it is the ordinary things, such as prayer and living the life of a surrendered will, that genuinely prepare each of us for the greater things. That was certainly true in Peter's case. He could in a flash of reaction whip out his sword (Mark 14:47), but a little time would send him scampering into the dark with the rest of the disciples (verse 50) and would eventually lead him to repeatedly swear that he was no disciple of Jesus (verses 66-72).

Perhaps things would have been different if Peter could have stayed awake in prayer. Perhaps his story would have taken a different course if he had realized that it is the less glamorous parts of our Christian lives that consistently prepare us for the more threatening ones.

54. Kissing Has More Than One Meaning

Mark 14:43-52
   ⁴³And immediately, while He was speaking, Judas (one of the twelve) arrived, and with him a crowd with swords and clubs, who were from the chief priests and the scribes and the elders. ⁴⁴Now the one who was betraying Him had given them a signal, saying, "The one I kiss, He is the one; arrest Him and lead Him away under guard." ⁴⁵And coming, Judas immediately approached Him, saying, "Rabbi," and he kissed Him. ⁴⁶And they laid their hands on Him and arrested Him. ⁴⁷But one of those standing by drew his sword and struck the slave of the high priest and cut off his ear. ⁴⁸And Jesus said to them, "Do you come out against Me as a thief, with swords and clubs to arrest Me? ⁴⁹Every day I was with you in the Temple teaching, and you did not arrest Me. But this is done so that the

Scriptures might be fulfilled." ⁵⁰*And they all left Him and fled.*
⁵¹And a young man followed Him, being clothed with only a linen gar-
ment over his naked body, and they seized him, *⁵²but he fled naked, leav-*
ing behind the linen garment.

The characters are all in place for Jesus' betrayal. First, we find Judas, positioned at last to complete the treachery that he had been working
toward since Mark 14:11. He had decided on the place and the procedure
of the betrayal. But one last detail remained crucial to the plan. In the confusion it was important that they arrest the right man. After all, there were
12 of them and in the shadows of the olive grove it would be easy to make
a mistake.

To Judas the solution was a simple one. He would do what he had
done so many times before—he would greet Jesus with a word of homage
and kiss Him on the forehead, a sign of honor to a respected Rabbi. In the
process, Judas turned the meaning of the affectionate kiss and the word of
respect on their head. Or as Halford Luccock puts it, he added "the last refinement of treachery" (Luccock, p. 885).

The description of the kiss is itself of interest. Mark 14:44 utilizes the
usual word *phileō,* which means to love or to kiss. But verse 45, in which
Judas actually gives the kiss, employs an enriched and intensified word—
kataphileō. The prefix *kata* transforms the kiss from meaning just any old
kiss to a special one. It means to " 'kiss warmly,' 'kiss affectionately' "
(Bratcher, p. 456). It is the type of kiss persons give to their beloved, special one—a kiss exchanged between two lovers. The compound word,
C.E.B. Cranfield suggests, "perhaps indicates a prolonged kissing designed
to give all the *ochlos* [crowd] a chance to see which person is to be seized
and to be ready to seize him at once" (Cranfield, p. 437).

Judas performed the ultimate in the reversal of word meanings when
he used the Greek word and action for love and affection as the sign of betrayal. Entering the garden that night with a twisted meaning, he left it a
contorted and tortured soul, apparently slinking off into the shadows after
his final act.

Mark has no more to say about Judas. Matthew tells of his disillusion-
ment and suicide (Matt. 27:3-10).

The second element in the list of characters that evening is the crowd sent out by the Sanhedrin ("the chief priests and the scribes and the elders" [Mark 14:43] being the three groups that made up the highest Jewish ruling body). Mark doesn't tell us much about the crowd except who sent it and that it came with swords and clubs. But John explains that Judas procured a cohort of soldiers captained by a tribune (18:3, 12). Such a unit would normally contain 600 men, although the number could have been fewer (see Barrett, p. 433). At any rate, it was a large force to capture one man.

And then we must not forget the disciples. One of them at first decided to put up a fight. Taking his sword he cut off the ear of a servant of the high priest (Mark 14:47). That is one man who probably never forgot that night, especially since Jesus performed His last recorded miracle by restoring his ear to him (Luke 22:51). One can only wonder if the healed man ever experienced the fuller healing of his soul. There is a good indication that he did, since the Gospel of John tells us that his name was Malchus (John 18:10). It is possible that John knew his name because he had later become a part of the infant church in Jerusalem and had shared his testimony with fellow believers.

Mark doesn't identify which of the disciples wielded the sword. But once again John does. It was the impetuous Peter (18:10), acting quite like his normal self. That is, responding without first thinking through the consequences. But then maybe he expected Jesus to follow his lead and take the opportunity to begin His role as a conquering Messiah on the order of King David. After all, the disciples still expected that scenario to play out. They just didn't know when. Because of that expectation it may be that all the disciples would have stood and fought if Jesus would have exhibited the awesome powers He had used earlier in His ministry against the forces of nature and disease. They had no doubt as to His ability to take control of matters if He so desired. In fact, they had even seen a flash of that power when, according to John, the crowd "drew back and fell to the ground" (John 18:6, RSV).

But Jesus didn't resort to His power. Instead, He allowed the mob to take Him captive. That was too much for the bewildered disciples. Any hope they may have still entertained collapsed, and "they all left Him and fled" (Mark 14:50).

Jesus, of course, is the central character in the scene. And He appeared to be completely at peace. In fact, rather than seeking to avoid Judas and the crowd, He went out to meet them (Mark 14:42). He even accepted Judas' loathsome kiss, making no effort to push him away. And He meekly submitted in the spirit of Isaiah 53 as they arrested Him, even though, as He told Peter, He could have summoned 12 legions of angels (Matt. 26:53; a Roman legion consisted of about 6,000 foot soldiers and 700 horsemen). Furthermore, He even restored the ear of the injured servant (Luke 22:51), demonstrating that He was following His own counsel to "love your enemies and pray for those who persecute you" (Matt. 5:44, RSV).

> J. C. Ryle sees a lesson in the fleeing disciples. "Let us learn," he writes, "to be charitable in our judgment of other Christians. Let us not expect too much from them, or set them down as having no grace at all, if we see them overtaken in a fault. Let us not forget that even our Lord's chosen apostles forsook Him in His time of need. Yet they rose again by repentance, and became pillars of the Church of Christ" (Ryle, p. 324).

And how, you may be thinking, *could Jesus be so calm when just a short time before He had been in agony in the Garden of Gethsemane because of what would soon befall Him?* The answer is that in Gethsemane He had finally and totally surrendered His will to that of the Father. He can now have peace in His hour of crisis because He knows He is doing what God expected of Him.

Each of us can have the peace that comes with the surrender of our will. But to surrender is a struggle. It is at that very point that the satanic conflict within ourselves is at its fiercest (see White, *Steps to Christ,* p. 43). And it is only through surrender that we can obtain the peace that Christ had as He passed through life's crises.

We find one final character in the cast present at Jesus' arrest—the young man wearing the linen garment who manages to barely escape, leaving his garment in the hands of the mob (Mark 14:51, 52).

We need to ask ourselves why those verses even appear in Mark's Gospel. All the gospel writers tell the story of the arrest but only Mark contains these two cryptic verses. While Mark omits many important details in the events surrounding Jesus' arrest in the apparent interest of brevity, he still takes time to tell us this trivial bit of information.

It in no way affects the course of events. The only reason for its inclusion is that it must have been of special interest to Mark himself. Robert Gundry points out that the young man "has often been identified with John Mark" (Gundry, p. 861). If so, it may be Mark's way of saying, "I was there" to his readers in the anonymous manner of the Apostle John, who used such phrases as the "disciple whom Jesus loved" and "that other disciple" to identify himself in the Fourth Gospel (John 21:7, 20; 18:15, 16; 20:2-4, 8, KJV).

And some biblical data supports the conclusion that Mark was the young man of verses 51 and 52. Acts 12:12, for example, indicates that the meeting place of the Jerusalem church was in the home of Mary, John Mark's mother. If that is so, it is a possibility that the upstairs room in which Jesus and the disciples ate the last supper was a part of Mark's home. Should that line of logic be true, then it may be that John Mark slipped out of bed and followed Jesus and the 11 disciples out to Gethsemane and was only discovered lurking in the shadows at the arrest. Absolute identification of the young man of verses 51 and 52 is impossible, but some such scenario is the only logical explanation as to why the generally parsimonious Mark took the trouble to add those verses.

Whoever he was, he was an eyewitness. But he was one who fled. James Edwards suggests that the very "lack of identity" of the young man "invites readers to examine their own readiness to abandon Jesus" in a time of crisis (Edwards, p. 441). With that challenging thought we will move to Jesus' trial before Caiaphas. ✗

55. Jesus Under Trial

Mark 14:53-65

⁵³And they led Jesus to the high priest, and all the chief priests and the elders and the scribes gathered together. ⁵⁴Peter followed Him from a distance, right into the courtyard of the high priest, and he was sitting with the guards and warming himself near the fire. ⁵⁵Now the chief priests and the entire council were seeking a witness against Jesus so that they might put Him to death, but they found none. ⁵⁶For many testified falsely against Him, but their testimonies were inconsistent. ⁵⁷Some stood and testified falsely against Him, saying, ⁵⁸"We heard Him say, 'I will destroy this temple made with hands and after three days I will build another not made with hands.'" ⁵⁹Yet even then their testimony was not consistent. ⁶⁰And the high priest stood up in the midst and questioned Jesus, saying, "Have You no answer for what these men are testifying against You?" ⁶¹But He was silent and did not answer anything. Again the high priest questioned Him, saying to Him, "Are You the Christ, the Son of the Blessed One?" ⁶²And Jesus said, "I am; and you will see the Son of Man sitting at the right hand of power and coming with the clouds of heaven." ⁶³The high priest tore his clothes, saying, "What further need do we have of witnesses? ⁶⁴You heard the blasphemy. How does it seem to you?" And they all condemned Him to be deserving of death. ⁶⁵And some began to spit on Him and to cover His face and to strike Him, saying to Him, "Prophesy!" And the guards received Him with blows.

The Jewish leaders at last have Jesus where they want Him, and they lose no time in their work. Their first task is to formulate a charge that will stick. For that purpose a portion of the Sanhedrin met at the home of Caiaphas the high priest.

Unfortunately for them, there would have to be a two-phase trial. The first stage was the ecclesiastical trial, when the leaders of His own people would judge Jesus. That would have been enough in many cases, but the Jews were seeking the death penalty, which the Romans had reserved to themselves.

By and large the Roman government allowed a great deal of local rule among conquered and subject peoples. They were especially generous in the matter of religion. The basic policy of Rome was not to interfere with local religion so long as it did not menace imperial power. Thus rather than destroying the Jewish Sanhedrin, the Romans utilized it to help maintain control in Judea. As a result, the Sanhedrin could try and punish religious offenses for all matters except those that demanded the death penalty (John 18:31, 32). Capital cases had to go before the Roman governor. As a result, following the ecclesiastical trial there would have to be a civil one in front of Pilate.

That second trial made it all the more important that the Jewish leaders come up with an adequate charge against Jesus. But that would eventually prove to be more than a little problematic, since those things about Him that most irritated the Jewish leaders Rome would not regard as worthy of death. So the task of the Sanhedrin was twofold. First, to formulate a charge amongst themselves, and then to word it in such a way that Pilate would have no choice but to act.

The trial before the Sanhedrin in Jesus' case functioned as a preliminary hearing or a grand jury. "Mark," R. T. France points out, "clearly does not want us to think of this as a fair and impartial trial. The aim is, quite simply, 'to put him to death.' The verdict is already decided, and the only problem is how to find suitable evidence to support it. But it seems that the authorities are eager to ensure that due process of law is seen to have been carried out" (France, *Mark,* Doubleday, p. 190).

In spite of their desire to give the impression that they were following due process, the Sanhedrin broke many of its own rules that would eventually be encoded in the *Mishnah.* In capital cases, for example, a guilty verdict required a second sitting of the court on the following day, both sittings had to take place during the daytime, and neither could be on the eve of a Sabbath or a festival (see m. Sanhedrin 4:1, 5). One modern law expert has documented nine legal errors in Jesus' trial (see Foreman, pp. 116-120). But in the minds of the Jewish leaders it was not the time to worry about the niceties of the law. They had a mission to accomplish, and they desired to do it quickly. As a result, they overrode their own laws, much like what even modern democratic nations do when their leaders define a problem as a "national security issue."

One of their most serious problems was that of adequate witnesses. It was an especially thorny issue since Jewish law explicitly called for at least two corroborating witnesses in capital cases (Num. 35:30; Deut. 17:6; 19:15). The difficulty in Jesus' trial was not a lack of witnesses, but one of orchestrating their testimony. Under cross-examination their witness was "inconsistent" (Mark 14:56).

For a while it appeared that the most fruitful line of attack might be Jesus' statements regarding the Temple (verse 58). After all, in both His words and actions He had offended the Jewish leaders on that topic. His cleansing of the Temple (Mark 11:15-19) had been a frontal assault on the foremost symbol of their religion, and Jesus had even gone so far as to claim that the Temple would be destroyed (13:2). Judas had certainly had time to share that tid-bit of information with the authorities.

Some of the witnesses concocted the story that Jesus had said that He would destroy the Temple and raise up another in three days (14:58). That

271

was not what Jesus had said but the rumor of it was widespread enough to stick in the popular mind, being repeated by passers-by as He hung on the cross (15:29). The basis for the misconception may have been a conflating of what Jesus said about the future destruction of the Temple with sayings related to His resurrection after three days in the tomb (8:31; 9:31; 10:34). But no matter what the origin of the rumor, it didn't stand up even in a prejudiced court (14:58, 59).

Up to that point, Jesus had been totally silent, perhaps reflecting the prophesy of Isaiah 53:7: "He was oppressed, and he was afflicted, yet he opened not his mouth; like a lamb that is led to the slaughter, and like a sheep that before its shearers is dumb, so he opened not his mouth" (RSV).

At least one student has suggested that His silence was offensive because the Jewish leadership perceived it as "a contempt of court" (see Martin, *Where the Action Is,* p. 133). Another has suggested that the Jews should have been thankful Jesus was silent. After all, He "had, again and again, impaled the scribes and Pharisees on the horns of an inescapable dilemma." He "had punctured his opponents with sharp questions for which there was no answer," and He "could have completely toppled over the flimsy scaffolding of lies erected against him. But he was silent" (Luccock, p. 890). Of course, He was well aware that *anything* that He said could be twisted and used against Him.

It was in the face of that maddening silence that Caiaphas took matters into his own hands, asking bluntly, "Are you the Christ, the Son of the Blessed One?" (Mark 14:61). The question itself was unlawful, since, according to Jewish law, defendants must not be asked questions that would incriminate them, and they were never to be compelled to testify against themselves (see Foreman, p. 118). However, that was just the type of question that Caiaphas employed.

Yet, surprisingly, Jesus broke His silence. The Man who had told people not to let anyone know who He was, was now telling the high priest in public. The Messianic secret had ended. Jesus admitted to being both the Messiah and the Son of God (Mark 14:62). The time had come when people could no longer misinterpret His mission as that of a political liberator.

Caiaphas now had what he needed. Claiming to be the Messiah was not a capital crime, but in his very carefully worded question the high priest had got Jesus to admit that He was the Son of God, and blasphemy was a death offense in Jewish thinking. Caiaphas was now ready for stage two of the trial (verses 63, 64).

But before moving to that topic we should note two things about Jesus. First, He was courageous. He knew that if He answered as He did He would die for it. Prudence and the law would have led Him to continued silence.

Second, even in that dark hour Jesus was confident in the future, claiming that Caiaphas would "see the Son of Man sitting at the right hand of power and coming with the clouds of heaven" (14:62). That part of the answer was unnecessary. It went beyond the high priest's question. But Jesus, building His reply on Daniel 7:13 and Psalm 110:1, had not the slightest doubt in His ultimate victory. Human beings might dishonor Him but God would honor Him.

And the dishonor was quick in coming as guards struck, spit at, and mockingly told Jesus to prophesy while His head was covered, an appropriate jest since "one who claimed to be Messiah was popularly expected to be able to identify his assailant by smell without seeing him" (France, *Mark*, NIGTC, p. 617).

The entire procedure is what sociologists refer to as a degradation ritual. Throughout the Gospel, Mark has presented Jesus as a person whose words and deeds were out of proportion to the honor status of a village craftsman. But now the authorities have Jesus arrested and even His core group—His closest followers—have deserted Him. The first stage of the degradation ritual takes place at the home of Caiaphas in the mocking episode of Mark 14:65. In the process, "he appears powerless to prevent" what is being done to Him, and "Jesus' lofty status in the eyes of the people begins to crumble." The process of removing His aura of honor will continue the following day. Jesus may make great claims for Himself, but the Jewish leaders will show who He is and demonstrate the fruits of blasphemy (Malina, pp. 412, 413, 215).

Although dishonor now quickly overwhelmed Him, He will regain honor eventually. Jesus told Caiaphas that He would return in glory and would be seen by those very Jewish leaders who were seeking to degrade Him (Mark 14:62). The book of Revelation picks up on that event: "Behold, he cometh with clouds; and every eye shall see him, and they also which pierced him" (Rev. 1:7, KJV). With that event we find the ultimate role reversal. "Jesus," James Edwards argues, "stands on trial before the Sanhedrin, but the Sanhedrin will stand trial before the Son of Man when he returns in glory. The Sanhedrin makes a charade of Jesus' ability to prophesy, but his prophecies all come true" (Edwards, p. 449).

Part of the gospel is that the great role reversal will not only take place in the life of Jesus, but also for each of His followers who have gone through various status degradation rituals across the ages. That was an especially important insight for those first readers of Mark who had so recently suffered under Nero.

χ

56. Peter Under Trial

Mark 14:66-72

⁶⁶And as Peter was below in the courtyard, one of the servant-girls of the high priest came, ⁶⁷and seeing Peter warming himself, she looked at him and said, "You also were with Jesus the Nazarene." ⁶⁸But he denied it, saying, "I do not know or understand what you are saying." And he went outside into the gateway [and a rooster crowed].* ⁶⁹The servant-girl saw him, and began to say again to those standing by, "This is one of them." ⁷⁰But he again denied it. And after a little while those standing by said to Peter, "Truly you are one of them, for indeed you are a Galilean." ⁷¹But he began to curse and to swear, "I do not know this man you are speaking about." ⁷²And immediately a rooster crowed a second time. And Peter remembered the word Jesus spoke to him, "Before a rooster crows twice, you will deny Me three times." And he broke down and wept.

------

*The last part of verse 68 does not appear in the earliest Greek manuscripts of Mark.

What we have in Mark 14:53-72 is a tale of two simultaneous trials— that of Jesus who stands before the most powerful person in Israel, the high priest, and that of Peter before a person with no power, a female servant. As Mark tells the story they are separate events with the first found in verses 53 to 65 and the second in verses 66 to 72.

Yet they are not separate, because in Mark's unique literary style he has created a sandwich around the trial of Jesus, with Peter's experience first being introduced in verse 54 but not resumed until verse 66, with the ecclesiastical trial of Jesus inserted between the two (verses 55-65). The sandwich is not only a tale of two trials but it is a story of two very different responses to the force of external pressure on human faith. And those responses may even reflect on the events in Gethsemane, where one Man prayed while the other slept, where one Man surrendered Himself totally to death on the cross while the other failed to face the events that would soon inundate both of them. In other words, the differences of results in the two trials were not the decision of a moment, but reflect the differing patterns of the habits of Jesus and Peter up to that time.

The first part of the sandwich occurs in Mark 14:54, in which Peter follows Jesus into the courtyard of the high priest so that he will have some knowledge of the trial of Jesus (verses 55-65). Verse 66 picks up the last part of the sandwich with Peter still in that same courtyard.

Caiaphas' house, like so many villas of that time and place, was apparently built around an open courtyard enclosed by the rooms of the surrounding house. The fact that Mark describes Peter as being "below" (verse 66) indicates that Jesus' trial took place in one of the rooms above the courtyard.

Perhaps the most remarkable thing about the incident is that Peter is there at all. Usually we fault Peter for his cowardice, but the fact that he followed Jesus, even if at a distance, says something about the man who had earlier in the evening pulled his sword in the face of a mob accompanied by a cohort of fully armed Roman soldiers. Mark tells us that all the disciples fled after Jesus' arrest (verse 50), but at least two of them—Peter and John—had had second thoughts and had gone to Caiaphas' home. That took courage.

So far so good for Peter. But then occurs the matter of the servant-girl who claimed that he was a follower of the Nazarene (Mark 14:67). And how did she make that deduction? It may not have been all that difficult. John tells us that he and Peter both followed the procession to Caiaphas' house, but that John had been allowed into the courtyard because he was known to the high priest while Peter was left outside the gate. So John went to the maid who kept the door and asked her to let Peter in. And, according to John, it was that very maid who first put the question to Peter (John 18:15-17).

Thus two disciples waited in the courtyard, but what a difference in their emotions. John, apparently well-known by the household as a follower of Jesus, showed no fear, while the "fearless" Peter almost lost his religious experience as he contemplated detection.

Why the difference between the two disciples? Perhaps it was the circumstances that led up to the maid's confrontation of Peter. As one author puts it, "the challenge took him by surprise. He felt himself in a trap. Besides, he had compromised himself. For while he had been sitting there at the fire he had tried to pass himself off as one of the crowd. I daresay they had been jesting about Jesus, making coarse jokes about Jesus, and Peter had listened to it all without protest, and perhaps affected to laugh with the rest. What could he do now he was thus challenged? What could he do but try to keep up the deception?" (Jones, vol. 4, p. 154).

In fear of discovery, he blurted out, "I do not know or understand what you are saying" (Mark 14:68). Mark's two Greek verbs for know in that verse may appear to be a redundancy, but they are not. "The first (oida)," James Edwards suggests, "tends to denote theoretical knowledge, and the second (epistamai) practical knowledge." Thus "Peter's denial . . . is a total denial—in theory and practice" (Edwards, p. 450).

The uncomfortable Peter decides to get out of the light of the fire and moves to another part of what is apparently a very crowded courtyard. But the maid spots him again, and Peter went through his second denial (Mark 14:69, 70).

By that time the servant girl's persistence had led to several suspecting that the cornered Peter was a disciple. Finally, a relative of Malchus (the man who had his ear chopped off by Peter) identified Peter because of his Galilean accent (14:70; John 18:26, 10). With the third accusation Peter completely unraveled and "began to curse and swear" that he didn't know Jesus—although we should note that the disciple couldn't bring himself to use Jesus' name, referring to Him as "this man you are speaking about" (Mark 14:71).

To curse and swear. Peter had gone about as far as he could go in denial. And what does it mean that he cursed and swore? We can imagine at least three possibilities. First, that he used profanity. That would have been bad enough, but the meaning is probably deeper than that. A second interpretation is that he swore by God's name that he didn't know Jesus, thereby couching his denial in the form of an oath that called God to witness as to its truthfulness.

The third possibility is even more damning than the first two. R. T. France argues persuasively that he may actually have cursed Jesus to prove he was not a disciple. "The Greek verb 'curse,'" France points out, "normally has an object: It is to curse someone, not just to utter profanities. Did Peter actually go to the length of uttering a curse upon Jesus to make it clear that he could not be his follower? Mark does not make it explicit, but that is the natural implication of the word he uses" (France, *Mark,* Doubleday, pp. 194, 195; France, *Mark,* NIGTC, p. 622).

Whatever the nature of the swearing and cursing, it was a significant betrayal of Jesus by His chief disciple. At that point, at least three things happened. The first was that the cock crowed again. Mark does not mention the second event, but Luke tells us that when the cock crowed Jesus "turned and looked at Peter" (Luke 22:61, RSV). It was at that point that the disciple remembered Jesus' prophecy that before the rooster crowed twice, he would deny Him three times (Mark 14:30).

"Even while Jesus is inside before the ruling priests who mock him and ask him to prophesy (14:65), Peter is outside fulfilling the very prophecy of Jesus that foretold Peter's threefold denial" (Evans, p. 467).

And what a look that must have been. Far from an "I told you so" kind of look, Ellen White tells us that it was one of "deep pity and sorrow, but there was no anger there" (White, *The Desire of Ages,* p. 713).

That look was more than Peter could bear. The third thing that took place in that instant of time was that the disciple wept bitterly (Mark 14:72). At that very point Peter's faith took a giant step forward. As G. Campbell Morgan points out, "his tears were evidences of the answer of his soul to the truth of his faith; and to the love which he had so cruelly insulted and desecrated as he denied his Lord" (Morgan, p. 313). Peter's tears demonstrated that he was indeed a follower of Jesus—and a repentant one at that. And Jesus knew their meaning. In one of the last verses in Mark Jesus highlights the fact that He wants Peter to accompany the disciples to meet Him in Galilee (16:7).

All of us need to learn several lessons from Peter's experience. The first is that Jesus' warning to Peter is not one for cowards, but rather to the bold and the brave. If Peter had been a coward, he would never have been in the courtyard. His problem was not fear but overconfidence in his own strength. He would never forget the lesson, later writing, "Be sober, be vigilant; because your adversary the devil, as a roaring lion, walketh about, seeking whom he may devour" (1 Peter 5:8, KJV).

A second lesson is that while none of us are above reproach, none of us are beyond God's grace.

λ

57. Jesus Under Trial Again

Mark 15:1-15

¹*As soon as it was morning the chief priests with the elders and scribes and the entire Council held a consultation, and having bound Jesus, they led Him away and delivered Him to Pilate. ²Pilate questioned Him, "Are You the King of the Jews?" And He answered him, saying, "You say so." ³The chief priests were accusing Him of many things. ⁴Then Pilate again questioned Him, saying, "Are You not going to answer anything? See how many things they accuse You of." ⁵But Jesus made no further answer. Pilate was amazed.*

⁶*Now at every feast he released to them one person who they asked for. ⁷Now there was one called Barabbas, imprisoned with fellow insurrectionists, who had committed murder in the uprising. ⁸And the crowd came and began to ask Pilate to do as he generally did for them. ⁹Pilate answered them, saying, "Do you wish that I should release the King of the Jews to you?" ¹⁰For he knew that it was because of envy that the chief priests had handed Him over to him. ¹¹But the chief priests stirred up the crowd that he should release Barabbas instead. ¹²Pilate again answered them, saying, "What then do you wish that I should do with the One you call the King of the Jews?" ¹³And again they cried out, "Crucify Him!" ¹⁴But Pilate said to them, "Why, what evil has He done?" But they cried out all the more, "Crucify Him!" ¹⁵So Pilate, desiring to satisfy the crowd, released Barabbas to them; and having flogged Him, handed over Jesus that He might be crucified.*

There was no time to waste. Roman legal proceedings began early so that by mid-morning the ruling class could embark on pursuits of leisure.

The interrogation of the evening is over, and now a large enough group of the Sanhedrin to form a quorum meets in the early daylight to "legally" formulate a charge against Jesus that they can present to the Roman governor.

The problem the Sanhedrin faces is that only the Roman governor can pronounce a death penalty. And it certainly wouldn't do to request Pilate to put Jesus to death on the basis that He had claimed to be the Messiah and the Son of God, that He had committed blasphemy. Pilate would have seen such charges as part of an internal Jewish squabble, and thus of no interest to the empire. But, given the Jewish way of thinking about the Messiah, they could give the title a political interpretation. After all, in the popular mind Messiah equated with king of the Jews, and a Davidic war-like one at that.

Mark doesn't tell us about the fancy footwork of the religious leaders in framing their official charge. But Luke does: "Then the whole company of them arose, and brought him before Pilate. And they began to accuse him, saying, 'We found this man perverting our nation, and forbidding us to give tribute to Caesar, and saying that he himself is Christ a king" (Luke 23:1, 2, RSV).

Now Pilate (governor of Palestine from 26-37 A.D.) did not represent Roman colonial government at its best. Philo (a Jewish contemporary of Jesus) described Pilate as "a man of a very inflexible disposition, and very merciless as well as very obstinate" (Philo, *Embassy to Gaius,* para. 301). Records of the day note no less than five occasions during which his insensitivity led to serious unrest among his Palestinian subjects, three times resulting in a massacre and a fourth with nearly the same result. Eventually the empire would remove him from office because of misgovernment (see Freedman, vol. 5, pp. 395-401). The last thing Pilate needed was another run-in with the Jewish leaders, especially during the inflammatory Passover season when the minds of the people were already thinking of exodus, liberation, and the overthrow of oppressors.

Immediately Pilate sized up both the religious leaders and Jesus. He easily concluded that Jesus was no political threat and that they were "envious" of Him (Mark 15:10). Pilate didn't beat around the bush, but at once asked Jesus if He was "the King of the Jews." At first glance Jesus' answer ("You say so") seems to be a strange one (verse 2). At most it was a guarded answer. He didn't admit to kingship, but neither did He deny it.

Exploring Mark

The reason for the ambiguity is that in one sense the charge was correct. After all, just a few days before (Mark 11:1-11) Jesus had ridden into Jerusalem in royal fashion in fulfillment of Zechariah 9:9. But, on the other hand, His kingdom was not a political one in the way that Jewish nationalists and Pilate thought of the topic. R. T. France claims that the truth of the matter is that "he is a king on a much wider stage than merely Jewish national politics, the Son of Man who will soon be seated at the right hand of God as sovereign over all nations. . . . So Jesus' answer probably means 'That is how you put it, but the truth is very different from what you are thinking'" (France, *Mark,* Doubleday, p. 197).

After His cryptic reply Jesus does not speak again in Mark until His agonized cry on the cross (Mark 15:34). Jesus could have developed a strong defense before Pilate that might have brought His freedom. But that was not His way. He had in Gethsemane surrendered to His Father's will, and He wouldn't stand in the way of its fulfillment now.

The fact that Jesus refused to defend Himself (15:5) amazed Pilate, but he saw no reason for the death penalty in His case. Fortunately, there was a way out. Every Passover season he freed one prisoner at the request of the Jews, and the crowd had begun to press that issue (verses 6, 8). Perhaps here was the answer, and Pilate suggested it, but they instead called for the pardon of Barabbas.

Mark described Barabbas as no ordinary criminal. Rather, he was a rebel who committed murder in a recent insurrection (verse 7). We have no knowledge of that specific uprising, but such events were common in an inflammable nation that chaffed under Roman rule. Barabbas may even have belonged to the *Sicarii* (meaning dagger-bearers), those radical Jewish patriots who pledged to murder and assassinate the Roman rulers and their collaborators whenever and wherever possible.

Whatever his exact connections, Barabbas was a type of nationalist leader that had great popularity in Palestine as a possible messianic-type liberator. It was not difficult for the Jewish leaders to manipulate the excitable crowd to demand the release of such a popular hero.

But what about the crowd? Hadn't a Jewish crowd that same week shouted Hosannas and provided Jesus with royal treatment on His triumphal entry into Jerusalem (Mark 11:1-11)? True, but this most likely was not the same mob of people. Rather, William Barclay suggests, "it may well be that this was a crowd which had assembled with the deliberate intention of demanding the release of Barabbas" (Barclay, *Mark,* p. 375). Whether that supposition is true or not, the religious leaders found an exploitable situation to their liking. They had no difficulty in fanning the popular clamor for the release of Barabbas (Mark 15:11).

The mood of the crowd was soon obvious to Pilate. It wanted the release of Barabbas and the crucifixion of Jesus (verses 11-14). And what a choice it was. Barabbas is an Aramaic name, *Bar-'Abba',* that means "son of the father." "In the ultimate irony of the entire degradation ritual, Jesus, the true Son of the Father, and Barabbas, the . . . criminal, have switched roles." Meanwhile, "as the crowd and rulers acquiesce, Jesus is reduced to a level of utter contempt, stripped, and crowned with thorns, with a scepter of reeds in his right hand. He is then mocked as 'king of the Judeans,' a degradation of Jesus and a public insult to the Judean crowd and its rulers (Matt 27:27-31; Mark 15:17-20). The ultimate humiliation, hanging naked in public on a cross, provides the occasion for the final public derision (Matt 27:39-44; Mark 15:29-32; Luke 23:35-38)." At that point the status degradation of Jesus would be complete (Malina, p. 413) and His crucifixion by Rome would later "severely damage attempts on the part of Jesus' followers to rehabilitate him" (Edwards, pp. 457, 458).

Pilate added his own sadistic touch to the civil trial. Before having Jesus crucified, he ordered a flogging (Mark 15:15). Roman flogging was a brutal ordeal in its own right. The whip had long leather strips with sharpened pieces of metal and bone studded here and there. Such an instrument could tear a person's flesh right down to the bone. Some victims never survived the ordeal. But that, in Jesus' case, was merely a preliminary.

In Mark 15:1-15 Jesus by His very silence forced a decision on Pilate and the crowd: Barabbas or Jesus. It was a choice between hatred and love, between a man of war and man of peace.

That early morning so long ago in Jerusalem still echoes in the world of today. Jesus still confronts each of us with choices every day. We still face the same alternatives. And too often it is the principles of Barabbas that capture our allegiance. Such is the underlying meaning of a world that continues to suffer from violence and wars 2,000 years after the crowd's fateful decision.

But such decisions are more than merely crowd choices. They are also personal. Even today I must decide between Barabbas and what he stood for and Jesus and the principles of the kingdom of God. Unfortunately, it is no more easy to choose the right today than it was that spring morning. And it's not made any easier by the fact that evil forces in the spiritual world seek to lead us toward the wrong choice.

58. The Only Volunteer
in the History of Crucifixion

Mark 15:16-32

¹⁶*And the soldiers took Him away into the courtyard (that is, the Praetorium) and they called together the entire cohort.* ¹⁷*They clothed Him in purple and placed upon Him a woven crown of thorns.* ¹⁸*And they began to salute Him, "Hail King of the Jews!"* ¹⁹*They kept striking Him on the head with a staff and spitting on Him, and bending their knees they bowed down before Him.* ²⁰*When they had mocked Him, they stripped the purple robe off of Him and clothed Him in His own garments. Then they led Him out, that they might crucify Him.*

²¹*And they compelled a passer-by, a certain Simon of Cyrene (the father of Alexander and Rufus), who was coming in from the countryside, so that he could carry His cross.* ²²*Then they brought Him to the place called Golgotha (which is translated as place of a skull),* ²³*and they tried to give Him wine mixed with myrrh. But He did not take it.* ²⁴*Then they crucified Him, dividing His garments by casting a lot for them to decide what each of them should take.* ²⁵*It was the third hour when they crucified Him.* ²⁶*The inscription of the charge against Him written over Him was, "The King of the Jews."* ²⁷*With Him they crucified two thieves, one on His right and one on His left.*★ ²⁹*And those passing by continually reviled Him, shaking their heads and saying, "Aha! You who would destroy the Temple and build it in three days,* ³⁰*save Yourself by coming down from the cross."* ³¹*Likewise, the chief priests also mocked Him to one another with the scribes, saying, "He saved others, but He is not able to save Himself.* ³²*Let the Christ, the King of Israel, now come down from the cross in order that we might see and believe." Those being crucified with Him also were insulting Him.*

★Verse 28 is missing from the earlier Greek manuscripts and reflects the content of Luke 22:37. It reads: ²⁸"And the Scripture was fulfilled which says, 'And He was numbered with the transgressors.'"

The Only Volunteer in the History of Crucifixion

It must have been great sport for the Roman soldiers. Garrison duty was boring, and here was an opportunity for some first-class entertainment. After all, it wasn't every day that a "king" fell into their hands.

Calling together the whole cohort (roughly equivalent to a battalion) of 600 men, they made the most of their opportunity. They mockingly clothed Jesus with the symbols of royalty—a purple robe and a reed for a scepter and a woven circle of thorns pushed down onto His head for a crown (Mark 15:16-20). Given the nature of common soldiers of the day, the mocking was undoubtedly anything but delicate and refined. It must have been "great fun" while it lasted. But soon a delegation of them led Him out to be crucified. Meanwhile, they were fulfilling Jesus' prophecy that when He came to Jerusalem the "chief priests and the scribes" would "condemn him to death, and deliver him to the Gentiles; and they will mock him, and spit upon him, and scourge him, and kill him" (Mark 10:33, 34, RSV).

It was the usual practice to have the condemned prisoner carry the crossbeam of his cross to the place of execution. And the route followed was the longest rather than the shortest. Crucifixion was psychological warfare, a form of terrorism. The Romans wanted as many people as possible to see it, so that the local population could take note of what happened to those foolish enough to challenge Rome's power.

Jesus apparently bore the crossbeam of His cross for some distance, but the night and morning of torture and flogging had taken their toll on Him. The soldiers, realizing His helplessness, glanced around for someone who they could press into service. It was not a happy task, and there were no volunteers. But when people felt the flat of a Roman spear on their shoulder they knew that they had no choice but to obey unless they also wanted to be treated as a rebel.

So it was that the eyes of the officer in charge fell on Simon of Cyrene (15:21). Cyrene was an important city in North Africa in present day Libya. He was probably on a Passover pilgrimage, one that he may have saved for years to afford. And now this.

But why, we need to ask, did the soldiers settle on Simon from the thronging crowd. The Bible doesn't say, but some suggest it was because of his strength, an obvious qualification. J. D. Jones, however, has put forth an intriguing possibility. "I prefer," he writes, "to account for Simon's choice in another way. It is possible that Simon in some way showed sympathy with Jesus. Coming in from the country and seeing this crowd surging out of the gates, curiosity may have impelled him to try to discover what the excitement was about. Edging his way through the crowd he would find himself face to face with Christ. It may be that just at that moment Christ fainted and fell beneath His burden, and some brutal act of the soldiers may have extorted from Simon some evident sign of sympathy. It was this, I suggest, that attracted the attention of the soldiers to Simon. They revenged themselves for Simon's indignant remonstrance by taking the Cross from Christ's shoulders and placing it upon his" (Jones, vol. 4, p. 205).

Such a view, of course, is speculation. But it is no conjecture to claim that it was the most important day in Simon's life, even though it may not have seemed so at the time. A hint at its importance appears in the words of Mark when he describes Simon as "the father of Alexander and Rufus" (15:21). Mark is the only one of the Gospel writers who mentions the name of the two sons. It is generally agreed that he did so for some reason. The most likely one is that it was a description of Simon that the believers in Rome could use to identify him. As noted in the introductory section of this book, Rome was the probable destination of Mark's Gospel. And in Paul's letter to the Romans we find a tantalizing piece of information perhaps related to Mark 15:21. "Greet Rufus," Paul wrote, "eminent in the Lord, also his mother and mine" (Romans 16:13, RSV). In addition, in November 1941 a burial cave in Israel used for Cyrenian Jews was found. It contains an inscription that reads, "Alexander, son of Simon" (Lane, p. 563). And some have even connected Simon of Cyrene with "Simeon who was called Niger" in Acts 13:1 (RSV), pointing out that Simeon is another form for Simon and that Niger was the regular name for a person of darker complexion who came from Africa, the location of Cyrene.

We have no compelling evidence that the Rufus of Romans, the Alexander of the inscription, or the Simeon of Acts were related to those mentioned in Mark 15:21. But as R. T. France observes, the mention of "Alexander and Rufus suggests that these two men were known to Mark's readers since they (and their father?) had become Christians, perhaps as a result of this involuntary involvement in the story of Jesus" (France, *Mark*, NIGTC, p. 641). God, after all, can use what appear at the time to be misfortunes in our lives for our blessing and good (see Rom. 8:28). Another way of putting it is that all the bad things that happen to us are not bad.

When the execution party reached the place of crucifixion, soldiers fixed the crossbar to the upright beam. They stretched the prisoner out on it and nailed Him to it. Then they raised the cross and dropped it with a flesh-tearing thud into the hole prepared for it.

Death on a cross, Martin Hengel writes, was not "just any kind of death. It was an utterly offensive affair, 'obscene'" in the fullest sense of the word. "Crucifixion was a punishment in which the caprice and sadism of the executioners was given full rein" (Hengel, pp. 22, 25). The physical torture of the crucifixion was not only the nails, but the inescapable burning of the Palestinian sun. The victim was immobile and therefore unable to fend off heat, cold, or insects. Since crucifixion affected no vital organs, death from fatigue, cramped muscles, hunger, and thirst usually came slowly, often after many days.

In Jewish understanding, anyone executed by crucifixion was rejected by his people, cursed by the law of God, and excluded from God's covenant with the Jewish people (Gal. 3:13; Deut. 21:23). To top it off, the Jews expected their Messiah to be a mighty conquering king, not a suffering criminal. No wonder Paul could refer to Christ's cross as a "stumbling block to Jews and foolishness to Gentiles" (1 Cor. 1:23, NIV).

"For the disciples who had followed Jesus to Jerusalem," penned Jürgen Moltmann, "his shameful death was not the consummation of his obedience to God nor a demonstration of martyrdom for his truth, but the rejection of his claim. It did not confirm their hopes in him, but . . . destroyed them" (Moltmann, p. 132).

The disciples were not the only ones present at the crucifixion who recognized the paradox of a crucified Messiah. Yet, unlike the disciples, the others did not remain silent. To the contrary, they heaped insults on the suffering Jesus. Mark mentions three distinct groups who did so: passers-by, the chief priests and the scribes, and the two criminals placed on either side of Him (15:29-32).

The mocking of the Jewish leaders is of special interest. "He saved others, but He is not able to save Himself. Let the Christ, the King of Israel, now come down from the cross in order that we might see and believe" (verses 31, 32). The paradox of the whole matter is that Jesus was the only person in the history of crucifixion who did not need to stay on His cross.

He could have used His divine power to get off of it. But He chose to stay on it and die in our place, to become "sin who knew no sin, so that in him we might become the righteousness of God" (2 Cor. 5:21, RSV). "I lay down my life," we read in John's Gospel. "No one takes it from me, but I lay it down of my own accord. I have power to lay it down, and I have power to take it again" (John 10:17, 18, RSV). Jesus had a choice. He decided to do God's will rather than His own—He chose to stay on the cross.

R. Alan Cole notes that the religious leaders' words in Mark 15:31 had "prophetic truth" in them when they said, "He saved others, but He is not able to save Himself." "If Christ wanted to save others," Cole points out, "then He could not come down from the cross; that temptation He had rejected first in the wilderness (1:13), then at Caesarea Philippi (8:33), and lastly in the garden of Gethsemane (14:36). To descend from the cross was not indeed a physical impossibility, but it was a moral and spiritual impossibility for the Messiah. If He did so, He would cease to be God's Christ, treading God's path of Messiahship; instead, He would become a mere human Christ, and such a Christ could never save the world. The only path by which to save others was to refuse to save Himself: in a way totally unexpected by them, the priests were correct" (Cole, p. 319).

59. The Meaning of Jesus' Death

Mark 15:33-47

³³When the sixth hour had come, it became dark over the whole land until the ninth hour. ³⁴At the ninth hour Jesus cried out in a loud voice, "Eloi, Eloi, lama sabachthani?" which is translated as "My God, My God, why did You forsake Me?" ³⁵Some of those standing by heard, and were saying, "Look, He is calling for Elijah." ³⁶And one ran and filled a sponge with vinegar, put it on a staff, and gave it to Him to drink, saying, "Wait, let us see if Elijah will come to take Him down." ³⁷And Jesus uttered a loud cry and died. ³⁸And the curtain of the Temple was torn in two from top to bottom. ³⁹And when the centurion who was standing in front of Him saw that He died that way, he said, "Truly this man was the Son of God."

⁴⁰There were also women looking on from a distance, among whom were Mary Magdalene, and Mary the mother of James the younger and

Joses, and Salome, ⁴¹who, when He was in Galilee, followed Him and served Him, and many others who had gone up with Him to Jerusalem.
⁴²When evening had come, since it was the preparation day, that is, the day before the Sabbath, ⁴³Joseph of Arimathea came, a prominent member of the Council, who himself was looking forward to the kingdom of God, and he boldly went in to Pilate and asked for the body of Jesus. ⁴⁴Pilate was amazed that He had died already, and summoning the centurion he questioned him to see whether He was dead already. ⁴⁵And finding out from the centurion he gave the corpse to Joseph. ⁴⁶And having brought a linen cloth and having taken Him down, he wrapped Him in the linen cloth and placed Him in a tomb that had been cut from rock, and he rolled a stone against the entrance of the tomb. ⁴⁷And Mary Magdalene and Mary the mother of Joses observed where He was laid.

The end had come. But it wasn't a day of brightness as the Jews had anticipated in their messianic musings. Rather it is one of unnatural darkness for three hours (Mark 15:33). Given the fact that Passover takes place at full moon, that darkness could not have resulted from an eclipse. That is, it was supernatural rather than natural. The Old Testament several times linked darkness with judgment (see, for example, Joel 3:14, 15; Isa. 5:30; 13:10, 11). Mark portrayed it as an aspect of the eschatological judgment of God, as in Amos 8:9: "'And on that day,' says the Lord God, 'I will make the sun go down at noon, and darken the earth in broad daylight'" (RSV).

The darkness of judgment wasn't only felt in the natural world. It also pressed down the soul of Jesus. At the end of His three hours on the cross He cried out in Aramaic, *"Eloi, Eloi, lama sabachthani,"* meaning "My God, My God, why did you forsake me?" (Mark 15:34). The words themselves came from Psalm 22:1, a messianic psalm that predicted the sufferings of God's Christ.

But they seem strange coming from the lips of the usually upbeat and cheerful Jesus. Why, we must ask, did He utter this cry? What is its significance?

The first thing that we need to note in forming an answer to those questions is that "this is, significantly, the only time in all the Gospels when Jesus does not use the term 'Father' to address God in prayer. A darkness has come between them" (France, *Mark,* Doubleday, p. 206).

A second thing to recognize is that the basis of Jesus' cheerful buoyancy throughout His life was His close relationship with His Father. "I am not alone," He claimed, "because the Father is with me" (John 16:32, KJV). "Believe me that I am in the Father, and the Father in me" (14:11, KJV). "I and my Father are one" (10:30, KJV). Up to this point in His life Jesus had confidence that His Father's smile rested upon Him, no matter how His outward circumstances appeared.

That brings us to the third thing we should keep in mind about Jesus' God-forsaken cry. That is that something had changed as He hung upon the cross. And in that shift we find the center of "the mystery of the Cross" (Jones, vol. 4, p. 225). At the core of the mysterious center itself we find Jesus encountering something totally new to Him. As William Barclay puts it, "Up to this moment Jesus had gone through every experience of life, *except one—He had never known the consequences of sin.* Now if there is one thing sin does, it is that it separates us from God. . . . That was the one human experience through which Jesus had never passed because He was without sin" (Barclay, *Mark,* p. 383). But on the cross "He made him who knew no sin to be sin on our behalf" (2 Cor. 5:21, NASB); "the Lord has laid on him the iniquity of us all" (Isa. 53:6, RSV); Jesus was giving "his life as a ransom for many" (Mark 10:45, RSV); He was drinking the "cup" of God's wrath that He had so dreaded in Gethsemane (14:36); and He deeply felt the results. For the first time in His life, as He died as our substitutionary "Lamb of God" (John 1:29), He felt separated from God. Through that process, which it is impossible for us to fully comprehend, Jesus laid the foundation for the salvation of sinners. For Him it was a time of unbearable agony.

Yet, and this is a fourth thing we should remember about Jesus' God-forsaken cry, He did not experience total hopelessness. After all, He still addressed God as "My God" (Mark 15:34). In His heart of hearts He knew that the separation would not be permanent.

The next thing that Mark records Jesus saying isn't even a word. Rather, he tells us that as He died He "uttered a loud cry" (Mark 15:37). The other two synoptic Gospels give us the same information (Matt. 27:50; Luke 23:46), but only John provides us with the words themselves. According to John, just before Jesus' death, He announced, "It is finished" (19:30, NIV).

That is undoubtedly the greatest single word (as it is in the Greek) ever uttered. "It is the cry," notes Barclay, "of the man who has completed his task; it is the cry of the man who has won through the struggle; it is the cry of the man who has come out of the dark into the glory of the light, and who has grasped the crown. . . . *Jesus died a victor and a conqueror with a shout of triumph on His lips"* (Barclay, *Matthew,* vol. 2, p. 408, italics supplied).

And that victory contains the meaning of the cross. Jesus who had lived a perfect life, became the spotless Lamb of God who in dying took away the world's sins (John 1:29).

That meaning we find symbolized in Mark 15:38, which tells us that at the moment of His death "the curtain of the Temple was torn in two from top to bottom." Note the phrase "from top to bottom." That curtain was approximately 60 feet in height. The directional description of its ripping signifies a supernatural act.

And the act itself symbolized two things. First, that the old system of ceremonies and sacrifices that pointed forward to Jesus' sacrifice on the cross (Col. 2:17) had been rendered obsolete, that the earthly Temple was no longer holy. The scene of action in the plan of salvation at that historical moment shifted to heaven, where a resurrected Jesus would minister as high priest for those who believe in Him (Heb. 8:1, 2). A second significance of the tearing of the curtain is that with Jesus as their advocate in heaven, every believer (and not just priests) would have direct access to the Father through the sacrifice of Jesus and through His post-resurrection heavenly ministry (Rom. 8:34; Heb. 4:15, 16; 7:25; 10:19-22).

Surrounding Jesus in Mark 15:33-47 were several people who have their own interpretations on the meaning of His death. First we encounter the curious bystanders who apparently confused Jesus' cry of "Eloi" with a plea for Elijah (Eli in Aramaic), who had been taken to heaven without seeing death (2 Kings 2:11). Many believed that Elijah would return in the last days to rescue God's people in a time of crisis. Seen in a positive light, the attempt to give Jesus a drink was to keep Him going till Elijah rescued Him. But more likely the whole event was merely one more round of cruel mockery, since probably few believed that God would send Elijah to rescue "the King of the Jews" from His cross (see Mark 15:36, 37). For them the death of Jesus was entertainment.

Then there was the centurion. He had undoubtedly participated in many crucifixions and witnessed people die the most agonizing of deaths.

But he sensed something different about this man, this death. As a result, we find an individual, who only a few minutes before may have been participating in cruel jesting now confessing at the moment of Jesus' death that "Truly this man was the Son of God" (verse 39). "The centurion," Craig Evans points out, "acknowledges that this crucified Jesus of Nazareth is the true son of God, not [the] 'divine' Caesar as the imperial cult would have it" (Evans, p. 512; cf. Edwards, p. 480). In that sentiment he echoed the same declaration God made at Jesus' baptism (Mark 1:11). But the Gentile centurion is the only human to make such a pronouncement in Mark. It was the way Jesus died and the circumstances surrounding His death that had led him to that conclusion. For the centurion Jesus' death was a revelation.

Mark's Christological Anchor Points

1. God—"You are My beloved Son, in You I am well pleased" (1:11).
2. Peter—"You are the Christ" (8:29).
3. The Centurion—"Truly this man was the Son of God" (15:39).

Another class of people around the cross were the women (Mark 15:40, 41)—Mary Magdalene, out of whom Jesus had cast seven devils (Luke 8:2); Mary the mother of Joses and possibly the less prominent James among the Twelve (called James the son of Alphaeus in Mark 3:18); and Salome, probably the mother of James and John (cf. Matt. 27:56). The disciples have largely run away or lurk at the edges of the action, thus Mark pictured the women as being better disciples than the men. At the time, however, the women didn't understand how to interpret the death of Jesus, but they were being positioned for their key role in the coming resurrection narrative (Mark 15:47; 16:1-8).

The last two characters in the drama surrounding Jesus' death were Pilate and Joseph of Arimathea. In Pilate's case the death of Jesus was merely puzzling in the sense that He had died so quickly (15:44), but for Joseph it was a life-changing event (verses 42-46). When Joseph, who had apparently been a secret disciple, boldly went to the Roman governor and requested the corpse of Jesus, he risked everything. He had no idea how the irritable Pilate would react to his request, but he knew for sure that he would lose his standing as a leader of the Jewish community and his membership in the powerful Sanhedrin. Had he been a poor man he may have come out in the open sooner. But he had much to lose. After all, the Jewish leaders had agreed that those who became followers of Jesus should be put out of the synagogue—excommunicated (John 9:22).

It was the cross of Jesus that transformed Joseph. Barclay writes that Joseph was one of those people "for whom the Cross of Jesus did what not even the life of Jesus could do. When he had seen Jesus alive he had felt His attraction, but had gone no further. But when he saw Jesus die . . . his heart was broken in love" (Barclay, *Mark,* p. 386). He, like the centurion, was a fulfillment of Jesus' words: "I, when I am lifted up from the earth, will draw all men to myself" (John 12:32, RSV).

Joseph discovered that no person can long remain a secret disciple. Eventually the secrecy will kill the discipleship or the discipleship will kill the secrecy. ✗

Part V

An Ending That Doesn't End

Mark 16:1-[20]

60. The Death of Death

Mark 16:1-8

¹And the Sabbath being past, Mary Magdalene and Mary the mother of James and Salome bought spices so that they might come and anoint Him. ²Very early on the first day of the week they came to the tomb as the sun rose. ³And they were saying to one another, "Who will roll away the stone from the entrance of the tomb for us?" ⁴And looking up they saw that the stone had been rolled away. (It was extremely large.) ⁵And having entered into the tomb, they saw a young man clothed in a white robe sitting on the right side, and they were startled. ⁶But he said to them, "Do not be startled. You are looking for Jesus the Nazarene, the one who has been crucified. He has risen, He is not here. See the place where they laid Him. ⁷But go tell His disciples and Peter, 'He is going before you into Galilee. You will see Him there, just as He told you.'" ⁸And they went out and fled from the tomb, for trembling and bewilderment had seized them, and they told no one anything, for they were afraid.

According to Luke the women had "rested" on the Sabbath, "according to the commandment" (Luke 23:56, RSV). The normal practice in the heat of Palestine would have been for them to anoint Jesus' body and prepare it for burial as soon after His death as possible. But He had died late on Friday, and even though the preparation was important, they waited until after their day of rest and worship was over. Thus it is that we find them going about the task around sunrise on Sunday morning (Mark 16:2).

But as they headed toward the tomb they had one worry. How could they possibly move the huge circular stone rolled across the entrance to the cave-like place of burial? (verse 3). Craig Evans writes that "it is ironic that not one of Jesus' male disciples is available to offer this assistance" (Evans, p. 539). They were apparently still in hiding. Mark's Gospel, in reflecting historical fact, doesn't have a great deal of positive things to say about the courage and fidelity of the disciples during the great climactic events of Jesus' life. It is the female followers rather than the disciples who take center stage at the death (Mark 15:40), burial (verse 47), and resurrection (16:1). Above all things, they desired to honor Jesus one last time. That action stemmed from their love and devotion to Him, since in their minds He was forever dead.

Thus it totally shocked them to find the stone rolled away and the tomb empty. The words of the angel who met them in the tomb, "He has risen" (verse 6), equally astounded them.

Those of us who read Mark's Gospel 2,000 years later may wonder why they were so surprised or even why God had to send an angel to tell them. After all, it is plain to any who can read that Jesus had predicted His resurrection at least four times (8:31; 9:9, 31; 10:34). But we need to be careful here. We approach Scripture with hindsight—we know how the story ends. But the first disciples didn't. To be sure, Jesus had foretold His resurrection. But to live after the resurrection event is to have a different kind of understanding than was possible before. All they knew was that dead people are dead. So it was with Jesus. Joseph of Arimathea had placed His lifeless body in his own tomb. And with that burial their hopes had perished.

But His resurrection and the angelic words, "He has arisen," would change both the face of history and perceptions of the nature of death. The resurrection is the core of the gospel, the centerpiece of the good news. We may tend to focus on the substitutionary death of Jesus for our sins as the gospel. But nothing is more pathetic than a dead savior. There is no hope there. Without the resurrection Christianity would have never existed. The resurrection is the hinge of history. Paul caught a glimpse of that truth when he wrote that Jesus Christ was "designated Son of God in power according to the Spirit of holiness by his resurrection from the dead." The resurrection alone gives us access to His grace (Rom. 1:4, 5, RSV). Again the apostle defined the gospel by the equally important facts that "Christ died for our sins in accordance with the scriptures, that he was buried, that he was raised on the third day" (1 Cor. 15:1-4, RSV). It is impossible to overestimate the importance of Jesus' resurrection.

"One thing is certain," William Barclay asserts, "if Jesus had not risen from the dead we would never have heard of Him. The attitude of the women was that they had come to pay the last tribute to a dead body. The attitude of the disciples was that everything had finished in tragedy. By far the best proof of the Resurrection is the existence of the Christian Church. Nothing else could have changed sad and despairing men and women into people radiant with joy and flaming with courage. The Resurrection is the central fact of the whole Christian faith" (Barclay, *Mark,* pp. 387, 388).

A Message From Jesus

"Do not be afraid. I am the first and the last, the living one. I am he who was dead, and now you see me alive for timeless ages! I hold in my hand the keys of death and the grave" (Rev. 1:18, 19, Phillips).

It is the fact of Jesus' resurrection that guarantees the resurrection of those who believe in Him. "For as in Adam all die, so also in Christ shall all be made alive" (1 Cor. 15:22, RSV). Because He rose from the dead, Christians are not like others who have "no hope" in the face of death. At the end of time "the Lord himself will descend from heaven with a cry of command, with the archangel's call, and with the sound of the trumpet of God. And the dead in Christ will rise first; then we who are alive, who are left, shall be caught up together with them in the clouds to meet the Lord in the air; and so we shall always be with the Lord. Therefore comfort one another with these words" (1 Thess. 4:13, 15-18, RSV; cf. 1 Cor. 15:51-57).

The reality of the risen Christ would transform the disciples from the cowering individuals of the Passover week to the courageous apostles we find in the book of Acts. It was also a heartening message to Mark's first readers who had suffered under the cruelties of Nero and who faced an uncertain future. And it is still the central hope of believers who live in the twenty-first century. *Jesus' resurrection spelled out the eventual death of death itself, while at the same time opening up the way of life everlasting to every person who accepts His gift. Now that is gospel, that is the ultimate good news.*

But Mark 16:1-8 is not only about the ultimate good news. The passage also had some very needed good news for the still hiding disciples. "Go tell His disciples and Peter," said the angel to the women, to meet with Jesus in Galilee (verse 7). Here is immediate grace in its most startling form. After all, the last we heard of the disciples in Mark was when they "all forsook him, and fled" (14:50, RSV). But the most moving aspect of Jesus' commission to the disciples through the angel is the words "and Peter." The last we heard from that wayward follower was when he cursed and swore that he didn't know Jesus, after which "he broke down and wept" (14:71, 72, RSV).

Peter must have gone through utter despair in the four days since he had betrayed Jesus. It is significant that of all the Gospel writers, only Mark records Jesus' special invitation to the fallen Peter. As noted in our introductory section, it appears that Mark collaborated with Peter in the writing of his Gospel. All the other Gospel writers may have neglected the words "and Peter," but Peter never could. Those two words shattered his despair. The Jesus who had earlier urged him to forgive 70 times seven (Matt. 18:22) was doing that very thing for His fallen disciple.

Here is grace. Jesus didn't give Peter what he deserved. To the contrary, He offered him what he did not deserve—forgiveness and restoration to the apostleship. As James Edwards points out, "if the word of grace from the resurrected Lord includes a traitor like Peter, readers of the Gospel may be assured that it includes those of their community who have also failed Christ" (Edwards, p. 495). And, we might add, that goes for clergy who have failed. We must never forget who Peter was and what he did. Yet Jesus forgave him. That is truly "Amazing Grace," grace that stretches the imagination of even the most generous Christians. Could we do what Jesus did? Or, more pertinently, would we want Jesus to do the same for us were we in Peter's position?

The most paradoxical part of Mark 16:1-8 is the failure of the women to do God's will in verse 8, the end of the second Gospel in the oldest and most reliable Greek manuscripts. R. T. France writes that "we can well understand the women's 'terror and amazement.' To go to a tomb looking for a body and to find there a living angel instead of the body would unnerve the strongest of us. What is not so easy to grasp is their fear and their silence. The message they have been given is one of hope and joy, and they have been specifically commissioned to pass it on to the disciples" (France, *Mark,* Doubleday, p. 213).

"Up to this point" in Mark's Gospel, Morna Hooker writes, "the women . . . have done well. . . . But at this point, even they fail. Their disobedience and fear demonstrate their inability to believe the good news. Throughout Mark's gospel, men and women have been blind and deaf to the truth about Jesus, and now at the end, when the divine message is delivered to the women, they are struck dumb, and fail to deliver it: 'they said nothing to anyone, for they were afraid.' Here is Mark's final irony. In the rest of the story, Jesus has commanded men and women to say nothing about the truth they have glimpsed, and they have frequently disobeyed. Now that the time has at last come to report what has happened, the women are silent!" (Hooker, p. 387).

Failure never seems to end. But, thanks be to God, there is apparently no end to grace either. Such is the message of Mark 16:7, 8.

61. The End That Is a Beginning

Mark 16:[9-20]

[⁹Now after He arose early on the first day of the week He appeared first to Mary Magdalene, from whom He had cast out seven demons. ¹⁰She went and announced it to those who had been with Him, who were mourning and crying. ¹¹When they heard that He was alive and had been seen by her, they refused to believe.

¹²But after that He appeared in another form to two of them as they were walking into the country. ¹³They went and reported it to the rest, but they did not believe them either.

¹⁴Later He appeared to the eleven as they were reclining at a table, and He reproached them for their unbelief and their hardness of heart, because they did not believe those who saw Him after He had been raised. ¹⁵And He said to them, "Go into all the world preaching the gospel to all creation. ¹⁶And the one who believes and is baptized will be saved. But the one who does not believe will be condemned. ¹⁷And these signs will accompany those who have believed: in My name they will cast out demons; they will speak with new tongues; ¹⁸they will pick up snakes, and if they drink any deadly poison it will in no way harm them; they will lay hands upon the sick and they will recover."

¹⁹The Lord Jesus, after having spoken to them, was taken up into heaven and sat down at the right hand of God. ²⁰And they went out preaching everywhere, the Lord working with them and confirming the word through accompanying signs.]

Exploring Mark

The more than 5,000 whole or partial copies of the Greek New Testament indicate a remarkable agreement as to the content of the New Testament. The most extensive disagreement, though, concerns the ending of Mark's Gospel. The problem is that the most reliable early Greek manuscripts end abruptly in mid-sentence in verse 8.

To compound the difficulty Mark 16:9-20 is only one of the endings found in existing Greek manuscripts. As translated above, verses 9-20 make up what scholars term the "longer ending" of Mark.

Other manuscripts add the "shorter ending" after verse 8: "But they reported briefly to Peter and those with him all that they had been told. And after this, Jesus himself sent out by means of them, from east to west, the sacred and imperishable proclamation of eternal salvation" (margin, RSV). In at least one manuscript the shorter ending concludes Mark, while in others it forms a bridge between verses 8 and 9-20. A few manuscripts insert the shorter ending after verse 14 (see Guthrie, pp. 89-93).

While the Greek manuscripts contain several endings for Mark, scholars of both conservative and liberal bents nearly unanimously agree that the original text of the Gospel as we have it ends in verse 8. Whereas some biblical scholars hold that verse 8 was the original ending, others convincingly argue that the original ending was probably lost. James Edwards, for one, writes that "several important arguments can be adduced in favor of the view that 16:8 was not the original, or intended, ending in Mark. First and perhaps most important, it is hard to imagine a Gospel that begins with a bold, resounding announcement of divine Sonship (1:1) ending on a note of fear and panic (16:8). The purpose of the centurion's confession in 15:39 is to bring Mark's readers to a confession of faith, whereas a conclusion at 16:8 leaves them in bewilderment. . . . One must . . . consider what effect the fear and bewilderment at 16:8 would have had on Mark's Roman readership as it grappled with faith in the midst of persecution. . . . An open ending [would not] be much encouragement to Mark's readers facing the savagery of Nero's persecution" (Edwards, pp. 501, 502).

We may never know what happened to the original ending. But the various ones that have been supplied seem to be aimed at rectifying the lack of a resurrection appearance by Jesus in Mark.

The longer ending of Mark 16:9-20 first appears in Greek manuscripts as early as the second century. It consists, as demonstrated in the box below, of material found in other New Testament passages.

New Testament Parallels to Mark 16:9-20

Verses 9-11: Jesus' appearance to Mary Magdalene and the refusalto believe her report.	The material in these verses is reported in John 20:11-18; Luke 24:11; 8:2.
Verses 12, 13: Jesus' appearance "in another form" to two unnamed disciples.	This incident is reported in Luke 24:13-35 as the walk to Emmaus.
Verse 14: Jesus' appearance to the 11 and His reproaching of them for their hardness of heart.	That event is paralleled in Luke 24:36-38; John 20:19-29.
Verses 15, 16: The command to preach the gospel in all the world, with instruction on baptism.	A parallel to the Great Commission of Matthew 28:19.
Verses 17, 18: The signs that would accompany the disciples.	The book of Acts records each one with the exception of drinking poison. For example, speaking in tongues is found in 2:4 and other places in Acts; in 16:18 Paul expels a demon; in 28:5 he shakes off a snake into the fire; and in 28:8 he heals the sick through the laying on of his hands.
Verse 19: Jesus ascension.	Recorded in Luke 24:50, 51; Acts 1:9-11.
Verse 20: The preaching of the apostles.	Reported in Luke 24:51, 52 and forms the subject matter of the book of Acts.

From the above box it is evident that we find nearly all the material in

Mark 16:9-20 in other parts of the New Testament. Thus even though it is probably a later addition to Mark, as R. Alan Cole points out, "the contents are in any case authentic." On the other hand, he argues that "it would be unwise . . . to build a theological position upon these verses alone" (Cole, p. 335). One result of those who have sought to build a theological position on the unique items of Mark 16:9-20 has been the rise of cults in the American South that center on the handling of poisonous snakes and the drinking of poisonous beverages as signs of faith. Most readers of Mark, however, would not agree with the conclusions or theological methodology of such groups.

Whatever our conclusions about the ending of Mark, it is quite clear that the 16:9-20 ending leaves readers in about the same place as Matthew's Gospel. Two ongoing conclusions jump out at us.

1. That Jesus has returned victoriously to heaven, where He functions at the right hand of God. Hebrews, among the New Testament books, especially expands on His right hand of God ministry, setting it forth as one of intercession for His followers here on earth (Heb. 1:3; 2:17, 18; 4:15, 16; 7:25; 8:1, 6; 9:12, 23, 24; 12:24; 1 John 2:1, 2; Rom. 8:34).

2. That the Holy Spirit has empowered Jesus' followers (disciples) on earth to preach and witness to the ends of the earth ("everywhere").

Thus in one way or another we have come to the end of Mark's Gospel. But it is not so much an ending as it is a beginning for both Jesus in heaven and His followers on earth.

X